Choice and Consent

This book of essays presents a feminist examination of the concepts of 'choice' and 'consent', as they operate within legal and political theory, jurisprudence, and across diverse areas of law. The concepts of 'choice' and 'consent' denote the activities of the autonomous, liberal (legal) subject and mark the boundary between public and private. Consequently, they are deeply gendered. This book of essays presents feminist analyses and critiques of the concepts and operations of 'choice' and 'consent'. The essays in the first two parts of the book focus on philosophical and jurisprudential issues surrounding consent and subjectivity, while those in the third part of the book provide detailed analyses of how choice and consent operate in particular areas of law, including criminal law, medical law, constitutional law, employment law, family law and civil procedure. The collection as a whole presents a dialogue between different feminist positions and approaches towards a common theme, and addresses larger questions, such as whether the concepts of 'choice' and 'consent' have consistent meanings and functions between different areas of law or whether they prove to be highly contingent when viewed across the broad field of law, and whether 'consent' can be rethought and infused with different meanings in a post-liberal feminist politics. *Choice and Consent* is unique in offering a sustained, critical analysis of key legal concepts. The international contributors bring different cultural persepectives as well as doctrinal and theoretical knowledge to the task.

Rosemary Hunter is Professor of Law at the Kent Law School at the University of Kent, United Kingdom.

Sharon Cowan is a lecturer in law at the School of Law at Edinburgh University, United Kingdom.

Choice and Consent

Feminist engagements with law and subjectivity

Edited by Rosemary Hunter and Sharon Cowan

Routledge
Taylor & Francis Group

LONDON AND NEW YORK

First published 2007
by Routledge-Cavendish
2 Park Square, Milton Park, Abingdon, Oxon OX14 4RN

Simultaneously published in the USA and Canada
by Routledge-Cavendish
270 Madison Avenue, New York, NY 10016

A GlassHouse book

*Routledge-Cavendish is an imprint of the Taylor & Francis Group, an
informa business*

Transferred to Digital Printing 2009

© 2007 Hunter, R., Cowan, S.

Typeset in Sabon by
RefineCatch Limited, Bungay, Suffolk

British Library Cataloguing in Publication Data
A catalogue record for this book is available from the British Library

Library of Congress Cataloging in Publication Data
Choice and consent: feminist engagements with law and subjectivity /
Rosemary Hunter and Sharon Cowan, [eds.].—1st ed.
     p. cm.
   Includes bibliographical references.
   ISBN13: 978–1–904385–85–1
   ISBN10: 1–904385–85–0
   1. Women—Legal status, laws, etc. 2. Women's rights. I. Hunter,
   Rosemary. II. Cowan, Sharon.
   K644.C46 2007
   346.01′34—dc22
   2007022607

ISBN10: 1–904385–85–0 (hbk)
ISBN10: 0–415–57446–3 (pbk)
ISBN10: 0–203–93738–4 (ebk)

ISBN13: 978–1–904385–85–1 (hbk)
ISBN13: 978–0–415–57446–4 (pbk)
ISBN13: 978–0–203–93738–9 (ebk)

Contents

Introduction

Rosemary Hunter and Sharon Cowan

The concepts of 'choice' and 'consent' denote the activities of the autonomous, liberal (legal) subject and mark the boundary between public and private, and consequently are deeply gendered. As such, it is hardly surprising that feminists have grappled with these concepts and have disagreed about the extent to which they have the potential to empower or to disempower women. This book of essays presents new feminist engagements with the concepts and operations of 'choice' and 'consent'.

The essays in the first two parts of the book focus on philosophical and jurisprudential issues surrounding consent and subjectivity, while those in the third part of the book provide detailed analyses of how choice and consent operate in particular areas of law. This concern with issues of both theory and practice recognises that choice and consent cannot be considered in a vacuum. In operation, the ideals of consent are often undermined for reasons of expediency, or because of a lack of attention to inherent power imbalances. The theoretical exercise of refiguring consent is meaningless and futile without a rigorous engagement with the operation of consent in practice, as mediated by particular actors as well as by legal, political and medical discourses, amongst others.

Although any discussion of the role of consent in law must inevitably address the criminal law relating to rape, this is by no means the only area in which choice and consent operate as central legal and philosophical principles. Thus, the essays also discuss health care law, family law, constitutional law and civil procedure. The authors ground their arguments and illustrate their points by reference to a range of local legal contexts, including England and Wales, Scotland, Canada, South Africa and Australia. These contextualisations exemplify both particular deployments of choice and consent within specific national and sub-national legal and political agendas, and the overarching status of choice and consent as defining attributes of the sovereign, self-interested, masculine, liberal subject.

Four major themes run through the book, each of which connects back to the central problem that the feminine subject does not conform to this liberal norm, which at the very least complicates – and potentially renders impossible – her exercises of choice and consent. The first theme is simply that of inequality – of Woman in psychoanalysis and political theory (Drakopoulou, Boshoff, Du Toit, van Marle), of men and women in traditional understandings of sexuality (Du Toit, Cowan) and the family (Boshoff, Hunter), of rape victims in the court-room (Douglas, Du Toit), and of women making decisions about reproduction and care at the beginning of life (Calder) and at the end of it (Biggs). On the one hand, this observed inequality can give rise to calls for women to be accorded equal treatment, for their autonomous decision making to be respected as Biggs argues in her chapter, or for their views about sexual encounters to be given equal prominence in law, as Cowan and Douglas propose. On the other hand, Du Toit, Calder and Hunter illustrate in their chapters some of the deleterious consequences for women when the law treats them *as if* they were autonomous, sovereign, liberal individuals when in practice they are not, and argue that law must take into account structural inequalities found in the very process of the formation of the individual subject, as well as in the material circumstances of lived experience, which impact on the quality of choices, consents and refusals.

This dilemma of how to respond to the inequality of Woman and of women gives rise to the second and third themes running through the book. The victim/ agency debate refers to the limited options liberalism provides for female subjects. Either they are conceived of as irrational, vulnerable victims and hence incapable of consent (or of non-consent as Du Toit shows in the con-text of South African rape law), or they can claim the status of atomistic, masculine subjects and are thereby, in the neo-liberal state, compelled to take full responsibility for the consequences of their private 'choices'. While Biggs makes an argument for women's agency in relation to end-of-life decision mak-ing, Boshoff, Du Toit and van Marle seek to deconstruct the victim/agency dichotomy by asserting that all subjects are unstable, contingent and intersub-jectively constructed rather than bounded, monolithic, sovereign agents. Hunter takes a different approach to critiquing the victim/agency dichotomy by posit-ing consent as divisible, so that rather than the subject being judged according to whether or not she can exercise consent, particular instances of consent may be judged according to whether or not they enhance or diminish their subjects.

This leads on to the third theme, which is the need to contextualise acts of choice and consent, to attend to the interrelated nature of choices and the context of gendered social relations in which so called choices are made. Choice and consent might be said to exist on a spectrum – from free and genuine agreement to pressure, coercion and force. As Cowan and Hunter argue, only by looking more closely at the context of choices can we see which choices reflect the genuine desires and wishes of those who have chosen. Calder also shows that attention to context necessarily includes consideration of the state's role in providing and supporting a range of meaningful choices, and the way in which economic and social conditions and constraints overlap, and together influence the choices women make.

The final theme of the book revolves around the question of whether the concepts of choice and consent can be rethought and infused with different meanings in a post-liberal feminist politics, as proposed by van Marle, Cowan and Hunter, or whether they should be decentred or completely replaced by something else, as Drakopoulou, Du Toit and Calder suggest. Is a feminist refiguring of consent possible? And if so, what would that refiguring involve? Can this question be answered in the abstract, or are different answers appropriate in different areas of law or different social contexts? More fundamentally, is this a choice that feminists ought to be making, or is a double gesture required? That is, as Boshoff contends, should we both acknowledge that it is necessary to conceptually undermine choice and consent as they are currently understood as liberal ideals, but at the same time explore how those concepts, as reinterpreted through a feminist lens, can offer 'occasions for respect' and perhaps even address wider issues of gendered power imbalances?

The book begins by historicising the concept of consent and its place within feminist discourse. In her introductory chapter, Maria Drakopoulou examines how consent became inextricably associated with notions of subjectivity and power, and how this association has been carried forward in feminist political theory and philosophy, and in feminist legal scholarship. She argues, however, that feminist inquiries into consent have tended to ignore the 'darker' side of consent, its association not just with freedom, but with subjection to the social order and the production of self-watching, governable subjects. In light of this, feminist scholarship could usefully challenge the processes of subjectification and threats to freedom represented by the concept of consent.

The book then moves to contemporary theorisations of choice and consent, beginning with chapters by Anél Boshoff and Louise du Toit, which both take a psychoanalytic approach to the issue of female subjectivity and the capacity for consent. Boshoff reviews the various possible consequences for women of the rejection of the Cartesian view of the subject, as put forward by Lacan, Irigaray, Kristeva, Butler and Derrida. She concludes that feminists should boldly reject the historically masculine version of subjectivity, and cautiously reformulate an ethical alternative, which would be capable of incorporating women as subjects and participants. Du Toit deals more specifically with the way in which rape law both assumes and undermines women's sexual subjectivity, by inquiring as to the presence of her consent while at the same time failing to allow her to become a consenting subject. Following Drucilla Cornell, she argues that the harm of rape is this very denial of the (woman) victim's individual subjectivity, both in the act itself and again in the courtroom. Thus, the role of law should be to protect the minimum conditions for each person's individuation and freedom to be a subject who can give or withhold consent.

In the following chapter, Karin van Marle turns to the relations between consent and politics, and argues for a rethinking and opening up of the concept of consent, so that it involves not just agreement to already established terms but real possibilities for dissent, refusal and difference. She explores the politics of friendship – as opposed to masculine sovereignty – as a possible framework for this enlarged notion of consent, drawing upon the work of Patchen Markell and Adriana Cavarero in particular. However, she also argues that Derrida's cautions about the tendency for friendship to collapse into (exclusive) fraternity need to be heeded by feminist scholars.

In the final chapter of the second part of the book, Sharon Cowan undertakes a jurisprudential analysis of consent in rape law, focusing on debates as to whether the harm of rape should be defined and consent identified by reference to the mind or the body. Cowan draws upon the work of feminist scholars Nicola Lacey, Monica Cowart and Michelle Anderson to deconstruct the mind/body dichotomy and propose a reformulation of the law of consent that would pay attention to embodied autonomy and respect the bodily and affective aspects of sexual intimacy.

The third part of the book opens with Heather Douglas's analysis of the role of the defence of mistake in Australian rape law. Douglas shows that even if a model of communicative consent is adopted to determine whether the alleged rape victim *in fact* consented, the defence of mistake shifts attention back solely to the subjective view of the perpetrator as to whether he honestly believed in her consent. Douglas illustrates this inexorable privileging of the perceptions of the perpetrator through two recent cases in the High Court of Australia, which followed the reasoning of the majority of the House of Lords in *DPP v Morgan*,[1] even despite legislative provisions that would have suggested a different result. This persistent deference to *Morgan*, she argues, will continue to frustrate efforts to reform rape law unless the defence of (honest even if wholly unreasonable) mistake is tackled directly.

Gillian Calder's chapter also concerns the frustration of law reform, in this case the unsuccessful efforts by Canadian feminists to reform the national maternity and parental leave benefits regime in order to enhance women's equality and improve their access to this important form of support for reproduction. Calder demonstrates how the rhetoric of 'choice' has continually thwarted efforts to improve the regime, and recently came close to destroying it altogether, by casting women's decisions to bear and care for children as matters of personal, private choice, thereby obscuring both the economic, social and legal conditions under which those 'choices' are made, and the state's interest in social reproduction. She argues that in this context, choice needs to be radically decentred, in order to deprivatise the debate and focus on whether the benefits regime actually meets women's needs.

By contrast, Hazel Biggs' chapter deals with situations in which women attempt to make what they perceive to be personal, private choices to die, but are unable to follow through with those choices due to paternalistic intervention by the medical establishment and/or the state. Biggs notes that much of the case law in the United Kingdom concerning end-of-life decision making has

---

1 *DPP v Morgan* [1976] AC 182.

involved women, and suggests that medical professionals and public authorities may have particular difficulties in respecting women's autonomy in these circumstances, because they are perceived as possibly irrational or vulnerable to duress or coercion. Rather, Biggs argues, the problem may simply be that women exercise their autonomy in different ways from the expected masculine norm. However, this should not mean that their choices are any less valid or worthy of any less regard than those of men.

In the final chapter, Rosemary Hunter draws upon her empirical research into protection order and family law proceedings to explore the construction of consent in relation to another 'vulnerable' group of women – in this case, survivors of domestic violence. While civil proceedings such as those examined are premised on a high level of dispositions by consent rather than adjudication, the validity of women's consent in the context of legal proceedings in which the other party is their violent (former) partner must be in question. Drawing on an early piece by US feminist legal scholar Ann Scales, Hunter argues that rather than viewing survivors of violence as either victims (incapable of consent), or agents (whose apparent exercises of consent are taken at face value), instances of consent should be viewed either as 'occasions of oppression' or 'occasions of respect', depending on whether they perpetuate violence and abuse, or conversely, support the woman's safety and autonomy. Thus, legal reforms in these areas should be precisely directed towards maximising occasions of respect and minimising occasions of oppression in the making of consent orders.

In offering a sustained, critical analysis of key legal concepts from an international perspective, this book seeks to shed new light on some long-standing problems and dilemmas in feminist legal theory and praxis. Clearly, the issues of female subjectivity and the appropriate conditions for women's meaningful political and legal participation as choosing and consenting subjects cannot be foreclosed. However, it is hoped that the following chapters will advance feminist debate across a broad field and provide fresh approaches to questions of choice and consent where they arise in philosophy, politics and law.

Part I

Historicising choice and consent

Chapter 1

Feminism and consent: a genealogical inquiry

Maria Drakopoulou

CONSENT, POWER AND THE FEMALE SELF*

The sheer diversity of the feminist engagement with consent is testament not only to the fruitfulness and inventiveness of feminist scholarship, but perhaps most importantly to the protean nature of the concept itself. Consent moves beyond disciplinary boundaries and through diverse territories within each discipline, attaching itself both to conceptual apparatuses and their practical applications. Privileged in accounts of the legitimacy of government and in normative ones concerning political obligation and citizenship, it has been posited as a fundamental principle of democratic ideology and social organisation, whilst as a qualifying element for the legality of specific acts it has proven itself foundational to areas of both private and criminal law.

In pursuing consent across such a rich variety of sites and citations, feminists have produced an impressive body of critical scholarship animated by an apparent discord between, on the one hand, the abstraction of consent's theoretical postulation as a constitutive element of the political, ethical and legal order, and, on the other, its pragmatic application in concrete social contexts. These critiques can be broadly divided into two categories loosely distinguishable along disciplinary lines. Most of those oriented towards political theory, ethics and philosophy interrogate the relationship between the rhetoric of consent and the everyday experience of women's personal lives wherein consent holds pivotal practical importance. In contrast, those undertaken by feminist legal scholars tend to focus on the micro-politics of consent, exploring law's treatment of consent in specific contexts such as sexual violence, prostitution, the trafficking of women for the purpose of sexual exploitation, and the relationships

* I would like to express my heartfelt thanks to Rosemary Hunter for her continuous support during the writing of this paper, for the discussions we had, but most of all, for her friendship.

between spouses.[1] Yet despite exhibiting considerable variation these encounters share a common, unifying characteristic: they scrutinise consent in reference to liberal individualism's vision of humanity. This is not to suggest that feminists engaged with issues of consent are necessarily advocates of liberal theory; rather that their writings apprehend consent as articulating a normative commitment to liberal subjectivity, one which privileges a specific representation, both of the consenting subject and the act of consent itself. The former is apprehended from the point of view of qualities that adorn the liberal self: a sense of self ontologically prior to any form of society and predicated upon an atomistic, disembodied, rational agency. The latter becomes more than a mere act of assent. According to the liberal ethic its essence lies in both its voluntarily nature and inner rationality, it being the outcome of individual judgement stemming from the subject's freedom of will and independent choice to maximise self interest, welfare or pleasure, and being limited only by the negative effects it has upon the interests of others.

Within feminist discourse this conception of consent as a function of liberal subjectivity has profound consequences, for not only does it fashion the substance and form of the discourse, it also shapes its direction and the solutions proposed to any problems the use of the concept poses. For example, feminist re-readings of the idea that the social contract forms the basis for political association challenge contemporary representations of modern democratic society as a post-patriarchal social and political order. They contend that women neither consented to the original social contract nor to the sexual contract said to have preceded it and according to which they voluntarily subjected themselves to men. Here, the very evocation of the notion of social contract is seen to sustain a veneer of equality that masks real and continuing structural inequalities between the sexes and to thereby represent much of women's social misery as 'consensual'. Drawing mainly upon data concerning sexuality and women's experience of family life, feminists argue that the current normative paradigms under which existing social institutions operate disqualify female experience and effectively negate the possibility of genuine choice for women. In so doing these paradigms are seen to make a mockery of the notion of female freedom of consent and to repudiate the classical liberal view that these institutions were consensually born amongst equal, free, rational individuals (see Pateman, 1980, 1988, 1997; see also Clarke, 1979; Coole, 1986, 1994; Frazer and Lacey, 1993: 70–77).

Similarly, feminist legal scholars ground their critiques of consent on juxtapositions of women's social and legal realities. For example, judicial interpretations of the legal requirement of female consent in cases of annulment of arranged or forced marriages, and likewise those of 'sexually transmitted debt'

---

1   This list is by no means exhaustive. There is a substantial critical feminist literature on consent in the area of obligations. See, for example, the work of Dalton (1985: esp. 1106 ff) and the special issue of *Feminist Legal Studies* (8/1, 2000) on 'gendered readings of obligations'.

involving wives as sureties, are seen as sustaining and reinforcing representations of women as immature or inexperienced, and as either too dependent on men, or as their victims in need of protection (Cretney, 1992: 537; Kaye, 1997: 46–47; Lim, 1996: 204–11; Diduck and Kaganas, 2006: 40–41). Such representations, in constructing women as submissive or victimised, in short, as bereft of the 'blessings' of the liberal self, are said to devalue and undermine the capability of real women to exercise meaningful consent. However, for others the legal recognition of women's consensual capacity, as, for instance, in regard to prostitution or being trafficked for the purpose of sexual exploitation, is to be applauded. They see it as conferring upon women the power of agency and the status of rational and autonomous actor, and hence, as affirming women's possession of the self-same liberal subjectivity credited to men (Sullivan, 2003: 76–79; Sullivan, 2004: 136–38; Doezema, 1998, 2005). Still others argue that law's formal adherence to the concept of consent as the decisive criterion of the legality of an act ignores the pragmatic constraints that harsh reality places upon women's consensual freedom and exercise of rational choice. For them, judicial indifference to or disregard of what they see as clear expressions of women's non-consent, for instance in cases concerning sexual violence, or where courts are insensitive to emotional pressure in situations where a woman acts as surety for husband or partner, serve to sustain male power over women and erase women's possibility for agency, independent choice and self-determination (MacKinnon, 1989: 176–83; MacKinnon, 2005: 242–48; Fehlberg, 1994: 474–75; Fehlberg, 1996: 693–94; Naffine, 1994: 24–31; Duncan, 1995: 368–44; Richardson, 1996: 382–83; Auchmuty, 2002).

Furthermore, not only do feminist interrogations of the concept of consent rest within the limits of the liberal legacy: so too do the solutions they propose to the problems they reveal. Any hope for change is either invested in proposals for a transformative normative politics or is directed towards pragmatic policy interventions. The first either embraces feminist attempts to remodel consent though remaining within the context of the contractarian tradition, or seeks to decentre and replace it as an analytical category of female experience with other, more suitable liberal values.[2] The second aims to remove structural

---

2   Feminist contractarians believe that although the concept of consent evokes images of disembodied and self-interested subjects, if exercised with respect for women's autonomy, equality and freedom, it can be successfully employed in the context of women's personal relationships. See, for example, Okin (1989), Hampton (1993) and Jaggar (1993). For an overview, see Brennan (1999: 874–79). Of those arguing that consent should be replaced by another liberal value, MacKinnon (1982, 1983) favours self-determination, Nedelsky (1989) favours autonomy, and Nussbaum (1999: 29–32) dignity. A substantial feminist literature embracing 'relational feminism' or 'the care perspective' advocates abandoning consent and liberal individualism altogether, but does not directly engage with the concept of consent. For a discussion of the impact of the 'care perspective' in political theory and moral philosophy, see Benhabib (1987), Hekman (1995) and Sevenhuijsen (1998). For a discussion in relation to law, see Sevenhuijsen (1991) and Drakopoulou (2000).

barriers preventing the flourishing of women's freedom and autonomy and to give 'true' meaning to the notion of female consent (Pateman, 1980, 1989; MacKinnon, 1982, 1983; Vega, 1988).

This entanglement of consent with liberal individualism's notion of self has become so pervasive within feminism that not only has the ability to consent come to signify the presence of the liberal female self, but a belief in the truth of this signification has come to provide the criterion for the feminist judgement on consent. For critics of contractarian stories of origin, consent is found wanting because its connotation of the liberal self is identified as a fiction; those emphasising the contextual obstacles to women's consensual freedom label the requirement for consent as misleading, not because consent erroneously manifests this self, but because the real-life situations in which it is sought are seen to be so complex as to fundamentally disrupt the signification process; and both positive and negative attitudes towards the law's demand for consent depend upon the critic's faith in this process. Here, questions concerning the validity of the concept are largely conflated with those of female subjectivity. Yet this is not the result of a consensus within the feminist discourse with respect to liberal subjectivity. Rather, it is because the attachment of consent to the liberal self registers the existence and operation of another important parameter, namely that of power. Put simply, consent and female subjectivity are bound together by issues of power: the power men exercise over women, women's power over themselves and their own lives, and the belief in the need to further empower women. Endorsement or rejection of consent is therefore predicated not only upon how effectively it communicates women as autonomous, rational and responsible political, social and economic actors, but also the anticipation of what will best affirm real women's agency and mastery over themselves and strengthen their equal standing in private and public life. Similarly, the solutions, strategies and measures that feminist considerations of consent have to offer are designed to reduce and redress systemic power imbalances between the sexes, both as a whole and within the particularity of individual circumstances.

In reading questions of consent as questions of female subjectivity and power, this chapter is not seeking to offer yet another exposition of the problems consent presents for feminist analysis. Neither is the intention to add to the solutions already suggested. Instead it poses the feminist discourse on consent as the object of inquiry and engages with questions about its nature and form. In short, it asks what precipitated the present configuration of this discourse. More specifically, it explores the conditions that allowed the apprehension of consent to become bound up with ideas of liberal subjectivity and the way in which they became indivisible from notions of power. In so doing, however, it proffers neither an exhaustive historical account of the concept of consent nor a causative explanation for its attachment to the liberal subject. It presents a genealogical inquiry (see Foucault, 1977) into the relationship of consent and selfhood, one which, in exploring hitherto unsuspected affiliations and seemingly insignificant elements, maps out the historical 'moments' at which significant shifts occur in the apprehension of the relationship of consent and selfhood, and thereby reveals the singularity of events responsible for the way in which consent is employed within contemporary feminist scholarship.

To this purpose the following text is divided into three parts. The first considers the initial valorisation of the concept of consent in Roman law and Stoic philosophy in the constitution of a hermeneutics of human action; the second traces a shift in the meaning of consent wherein as a key element of a religious or civic subjectivity it became a necessary condition of the creation and legitimacy of the order of the social – a shift revealed in the texts of the radical reformers and natural law lawyers of the 16th and 17th centuries; and the third, secured by the historical footholds provided by the preceding two, accounts for consent's association with notions of power and offers an appraisal of the modern feminist discourse of consent, the affiliations and aspirations it bears, and a critical evaluation of the possibilities it promises.

CONSENT AND THE HERMENEUTICS OF HUMAN ACTION

Derived from the Latin verb *consentire*, meaning to share physically, emotionally or intellectually, the word 'consent' originally emphasised the inter-relational element present in all instances of compliance and communicated an act of voluntary agreement. It was this apprehension of consent as the objective, 'neutral' descriptor of mutual concurrence which marked its adoption and use during Greek and Roman antiquity, both in judicial and philosophical accounts of human action.

As early as the period of the Republic, in Roman law the presence of consent comprised the sole requirement for granting legal status to a number of everyday activities, ranging from marriage and the formation of partnerships, to hiring, purchasing and sales. For example, a distinct category of legally binding contract demanded no other condition or formality besides having been agreed, and was equally easily invalidated by consent to the contrary (Sohm, 1907: 374, 396–408; Schulz, 1951: 524–26; Buckland, 1957: 251–54, 277–78, 348).[3] Similarly, engagements and marriages, which were likened to consensual contracts by Gaius (*Digest* 20.1.4), were legally validated or dissolved simply by the informal declaration of consent from the interested parties (*Digest* 23.1.4, 23.2.2, 35.1.15).[4] Such legal privileging of consent stemmed from jurists' efforts

---

3   This category of consensual contract had no counterpart in Greek law, where the legal recognition of contract was premised upon its performance and not simply upon the presence of consent (Πανταζόπουλοφ, 1968: 61–62; Cohen, 2005: 298–99; Rupprecht, 2005: 335–37).

4   Of course, the requirement for consent did not necessarily mean that of the bride and groom. For example, in early Rome it was that of the *pater familias* (Treggiari, 1991: 16). For a discussion of the significance of consent in Roman marriage and cohabitation, see Reynolds

to project legal meaning onto conventional articulations of human volition bearing particular significance for the individuals directly involved and the wider community. Consent was therefore understood very much in a pragmatic way, functioning in law, as it did in common language, as a sign of agreement, with its juridical exercise connoting voluntary participation of parties in a specific action and their assent to its legal effects. Indeed, the overwhelmingly practical nature of this engagement is attested to by the absence of any definition in law as to what the term 'consent' actually meant. It was there to be objectively discovered in each instance and was a matter of fact rather than legal principle.[5]

Outside law the first major employment of consent as a key concept took place in schools of Hellenistic philosophy, most notably that of the Stoics.[6] Here, in contrast with other philosophers who identified reason alone as being in charge of purposive activity, the Stoics posited a cooperation of reason with 'assent' (συγκατάθεσις) (Long and Sedley, 1987: 40b, I, h3, k3, o).[7] They understood the process as involving two additional elements, 'presentation' and 'impulse', which together with 'assent' and 'reason' were considered to be powers of the soul inhabiting the heart and to operate in combination to generate human action.[8] The first of these, 'presentation', referred to the stimulus received, and, as the impression of the external world upon the soul, comprised the force providing the direct cause of action. However, in being mere impressions of the external world, presentations in themselves could not constitute objects of consent. It was only when transformed into language as words and concepts to be clarified and built upon through discursive thought to form

(1994: 22–30), Sohm (1907: 456–57) and Treggiari (1991: 146–47, 70–76). For a discussion of the coercion of consent, see Saller (1993). In Greek law, consent was also crucial to betrothal and marriage, but only the consent of the fathers of the bride and groom (Sealey, 1990: 25–26, 86–88; Cantarella, 2005: 246–47; Maffi, 2005: 254).

5 Similarly, notions of duress, fraud and mistake, although acknowledged as defences in consensual contracts, were never explained in terms of any theoretical understanding of what constituted consent (Gordley, 1992: 33).

6 It was in the teachings of Chrysippus in particular (circa 280 BC) that the concept of consent held a pivotal position (Inwood, 1987: 54; Kahn, 1988: 245; Sandbach, 1994: 121).

7 In this chapter I am using the concepts of consent and assent interchangeably. They both have a common etymological root, although consent seems to emphasise more an inter-relational element. However, later in the Middle Ages, consent as a concept was used in relation to the will, while assent was used in relation to the intellect (Aquinas, 1265–74/1970: Ia.2ae.15.3). A similar distinction is preserved in the *Oxford English Dictionary*.

8 The Stoics perceived the soul as having a material existence. It was thought to be a 'breath', a compound of air and constructive fire integrated throughout the body (including flesh, bones, sinew, etc) and to which it gave life, warmth, growth and maintenance. However, the soul was also believed to possess a commanding part (the *hegemonikon*), which was the seat of reason, assent, impulse, passion and sensation (Long and Sedley, 1987: 53h, k-m). For an exposition of the Stoic sources on the soul, see Long and Sedley (1987: 53); for a discussion of the Stoic concept of the soul, see Sandbach (1994: 82–85) and Long (1982).

and inform meaningful propositions that they ceased to provide more than a mere awareness in the subject. Only then did they enter the realm of human reason as rational propositions, become evaluated as objects of assent, and the impulse they generated be granted or refused (Long and Sedley, 1987: 33c, d; see also Inwood, 1987: 57–60). Whereas in animals the impulses were thought of as mechanical, instinctive responses to the impressions wrought by the environment, in humans they were seen as mediated by the mental act of assent, the rational approval of one's impression and the course of action it suggested.

As in law, the Stoic's 'isolation' and incorporation of consent was predicated upon its function as an objective descriptor, although here it did not indicate agreement between persons about the performance of specific acts. Instead, in being posited as the *locus* wherein the rationality of the action-guiding process was manifested, it connoted accord between reason and the voluntary execution of *any* act, a concurrence deemed necessary to all activities appropriate to achieving one's ends. Therefore, whether the context was legal or philosophical, the centrality of consent essentially depended on its instrumental value, with its 'discovery' dictated by the logic of an interpretative account, it being incidental to a legal or philosophical hermeneutics of human action. In being incorporated in this way, consent did more than signify acts as consensual; it also distinguished them from others and, in so doing, provided an analytical category of human action.

Within Roman law this analytic significance of consent lay in the separation and differential legal treatment of certain consensual acts, with justification for this distinction being found, not solely in the nature of the act, but also in its association with the nature of its subject. Specific acts were seen as 'natural' and peculiarly suited to humankind because their performance was either in accord with human physical characteristics or was associated with the rational ordering of their general interests and consequently necessary to humanity's common welfare. In being considered essentially natural, these acts produced self-evident obligations requiring no further explanation as to why they were actionable other than that they were expressions of the universality of the human condition.[9] Indeed, this connection is attested to by their being grounded upon nature's law, the law common to all living things, or resting within the jurisdiction of *ius gentium*, the law established by natural reason and applicable to all persons, not only the Roman citizens (*Digest* 1.1.1.3, 23.2.1, 1.1.9, 19.2.1, 18.1.1.2; Gaius, 1988: 33.154; Cicero, 1975: I.4.11–13). So in endowing commonplace, informal, real-life consensual activities with legal form, jurists did

---

9   In stating that these obligations were natural, the Romans did not consider them to derive from a natural or divine order which they thought superior to the *ius gentium*. For a discussion of the Roman conception of natural law and its relation to *ius gentium*, see Levy (1949). This distinction between natural obligations arising in the *ius gentium* and civil ones arising in civil law continued in the writings of the medieval jurists (Gordley, 1992: 41–45).

more than engage in a legal hermeneutics of action; they also embraced a hermeneutics of the self, for within the interpretative claims they articulated about human action there resided the truth of the acts themselves and, most importantly, that of the performing subject.

Unlike the jurist, for the Stoic philosopher the analytic significance of consent lay not in separating 'naturally' consensual acts from others: the very assertion that a moment of assent prefaced every voluntary action precluded such distinctions. Also unlike the jurist, the Stoic philosopher's adoption of assent provided no testament to the indisputable rationality of a particular act: assent always connoted agreement with reason and so demonstrated the rational quality of *all* human activity.[10] Yet despite the capacity to assent being the property of all humans, it was conditional upon age, natural aptitude and intelligence, with its lack, presence, or quality distinguishing the activities of animals from humans, adults from young children, and the intelligent from the simple (Long and Sedley, 1987: 41a).[11] Moreover, any 'decision' to grant or withhold assent, in being the actor's 'internal' response to the action suggested by the 'impulse', was within the person's control, being formed and informed by personal circumstances, nationality, profession, gender, social and familial status, as well as by individual habits, beliefs and education, and thus the expression of the actor's personality and character (Rist, 1969: 34; Long, 1991: 118; Long, 2000: 164–72). Assent was now transformed into a highly individualised measure of human activity, separating and selecting acts in accord with one's better judgement, reason, virtue or vice, while rejecting all others.

This apprehension of assent did not, however, signal a belief in the agent's liberal choice of action, as it has been suggested (see, e.g. Kahn, 1988: 244; Taylor, 1989: 137). Central to Stoic philosophy was the notion of fate, of Zeus's will, securing the certainty that accompanied the 'natural arrangement of all things', a providentially ordered plan according to which the world and everything in it followed a pre-ordained path (Long and Sedley, 1987: 20e, h, f, 38e, g, 54b, v, 55, 70g; see also Gould, 1974; Sandbach, 1994: 79–82). Hence, in addition to the capability for assent being determined by fate, fate also marked the life and experience of the agent and thereby directed and shaped assent's choice of action. That the agent could not help but act as s/he did negated neither the

---

10 The Stoics maintained a monistic theory of human activity according to which the process of generating voluntary action was always rational. In contrast, Aristotle and Plato acknowledged two distinct faculties, reason and the passions, both of which were instrumental in the production of activity. Conduct guided by the passions and sensual appetite and not by the intellect and deliberation, though voluntary, was considered to be irrational.

11 Children below 'the age of reason', those under seven years old (full acquisition did not take place until the age of 14), were said to lack the power of assent. Like animals, they could not help but yield to the power of presentations (Inwood, 1987: 72–75; Sandbach, 1994: 3). Similarly, a lack of education or ignorance was also thought to produce only a 'weak' assent (Annas, 1990: 187–88).

fact that it was s/he who acted nor the praiseworthy or shameful nature of this act; it did nothing to diminish ethical responsibility for the failure or success to act in agreement with one's own particular humanity. Although bound by divine will, assent's choice of acts marked the ethical quality of these acts, with the only freedom to assent being exercised in the responsibility to fulfil the potential of one's own nature, a freedom often defined as the 'freedom to obey God' (Seneca, 1932: 15.7; Diogenes Laertius, 1925: II.7.147).[12]

Operating at the intersection of cognition and moral life, assent therefore functioned both as an objective criterion of human conduct, distinguishing acts by assigning them to different developmental stages of life, and as a subjective one, authorising acts agreeable with the actor's natural and social potentials. In so postulating consent as a generic principle of human activity and in associating it with the individual's ethical and social *persona*, the Stoic philosopher, in a similar way to the jurist, engaged in an interpretative account of human action while at the same time articulating knowledge claims about the truth of the consenting subject. Here then, as in law, a hermeneutics of action was intimately linked to a hermeneutics of the self. For Roman lawyers and Stoic philosophers alike, knowledge of the truth of the self resided not in *a priori* posited ontological qualifications, but in the very acts the self performed. Only in the nature and quality of the assented acts, in the degree of maturity and wisdom they exhibited, could the universal, natural and concrete, singular humanity of the subject be laid bare.[13]

Thus was the appreciation of consent in antiquity, though anthropological in nature, not anthropocentric in focus. Neither the legal nor philosophical accounts of consent were driven by subjectivist concerns or claimed constituency to a metaphysics of the subject. No reference was made to a 'thinking thing', a unity of consciousness and self-consciousness, which, in being sole author of its own volitions, possessed freedom of will and moral autonomy; this would be the subject much post-Cartesian philosophy would come to cherish so highly. Instead, being validated as a qualifier of purposive conduct within a legal and philosophical hermeneutics of action, which was also espoused to a

12 This apprehension of freedom as obedience, which may be seen as prophetically announcing the coming of Christianity, is powerfully evidenced in Cleanthes' famous *Hymn to Zeus*. Cleanthes was a student of Chrysippus. The text of the *Hymn* may be found in Long and Sedley (1987: 54i).

13 This interpretation of the self through its acts was perhaps most clearly evidenced in Stoic admonitions to review one's own actions through a process of personal introspection, often represented as a form of inner dialogue functioning as a means of recollecting one's own acts and measuring them against what ought to be done so that a closer correlation between personal character and future purposive action would be secured. For examples of the process of thinking as an inner dialogue, see Epictetus (1928: 1.1.7, 2.1.4, 2.22.29, 4.6.34), Seneca (1995: iii.12.2–4, 26.3–5, 36) and Marcus Aurelius (1989: xii.18). For a further discussion of the Stoic conception of the inner dialogue, see Gill (1998: 56–60, 226–32), Inwood (1987: 81–85), Long (1991: 111–20) and Foucault (1993: 206–7).

hermeneutics of the self, consent was not only a necessary condition of the former, but it also became a constitutive part of the latter.

In the centuries to come, the apprehension of the relationship of consent and selfhood remained essentially unchanged, although St Augustine's 'invention' of the human will as an independent faculty of the mind modelled upon that of God tarnished consent's centrality in the process of the generation and ethical qualification of human action.[14] Not only was the will the sole 'mover' of all intellectual and practical activity, but because all activity lay within its power, it was also the *locus* of the actor's ethical responsibility.[15] Whether thought of as free to do as it wished, as aided by rational deliberation, or as irrevocably wounded by original sin, vulnerable to concupiscence, and thus in need of God's grace, it was in the nature and quality of the acts to which the will assented that the knowledge and truth of the self was to be sought (Augustine, 387–88/1964: I.xiii, xvi.117, II.i.5, II.xviii, III.ix, xx; Augustine, 427/1964: 4; Aquinas, 1265–74/1970: Ia.82.3–4, 83.4, Ia.IIae.15, Ia.IIae.77.3). Consensual acts were hence no longer differentiated into natural and juristic ones or into those whose performance may or may not fail to conform to the individual actor's 'fated' nature. They provided no testimony as to the humanity, personality or character of the performing subject, but instead, being bearers of its intentions, secret thoughts and innermost desires motivating its decision to act, were the marks of the presence or lack of a sinful will. Whether actually performed or just wished therefore, they needed to be deciphered; they must be closely examined and interrogated so that the disposition of the actor's will was established and the truth of the Christian self revealed. So within the voluntaristic tradition of the Middle Ages, consent, although continuing to partake in a process embracing explications of the 'mechanics' of human action and of the performing subject, now loses its 'autonomy' and resides in the shadow of the human will. Still communicating an act of agreement, it does so neither as an objective descriptor of the nature of an act nor as a power of the rational soul sharing equal standing with reason: it does so as a representation of the human will, with actions 'called voluntarily from the fact that we consent to them' (Aquinas, 1265–74/1970: Ia.IIae.15.4).

---

14 It has been argued very persuasively that a concept of will as a distinct faculty was unknown to ancient Greek philosophers and that it only emerged in the writings of St Augustine (Dihle, 1982: 20–67, 123; Kahn, 1988: 234–47). For a discussion of the concept of will in Hellenistic and Latin philosophy, see Gilbert (1963) and specifically in Augustine, see Dihle (1982: 123–44) and Spencer (1931: 473–76).

15 Of course there were different epistemological accounts of the role of the will in the attainment of knowledge, ranging from that of Augustine, who posited will as the source of all thought, to Aquinas, who accepted the Aristotelian cooperation of will and reason; although even for Aquinas, the will was the prime mover of all powers of the soul. For a discussion of the voluntaristic nature of Augustine's theory of knowledge, see Cushman (1950) and for the relationship of will and reason in Aquinas, see Gilson (2002: 236–48).

CONSENT AND THE DEONTOLOGY OF ORDER

The 16th and 17th centuries witnessed a radical shift in the way consent was apprehended. Although still associated with the faculty of will, consent ceased to be privileged solely as the mark of its disposition, and consensual acts became more than merely evidence of the soul's struggle to choose godly pursuits over earthly pleasures. Expanding beyond the interiority of the self to embrace the external world, consent became bound up with the subject's worldly being and took on a pivotal role in the constitution of any of the multiplicity of visions of social order offered by the times; those theocratic and salvational, as articulated in the teachings and experiments of the radical reformers, and secular ones of a moral and political nature advocated in the 'civil philosophies' of the modern natural law thinkers.[16] This is not to suggest that a socially oriented appreciation of consent had been entirely unknown during the Latin Middle Ages. It had been widely employed in medieval ecclesiology and the political theories of the scholastics, where in representing community will it had been closely associated with notions of secular and religious government. As either assemblies of the people or bodies of the faithful, communities had been seen to possess a corporate personhood, and hence to enjoy a common, singular will to enter into agreements binding upon each and every member.[17] Yet this form of consent had not been essential for the appointment of legitimate authority because existing hierarchical political arrangements, together with each person's place within them, were unquestionably accepted as divinely ordained. The community's granting of consent was of procedural significance only, simply affirming the natural necessity of rule, together with people's obligation of obedience and voluntary submission to a ruler whose legitimacy was already established; it was a result rather than cause of legitimate government[18] (Kern, 1948: 69–70; Ullman, 1975;

---

16 The term 'radical reformers' was used in opposition to 'magisterial reformers', notably Luther, Calvin and Zwingli, who, in seeking protection from the civil magistracy, acknowledged its authority. Although Anabaptists formed the core of the 'radical reformers', this so-called 'left wing' of the reformation was by no means homogenous. For a discussion of these groupings, see Troeltsch (1956: II.691–700), Williams and Mergal (1957: 20–35, 1962: xxiii–xxxi), Bainton (1963) and Baylor (1991: xi–xvii). For a discussion of the appeal of the radical reformation in England, see Daw (1917) and Troeltsch (1956: II.706–14). The term 'civil philosophies' is Hunter's (2001), describing the 17th century body of juristic and political thought, which employed a secularised concept of natural law and which attempted to desacralise ethics and politics. For a discussion, see Tuck (1987, 1993: xiv–xv), Hunter (2001: 63–65, 366–68) and Hochstrasser and Schröder (2003: ix–xvii).

17 The idea of society as a corporation was a medieval development of the Roman law concept of partnership (*societas*). For a discussion, see Tierney (1982: 19–28) and Maitland's 'Introduction' in Gierke (1938: xviii–xliii).

18 While legitimating reasons could be virtue and courage, the service of the common good, divine descent, sacral status, or blood lineage, the necessity of government was grounded in scripture or Roman law (Paul, Romans: 13.1; *Digest* 1.1.5, 8). A doctrine of popular sovereignty,

Gough, 1963: 41, 46–47; Tierney, 1982: 39–41; Oakley, 1983: 324). With its new incarnation however, consent was no longer to be perceived of in a corporate sense, nor was its social relevance realised in its facilitating a procedural step in the establishment of government. Instead, in embracing the life of every individual member of the community, it became central to what Taylor (1989: 13–14, 23) describes as the Protestant Reformation's 'affirmation of ordinary life'.

Reformation calls for a new way of living that revived the communal ways of the Apostolic Church, with its commitment to teaching and living the Gospel, rested on the belief that whoever answered the call entered into a covenant with God in the hope of becoming the 'elect' of His love and mercy; those for whom the promise of salvation and eternal life would be fulfilled.[19] Founded in Christ's suffering and death, this covenant, a sign of divine justice manifesting the will of a provident and omnipotent Lord, was central to all reformation theology, both magisterial and radical alike (Calvin, 1949: II. vi; Calvin, 1540–64/1958: Gen. 17.7, 25.33, Heb. 9.15, John 3.16, Mt. 10.6; Zwingli 1525/1981: 99–100).[20] For the magisterial reformers, since establishing a saving relationship with God was a matter of divine predestination and election, the offer of the covenant was neither grounded upon the dignity of human nature nor depended upon merits evidenced in the possession of unassailable faith or the practice of good works; it relied on God's grace alone. Consequently, its fulfilment required neither rational deliberation nor the presence of a free will on the part of the believer (Calvin, 1949: II.ii.10–13, III.ii.11–12; Calvin, 1540–64/1958: Dan. 9.4, Mal.1.1, Rom. 11.34, John 6.40; Zwingli 1525/1981: 118–137).[21] For

according to which legitimate government, whether secular or ecclesiastical, should be established by popular consent and could be withdrawn at will from an incorrigible ruler, emerged in the conciliar movement of the 14th and 15th centuries, and was developed in the writings of scholastics such as Bartolus of Saffoferato, John of Paris, William of Ockham, Nicolaus of Cusa, Marsiglio of Padua, Pierre d'Ailly and Jean Gerson. For a discussion, see Gierke (1938: 36–41), Kern (1948: 117–33), Watanabe (1972: 221–25), Oakley (1981: 791–800, 1983: 314–23) and Tierney (1982: 56–65).

19 For a discussion of the history of the theological concept of covenant, see Elazar (1996: 19–37).

20 With the exception of Luther, the magisterial reformers developed a fairly homogenous concept of covenant. Luther's doctrine of justification by faith alone, perhaps best evidenced in the severe soteriological limitations he placed on human conscience, was not congenial to the development of covenantal theology. For a discussion of Luther's concept of covenant, see Ozment (1969: 139–58) and for one of conscience, see Drakopoulou (2001: 354–56).

21 For the magisterial reformers, faith and the willingness to abide by the Word were not thought of as the causes of electing grace, but rather they were its merciful gifts, breathed into the Christian soul by the Holy Spirit. They signified the regenerate Christian's spiritual communion with the Holy Spirit and offered peace and assurance to the open, repentant heart, which, surrendering total control of everyday life to follow the Word, hoped to receive God's saving grace. The magisterial apprehension of faith was reflected in the Confession of Faith of Protestant Churches of France (1559, cited in Popkin, 1979: 9) and in the Westminster Confession of Faith (1646, Chapters VII and IX). For a comparison of the theologies of

the radical reformers, however, the covenant was a voluntary and mutually binding agreement according to which the faithful had to earn their place at His table by a total and free commitment of will to a complete regeneration of the Christian self (Müntzer, 1524, cited in Gritsch, 1989: 57–61; Denck, 1526/ 1957: 94, 96, 100–1; Hubmaier, 1527/1957: 124–32; Hut, 1520–27/1991: 162– 63; Hofmann, 1533, cited in Williams, 1962: 263, 285; Riedemann, 1545/1968: 146; Karlstadt and Grebel, cited in Pater, 1984: 152).[22] This could not be achieved purely with a spiritual preparation of one's soul to receive the Divine. Although faith was indispensable, this regeneration also required material rebirth through voluntary immersion in a novel form of social existence the 'truly converted' practised in communities the radical reformers established for this very purpose. The human side of the covenant thus involved a free and voluntary agreement to assume a strictly disciplined life, which, although lived on earth, partook of the heavenly fabric. Only here, in a society separated from the godless world and its degenerate established churches, its state, laws, courts and oaths, as well as its wars and violence, could the 'brethren' who broke bread together pursue a pure, honest life in full accord with His word (Sattler, 1527/1968; see Troeltsch, 1956: 694–99 and Clasen, 1972: 152–209).[23] Fulfilment of the covenant, and hence redemption of the Christian self, then depended not only on adherence to the prescriptions of an ethical and otherworldly salvational order, but also on actually enacting them within a congregation of equals that transcended the boundaries of the institutional Church.

Agreement to this double pledge demanded an act of verification that clearly and unambiguously communicated the individual believer's consent as being freely given. This act, likened to a 'signature' to the terms of the covenant, was the request and performance of baptism (Troeltsch, 1956: II.695–96; Williams and Mergal, 1957: 21; Hillerbrand, 1971: 73; Clasen, 1972: 95–106; Hostetler, 1974: 7–8; Baylor, 1991: xvii). However, the radical reformers, in seeing children as having neither the maturity nor will to understand the meaning and significance of the covenant and hence as being unable to consent to it either truly or freely, believed strongly that baptism should only be available to adults

---

Luther and Calvin, see Troeltsch (1956: 576–92) and for a discussion of the differences in the theologies of Luther, Calvin and Zwingli of their doctrines of predestination, election and Christian faith, see Locher (1981: 182–210).

22 Indeed, John Tauler, a German mystic of the 13th century whose views influenced many radical reformation leaders, saw the covenant as a business agreement; a 'fair bargain' with God (Ozment, 1969: 32). For a discussion of his influence on Thomas Müntzer, one of the most notorious radical reformers, see Friesen (1990: 6, 14–20, 48–50) and Gritsch (1989: 13).

23 Michael Sattler (circa 1490–1527), a leader of the Swiss and South German Anabaptism, was the main author of The Schleitheim Confession of Faith, the oldest creedal statement of the Anabaptists proclaimed in a conference of the Swiss Brethren (1527), in which the radical reformers' views on social life are clearly set out.

(Hut, 1520–27/1991: 161; Grebel, 1524/1991: 127–28; Manz, 1525/1991: 98–100; Sattler, 1527/1968: 131; Karlstadt, cited in Sider, 1974: 292–93). Adult baptism was thus vested with an importance far in excess of its conventional sacramental meaning, and the role of consent thereby ascribed unprecedented social value. Posited as the single, indispensable requirement for novices seeking membership of a covenantal society, it provided the foundation upon which such societies were constituted, and as such became firmly attached, not only to a vision of a spiritual life, but to a specific social reality. Whilst faith led the soul in the battle against the corruption and sinfulness of the fallen human nature, it was the free choice to comply with the norms and rules of the community which guided and strengthened the earthly battle against the flesh.

This close association of consent with social order was to prove to be more than a peculiarity of the mind of the Reformation. Perennating into the next century, it would capture the intellectual tradition of the civil philosophies of modern natural law theory, and thereby fortified and consolidated, would endure to the present day. This is not to suggest a direct lineage, with transmission of an unadulterated intellectual inheritance; rather, to emphasise that despite their apparent irreconcilable opposition, with the former offering blueprints of 'kingdoms of God on earth' and the latter reconfiguring designs of the secular, they nevertheless shared a common understanding and use of the concept. Both claimed the individual subject of consent to possess a will freed from its 'bondage' to sin and asserted its capability to choose good and useful acts without committing the sin of pride (Grotius, 1604/1950: 18–19; Hobbes, 1642/1998: II.I.8; Hobbes, 1889/1969: 12.3–8; Pufendorf, 1673/1991: I.9, 11).[24] Similarly, for both, the presence of consent represented more than a general freedom of will. It also marked the willing commitment of the subject to a specific order of being and signified the ascendancy of the artificial and social over the natural and free. Choosing the exclusive, highly organised mode of life practiced in the voluntary and self-selected communities that the radical reformers espoused was therefore neither a renunciation of temporal life in favour of a holy one of solitude and contemplation, nor the expression of a preference for one social form over another. Instead, the abandoned order was seen as mirroring the natural condition of fallen humanity, and, with the fundamental nature possessed by all Adam's descendants being corrupt, depraved and full of lust, the world inhabited by Christians bereft of divine similitude

---

24 Magisterial reformers believed that individuals possessing corrupted cognitive and volitional powers could not contribute to their own salvation because this would ascribe to the individual that which belonged to God. This led them to condemn any claims that charitable acts resulted from free will which were due to self-love and pride (Luther, 1525/1957; Zwingli, 1525/1981: 83–84, 95–96, 118–19, 271–78; Calvin 1536/1949: II.3.4). Such ideas permeated theological debates on the freedom of will, notably those between Pelagius and Augustine (5th century) and between Erasmus and Luther (16th century).

was simply a natural order of carnal servitude, darkness and sin (Hut, 1520–27/ 1991: 164, 166; Grebel, 1524/1991: 42; Sattler, 1527/1968: 132). Similarly, in those visions of order advocated by the civil philosophies, the choice to live in a community grounded upon the consent of its members was predicated upon the rejection of a life of absolute freedom in the state of nature (Grotius, 1604/ 1950: 9–11, 19–21; Hobbes, 1651/1991: XIII; Hobbes, 1642/1998: I; Pufendorf, 1673/1991: I.3). So whether imagined as a 'community of saints' or as a carefully delimited domain of profanity inhabited by secular selves, the social order being envisaged was constituted as a concatenation of individually articulated wills of equal standing; wills which, in voluntarily consenting to the terms of a founding covenant, pact or contract, breathed life into the consensual artifice.[25]

This demarcation between, on the one hand, a natural mode of being associated with a space prior to history and apart from society, and on the other, an artificial one contingent upon human volition and associated with the order of the social, gave rise to two distinct modes by which consent and its relation to selfhood was apprehended. As the representation of the will's elective capabilities and freedom of action, consent communicated intrinsic, essential properties of the ontologically defined self. Yet, although marking generic features of humanity, it was no longer valorised as central to a hermeneutics of action. Consent acquired meaning and significance as an articulation of the natural, base self, such that it provided testimony to the individuality of a will both unique and free to choose any possibility set before it. What drove individual consent to adopt a course of action was neither fate, an *a priori* recognition of the common good, nor obedience to divine commandments; for, whether the creation of an omnipotent and benevolent God, or 'self-begotten', as with Milton's rebel angels in *Paradise Lost*, this base self, always ontologically posited prior to the social, inhabited a natural state of anomie wherein it cared little as to the wicked or virtuous nature of the acts it performed. Here, equal among equals, it fashioned a solitary trail, guiding its actions towards the achievement of private ends dictated by its passions, desires or needs, and aided only by the precepts of nature that experience and the exercise of reason revealed (Hubmaier, 1527/1957:16–124; Hobbes 1651/1991: I.13; Hobbes, 1889/1969: I.14.1; Pufendorf 1672/1729: II.ii.3; Pufendorf, 1673/1991: II.1.3–8; Locke 1698/ 1989: II.ii.4–7).[26] Thus immune to ethical concerns and endowed with a strong subjective quality, consent was now posited as a natural and anthropocentric

---

25 For a discussion of parallels between the covenant and the social contract, see Oestreich (1982: 135–54).

26 The distinctive feature of modern natural law theory is that natural law is thought of as deriving from human rather than divine origin. For a discussion, see Hochstraser and Schröder (2003: ix–xvi) and Scattola (2003). For a discussion of the radical reformers' views on the possession of freedom of will and reason as an inward experience of the divine guiding life, see Jones (1914: xxii–xxxviii).

concept, one whose moral significance derived not from its abstraction as a representation of the ontological possibilities of human nature, but from its concrete, specific function as a means to some individual end freely chosen and pursued by the consenting subject.

In addition to this natural and anthropocentric apprehension, consent, remaining faithful to its etymological root, also communicated an act of voluntary agreement. As an objective descriptor of human action it was concerned with the effects rather than the function of the individual will; with the very meaning and significance of consensual acts. This normative understanding of consent and its subject could neither boast ontological primacy nor dwell in an anomic state because herein the actual performance of consensual acts would necessarily be found wanting. Given freely by the natural Christian self living in a fallen world seething with animal desires, consent could easily and unwittingly take the devil's path, whilst for inhabitants of a natural order in which unfettered wills chose as they pleased, it was prey to multifarious, often contradictory, passions and desires, and hence was of accidental and fleeting efficacy. So, although in the state of nature consensual acts remained a possibility, the lack of any will superior to that of the natural self rendered their security conditional upon the strength, cupidity, self-interest or self-love of all other agents living in natural equality with the performing subject (Hobbes, 1642/ 1998: II.11, 13, V.1; Hobbes, 1651/1991: I.15.71; Pufendorf, 1672/1729: II.ii.3, VII.i.4; Pufendorf, 1673/1991: I.1.11–12, I.3.4–5, II.1.9–10). Accordingly, since the social order alone possessed the means of ensuring respect for the performance of voluntary acts by directing, suspending or moderating the freedom of human will, this normative apprehension of consent could only be envisaged as an occurrence of the social. Consensual acts thereby acquired an unprecedented significance. They provided the key to the founding covenant, but also bore responsibility for forging the bonds between the Christian or civic self and the order of the social.

The imperatives authorising and justifying the creation of the social were predicated neither upon previously extant principles concerning the common good nor teleological injunctions about the natural or ethical condition of humanity. Whether that which moved the individual will to enter the original covenant was hope of salvation, the feebleness of human nature, or the desire for self-preservation, it was recognition of the necessity to transgress the state of nature that precipitated the need for the social, whilst it was the voluntary and free nature of the consent that provided its moral legitimacy. Therefore, the only social and ethical bonds the social could legitimately claim were of instrumental value, being aimed at the willing acceptance of and compliance with the moral entities the social artifice invented, namely, the nexus of public and private rights, duties and obligations, which, in functioning as 'bridles of natural liberty', directed the natural self's freedom of choice and action (Hobbes, 1651/1991: I.xiv; Hobbes, 1642/1998: II–III; Pufendorf, 1672/1729: I.vi; Pufendorf, 1673/1991: I.ii.I.2, 15; Selden, 1689/1927:

36–37).[27] Without such impositions neither self-restraint in regard to self-interest, self-control over one's own passions and desires, nor the cooperation or orderly conflict of individual wills could be achieved, and consequently, neither lawfulness and peace nor the justice of the social could be maintained.

Duties and obligations were fulfilled in the ordinary, everyday performance of voluntary acts, in the ready exercise of acts of obedience to one's superiors, and it was in the voluntary honouring of contracts, those private agreements forming the sole *locus* of the birth, renouncement or transference of rights, that the triumph of the social over the natural was nurtured and its moral legitimacy preserved. Hereafter, consensual acts bore no truth of the performing subject. Situated within a web of hierarchically structured positions, with each anchored in and identified with the performance of specific duties and obligations and the possession of corresponding rights, the artificial, socially created Christian or civic self, now found its truth as the bearer of the sum of rights and responsibilities assigned to the office it voluntarily assumed. Moulded by requirements of this 'office', whether that of preacher, faithful or regenerate, magistrate, master, father, husband or monarch, slave, mother, wife or daughter, the social individual was defined, evaluated and judged according to the mode, manner and degree to which s/he performed specific obligations, fulfilled particular duties and exercised rights whilst respecting those of others.

With the 17th century drawing to a close, the ancient and scholastic conceptual unity of an anthropological and a normative understanding of consent thus finally broke down. Unleashed from its past and no longer tied to a hermeneutics of action and of self, consent, newly bound to an ontology of the self and a deontology of order, would now linger unhindered into its future.

POSTSCRIPT, OR CONSENT AND THE *NOMOTECHNICS* OF THE SELF

No longer part of the 'great chain of being', that ontological scale upon which everything once had been carefully graded according to its degree of 'perfection', liberated from moral prescriptions of the medieval teleological universe, the subject of the anthropocentric understanding of consent became endowed with an unlimited, autonomous freedom 'to act in accordance with his own will' and thus to be 'subject not to another's will but to his own' (Lovejoy, 1936: 58–59; Huizinga, 1955: 46–55; Grotius, 1604/1950: 18). Freely exercising the will's elective capacity, individual agents could now initiate, decide upon or veto any course of action they wished; although as lone authors of these actions they bore moral responsibility for them as well (Grotius, 1625/1957: I.iii.viii; Hobbes, 1651/1991: XXI.108; Pufendorf, 1673/1991: I.i.10, I.7.5; Locke, 1698/

---

27 For a discussion of Selden's ideas of consent, contract and obligation, see Tuck (1979: 82–100).

1989: I.ii.7).[28] This requirement that individual consent be freely given also demanded an elective process untrammelled by 'alien elements'; for any influence, even the merest hint of coercion, would be seen as morally wrong because it wounded the agent's autonomy. Thus, despite being held common to all humanity, possessed by each individual in equal measure, consensual freedom, in embodying the right to exclude all other wills from one's own decision-making, also acquired a distinctly personal and private nature.

Whether God's benevolent gift to the first humans, a merciful offering to aid in the redemption of the fallen self, or an individual right inscribed in nature's laws, for radical reformers and civil philosophers alike this freedom of the will's choice was fundamental to their understanding of human nature.[29] As a 'natural freedom' it was akin to the exclusive ownership of property, such that each individual, as the sole and original source of this freedom, enjoyed the right to not only 'dispose' of it at will, but to legitimately prohibit external attempts to intervene in it (Grotius, 1604/1950: 18; Grotius, 1625/1957: I.2.1.5, I.17.2; Pufendorf, 1673/1991: I.12.3; Lilburne, 1646/1938; Lilburne, 1647/1964: 2–5; Locke, 1698/1989: II.V.27).[30] Although invariably extended to embrace the person and their life as a whole, this equation of natural freedom with property ownership (*dominium*) enunciated a novel understanding of the relationship between consent and selfhood, one clearly manifested in the practices of the radical reformers and explicitly theorised in 17th century thought (see Buckle, 1991: 35–52, 161–79; Tully, 1982: 95–124). Here, consenting subjects claimed total proprietorship of all they called their own (*suum*) alongside the right to prevent its possession by any other.[31] In so doing, they were not only possessive owners, as many have argued, but they were also vigilant and watchful owners, standing sentinel over the essential possessions recognised as theirs.[32] Where

28 Although there was a difference of opinion as to whether the freedom of will included the freedom to will, there was common agreement amongst radical reformers and natural law philosophers that a freedom of will to choose existed. For a discussion of this in relation to Scholastic and contractarian thought, see Riley (1982: 5–16). Perhaps the most controversial philosopher on this point was Hobbes. His writings include contradictory passages, some supporting, others negating the freedom of will. For a discussion of Hobbes's views on the will, see Damrosch (1979) and Riley (1982: 23–33).

29 Some radical reformers saw the freedom of will to be a divine gift given in the Creation, and as lost with the fall, only to be reinstated with the spilling of Christ's blood on the cross; others saw it as a permanent possession (Denck, 1526/1957: 91; Hubmaier, 1527/1957: 114; Pater, 1984: 128–31).

30 This understanding of property (*dominium*) as an exclusive form of private ownership dominated the writings of 17th century natural law theories. For a discussion of this point in relation to Grotius, see Tully (1982: 68–72).

31 Grotius' definition of the *suum* is 'A man's life is his own by nature (not indeed to destroy it but to preserve it) and so is his body, his limbs, his reputation, his Honour and his Action'.

32 For the description of what constitutes possessive individualism, see Macpherson (1962: 263–65). For a critique of Macpherson's understanding of possessive individualism, see Tully (1993: 71–95). For a feminist critique, see Pateman (2002).

freely given by the autonomous, natural self, consent served to ethically justify the 'creation' of the social. Yet the possessive self's concern to maintain proper respect for his or her material property and 'natural freedom' necessitated and sustained a voluntary acceptance of the socially instituted 'fountains' of authority. Safeguarding this possessive self's property thus fuelled the watchful self's right to judge the authority and the mode of government it had consented to and to respond accordingly. So the freedom to grant or withhold consent not only sanctioned the consenting subject's right to interrogate and critique the true nature of the acts of the sovereign authority, but, in light of the watchful owner's obligation of self-defence, it also explicitly granted a mandate to resist them whenever necessary.

Although specific attitudes to the Sword and baptism provided the main division between magisterial and radical reformers, questions of consent, government and resistance were centrally important to both.[33] Mainstream reformation leaders, those who believed that the power of the sword ordained by God and passed from Adam to his sons maintained the worldly order by punishing evil and protecting good, saw the essential duties of the Christian as revolving around obedience and non-resistance. True, many did cast doubt upon such duties and advocated the right to resist any government which ceased to enjoy its subjects' consent, but this was a right granted to magistrates in response to a tyrant Prince, rather than one belonging to every private person (Luther, 1523/1991: 4–10, 34–43; Calvin, 1536/1991: 50–56, 74, 78–82; Zwingli, 1523, cited in Stayer, 1976: 61–65; Mornay, 1579/1969: 146–56, 167–68, 180–97; Beza, 1574/1969: 101–10,131–35).[34] For the radical reformers, the faithful, in voluntarily espousing a separatist mode of life, neither participated in civil government nor asked for its justice, and therefore owed no such duty of obedience to the godless secular and religious leaders they labelled as violators of God's will and law. Consent to enter the polity of Christians and conduct their lives according to its norms, rules, practical values and principles, constituted an act of faith based on a conscious and free decision. It was also testimony to their individual power to act and choose without 'external' influences upon their preferred mode of life. So whenever their capacity to freely grant consent

---

33 'Sword' was a term that designated the worldly order. Luther supported a sharp distinction between the jurisdictions of temporal and spiritual government and defined the sword in the widest sense as embracing all secular authority and the laws, rights and offices associated with it (Luther, 1523/1991: 22–34). For a discussion of Luther's ideas, see Stayer (1976: 33–44). Calvin's ideas, initially very similar to Luther's, gradually fused the two into a theocratic model of government which he instituted in Geneva. For a discussion of Zwingli's ideas, see Stayer (1976: 49–69).

34 For a discussion of Calvinist theories of resistance, see Skinner (2000: 189–238) and Kingdon (1994: 193–218). Although I engage with Protestant theories of reformation, these issues were so widely debated that they were also pivotal in writings of the Catholic Counter Reformation. For a discussion, see Salmon (1994: 219–53).

was endangered, questioned or disputed, as private persons they had a right of resistance and self-defence. Hence did zealous consent to a regenerate life often acquire considerable political force, not simply inducing castigation and critique of worldly authorities, but precipitating acts of civil disobedience, active resistance or even revolutionary violence (Karlstadt, 1524/1991, and in Pater, 1984: 124, 145; Müntzer, 1524/1991: 27–32; Hubmaier, 1527/1991: 206; Anonymous, 1525/1991: 103–10, 118–24; Lilburne, 1645/1965: 261, 291; Lilburne, 1649/1964: 402–13; Overton, 1646/1976).[35] Couched in religious language and frequently interwoven with eschatological arguments and apocalyptic visions, the writings of radical reformers advocated 'grass-roots', egalitarian, often communistic, ways of life grounded upon the individual consent of the faithful, and cast a critical eye on the political and social institutions of the time. Provision of real-life alternatives gave this stance material hypostasis and, together with their writings, imbued considerations of consent with questions of power and truth. Celebrating the right of consenting subjects to question the nature and extent of political authority and existing practices, they asserted their individual power to resist and thereby provided the first locus of modern political critique.[36]

Over a century later, although proffered in a different language and different spirit, modern natural law theory once again placed consent at the heart of a critical discourse which also bound the consenting subject to notions of power and truth (see Foucault, 1996: 385–86). Civil philosophers, in emphasising the individuality and freedom of the will, were essentially seeking to construct a novel moral basis for political authority and obligation rather than challenge it (see Tully, 1993: 9–10; White, 1996: 11–26; Hunter, 2001: 150–51; Hunter and Saunders, 2002: 3–5).[37] Their efforts to construct models of unified and secular sovereignty inevitably engaged with the nature and origin of political power,

---

35 For a discussion of the views on the sword of the German Anabaptist leaders Hubmaier, Denck and Hut, see Stayer (1976: 133–66). The revolutionary action advocated by some German radical leaders led to the Peasants' War in Germany (1524–26), which was the largest popular revolt in Europe prior to the French Revolution.

36 Although it could be argued that such radical individualism was already evident in a particular strand of Christian thought, namely mystics and spiritualists, and reaching back into the Cistercian and Franciscan traditions, this emphasis on the individuality of will in relation to political and social questions is characteristic of radical reformation thought. For an example of blueprints of community, see Gaismair (1526/1991) and Hergot (1527/1991) and for a discussion of the Hutterite communities which advocated communal ownership of property, see Clasen (1972: 210–97) and Hostetler (1974: 5–59).

37 Hunter and Saunders (2002: 1–5) argue that modern natural law theory, what they call 'post-scholastic', as an intellectual reaction against Catholic scholasticism and its varied strands, comprised different strategies for justifying political authority. They identify as common themes permeating these strategies their juridical and political nature and their de-transcedentalism, i.e. the rejection of the metaphysical basis of civil law and political authority.

alongside issues of legitimacy, its reasonable limits and the corresponding rights of the subject. Although lacking the radical reformers' critical thrust, they still discussed and theorised widely on religious tolerance, the exercise of the right of conscience and resistance (Locke, 1675–79/1997: 230–35, 246–48, 267, 276; see also Laslett, 1989: 34–36, 79–93; Tuck, 1991: xviii–xxv; Tully, 1991: xvi–xxiv).

The bare, sovereign self, the atomistic individual so often postulated as ancestor to our modern liberal self, s/he who, in triumphantly entering upon the stage of history, captures it in a critical gaze, does, however, possess a darker, more sinister side. Posited as the only source of outward action, and in enabling autonomous agents to direct their own bodily movements and personal conduct, the natural self's freedom of will also shapes the empirical world they have chosen to live in and allows the possibility of voluntarily shying away from exercising this freedom. The original voluntary agreement that animated the social, its laws, norms and its system of punishments was, both for radical reformers and civil philosophers, an act of profound resignation; for it was not an act celebrating the consenting subject's natural freedom, but rather an act of its transgression. This freedom was exchanged for a Christian or civic liberty which bore the yoke of normative prescription; for even though the choice to abandon the natural was not imposed externally but resulted from self-reflective inquiry, the autonomous, possessive and watchful subject of consent had now to give way to a watched and, at the same time, self-watching subject (Pufendorf, 1672/1729: I.i.3–4; Locke, 1698/1989: II.vi.63). Whether envisaged as in thrall to the flesh, permanently at war with all others or as weak and incapable of safe existence, a realisation of the bare self's lack of resources of orderliness, self-help or self-protection led to a free choice of self-effacement. The watched and self-watching subject that rose in its place could henceforth only be the subject of the normative and juridical understanding of consent, never that of a natural and anthropocentric one. However, despite its contrasting so markedly with the free and *sui iuris* natural self, this social and disciplined subject was similarly located within a discourse on power, truth and subjectivity.

This discourse neither asserts possession of critical power, the right to question truth, nor criticises the imposition and exercise of sovereign power and its right to define what is to be true. Instead, it speaks of a true liberty whilst simultaneously exhorting obedience and advocating artificial chains, bonds, penalties and moral impositions, all of which it sees as emanating from the subject's consensual acts (Hobbes, 1642/1998: XIII.15–17; Hobbes, 1651/1991: XXI.108; Pufendorf, 1673/1991: I.2.5–8). Premised as the first and ultimate source of the power that is exercised in the social order, the subjects of consent become themselves the recipients of this power. Bound by their own consensual acts, without signs of indocility, they willingly abide within the limits of social liberty and come to govern their own conduct according to the prescribed normative requirements: those duties, obligations and rights attached to the 'social offices' they have freely accepted to occupy.[38] Here consensual acts, acquiring a life of their own, are transformed into little more than social practices of subjugation. They themselves are the embodiment of power, but a power without a face, a power which neither belongs to nor is exercised by subject or sovereign. Instead it is an evasive, insidious power, one which relies on its ability to affect conduct, and one which resides in the web of consensual acts that authorise, sustain and legitimise the social. It is a power that pervades the social body as veins do the corporeal, and a power whose effects bear upon all actions and interactions to produce the socially governed and self-governing self (see Foucault, 1982: 218–22).

It is my contention that the double apprehension of consent, as natural and anthropocentric and as normative and juridical, together with the discourses on power and truth it set in motion, announces both the concept's modern and feminist history; the feminist critic's location and interrogation of consent within a discourse on power, truth and subjectivity. It allows for the granting and withholding of consent to function as an axis of freedom and to empower critique, whilst also activating conditions of domination and self-subjugation.

Whether engaging with the employment of consent in theoretical discourses or with its function in social and legal practices, the feminist scholar, in associating the concept with the possession of liberal subjectivity so remindful of the natural bare self, is not just beguiled by the promise of its optimistic imaging. In predicating her critique or endorsement of the concept upon its ability to bestow essential, intrinsic qualities of the natural self upon the female subject, she seeks to appropriate for herself those possessions of freedom, agency and autonomy, and thereby assert her right as both possessive and watchful owner to question the truth of social and political discourses and judge social institutions and practices. For her, consent's seduction, therefore, lies not only in its enticing promise of the riches of the possessive self, but also in the critical power and right of resistance enjoyed by the watchful, owning self. However, amidst our efforts to claim possession of that which history and culture have for so many centuries denied us, we can lose sight of the possessive and watchful self's 'other' side, the watched and self-watching governable self, the consenting subject of the social order. And in granting consent its mythical status as the fundamental guarantee of freedom within the social, we remain immune to its starker side, its function as a threat to our freedom.[39]

In concluding this brief genealogical inquiry into the concept of consent and its bearing upon feminist scholarship, I realise that I may have opened myself to

---

38 The predominance of contract as the basis of social relationships, especially marital relationships, is discussed in considerable detail in the thought of the times. For a feminist discussion of the concept of contract in marriage, see Shanley (1982).

39 For a discussion of consent's 'darker side' in the context of sexual violence, see Gotell (2007).

the criticism that I have covered too much ground in too little a space and consequently have omitted much. This may indeed be the case, yet I would still maintain the position that the radical shift I have identified in the meaning and understanding of consent which took place in the thought and practices of the 16th century radical reformers and 17th century civil philosophies, did indelibly mark its future, laying down the conditions that made possible the specific form and priorities of the modern feminist explorations of consent. This is neither to deny the concept's subsequent history in political theory and philosophy, for example the works of Rousseau, Kant and Hegel, nor to devalue significant feminist work on this area (see Hampton, 1991). It is rather to impress upon the reader my view that feminist inquiry, even when attempting alternative readings of consent, does so in order to claim possession of the natural and metaphysical self, which, whilst boasting ontological primacy and celebrating its freedom, autonomy and agency outside history and society, at the same time entrusts its possessions to the keep of the social. By emphasising this modern direction of feminist engagement with consent and as a way of bringing my argument to a close, I want to pose the question: Do we really need to centre our inquiry into consent on the natural self and the liberal subjectivity it promises? It might be that the problem is neither one of a lack of recognition of we women as free, autonomous agents, nor the disempowerment this is thought to precipitate. Maybe the problem is that female subjectivity is nothing more than the historical correlation of processes of subjectification built into our history, social technologies prescriptive of the 'laws' of the self, such as the structure of consensual acts associated with the normative understanding of consent. So perhaps the solution lies in our first being able to historically locate such 'nomotechnics' of the self, then attempting to change them.

BIBLIOGRAPHY

Annas, J., 'Stoic epistemology', in Everson, S., ed., *Epistemology*. Cambridge University Press, Cambridge 1990, pp.184–203.

Anonymous, 'To the assembly of the common peasantry', in Baylor, M., ed., *The Radical Reformation*. Cambridge University Press, Cambridge 1525/1991, pp.101–29.

Aquinas, T., *Summa Theologiae*. Blackfriars, London 1265–74/1970.

Auchmuty, R., 'Men behaving badly: an analysis of English undue influence cases', *Social and Legal Studies*, 11, 2002, pp.257–82.

Augustine, St, *On Free Choice of the Will*. Bobbs-Merril, Indianapolis 387–88/1964.

Augustine, St, 'Retractations', in *On Free Choice of the Will*. Bobbs-Merril, Indianapolis 427/1964.

Bainton, R.H., 'The left wing of the Reformation', in Bainton, R.H., ed., *Studies in the Reformation*. Hodder & Stoughton, London 1963, pp.119–29.

Baylor, M.G., *The Radical Reformation*. Cambridge University Press, Cambridge 1991.

Benhabib, S., 'The generalized and the concrete other: the Kohlberg-Gilligan controversy and feminist theory', in Benhabib, S. and Cornell, D., eds, *Feminism as Critique:*

Essays on the Politics of Gender in Late Capitalist Societies. Polity Press, Oxford 1987 pp.77–95.

Beza, T., 'Rights of magistrates', in Franklin, J.H., ed., *Constitutionalism and Resistance in the Sixteenth Century*. Pegasus, New York 1574/1969, pp.97–135.

Brennan, S., 'Recent work in feminist ethics', *Ethics*, *109*, 1999, pp.858–93.

Buckle, S., *Natural Law and Theory of Property: Grotius to Hume*. Clarendon Press, Oxford 1991.

Buckland, W.W., *A Manual of Roman Private Law*. Cambridge University Press, Cambridge 1957.

Cantarella, E., 'Gender, sexuality and law', in Gagarin, M. and Cohen, D., eds, *Cambridge Companion to Ancient Greek Law*. Cambridge University Press, Cambridge 2005, pp.236–53.

Calvin, J., *Institutes*. James Clark, London 1949.

Calvin, J., 'On civil government', in Höpfl, H., ed., *Luther and Calvin on Secular Authority*. Cambridge University Press, Cambridge 1536/1991, pp.47–86.

Calvin, J., *Commentaries*. SCM Press, New York 1540–64/1958.

Clark, L., 'Women and Locke: who owns the apples in the Garden of Eden?', in Clark, L. and Lange, L., eds, *The Sexism of Social and Political Thought*. University of Toronto Press, Toronto 1979, pp.16–40.

Clasen, C.P., *Anabaptism: A Social History 1525–1618*. Cornell University Press, Ithaca 1972.

Cicero, *De Officiis*. Harvard University Press, Loeb Classical Library, Cambridge MA 1975.

Cohen, E.E., 'Commercial law', in Gagarin, M. and Cohen, D., eds, *Cambridge Companion to Ancient Greek Law*. Cambridge University Press, Cambridge 2005, pp.290–302.

Coole, D., 'Rereading political theory from a woman's perspective', *Political Studies*, *34*, 1986, pp.129–48.

Coole, D., 'Women, gender and contract', in Boucher, D. and Kelly, P., eds, *The Social Contract from Hobbes to Rawls*. Routledge, London 1994, pp.191–210.

Cretney, S., 'The little woman and the big bad bank', *Law Quarterly Review*, *109*, 1992, pp.534–39.

Cushman, R.E., 'Faith and reason in the thought of St Augustine', *Church History*, *19*, 1950, pp.271–94.

Dalton, C., 'An essay in the deconstruction of contract doctrine', *Yale Law Journal*, *94*, 1985, pp.999–1114.

Damrosch, L., 'Hobbes as a Reformation theologian: implications of the free-will controversy', *Journal of the History of Ideas*, *40*, 1979, pp.339–52.

Daw, E.B., 'Love fayned and unfayned and the English Anabaptists', *Proceedings of the Modern Language Association*, *32*, 1917, pp.267–91.

Denck, J., 'Whether God is the cause of evil', in Williams, G.H. and Mergal, A., eds, *Spiritual and Anabaptist Writers: Documents Illustrative of the Radical Reformation*. The Westminster Press, Philadelphia 1957, pp.88–111.

Diduck, A. and Kaganas, F., *Family Law, Gender and the State*. Hart Publishing, Oxford 2006.

Digest in Scott, S.P., ed., *The Civil Law*. The Central Trust Co, Cincinnati 1973.

Dihle, A., *The Theory of Will in Classical Antiquity*. University of California Press, Berkeley 1982.

Dioegenes Laertius, *Lives of Eminent Philosophers*. Harvard University Press, Loeb Classical Library, Cambridge MA, 1925.

Doezema, J., 'Forced to choose: beyond the voluntary v forced prostitution dichotomy', in Kemadoo, K. and Doezema, J., eds, *Global Sex Workers: Rights, Resistance, and Redefinition*. Routledge, London 1998, pp.34–50.

Doezema, J., 'Now you see her, now you don't: sex workers at the UN Trafficking Protocol negotiations', *Social and Legal Studies*, 14, 2005, pp.61–89.

Drakopoulou, M., 'The ethic of care, female subjectivity and feminist legal scholarship', *Feminist Legal Studies*, 8, 2000, pp.196–226.

Drakopoulou, M., 'Equity, conscience and the art of judgement as *Ius Aequi et Boni*', *Law Text Culture*, 5, 2001, pp.345–75.

Duncan, S., 'Law's sexual discipline: visibility, violence and consent', *Journal of Law and Society*, 22, 1995, pp.326–52.

Epictetus, *Discourses*. Harvard University Press, Loeb Classical Library, Cambridge, MA 1928.

Elazar, D.J., *Covenant & Commonwealth*. Transaction Publishers, New Brunswick 1996.

Fehlberg, B., 'The husband, the bank, the wife and her signature', *Modern Law Review*, 57, 1994, pp.467–75.

Fehlberg, B., 'The husband, the bank, the wife and her signature – the sequel', *Modern Law Review*, 59, 1996, pp.675–94.

Foucault, M., 'What is critique?' in Schmidt, J., ed., *What is Enlightenment? Eighteenth Century Answers and Twentieth Century Questions*. University of California Press, Berkeley 1996, pp.382–98.

Foucault, M., 'About the beginning of the hermeneutics of the self: two lectures at Dartmouth', *Political Theory*, 21, 1993, pp.198–227.

Foucault, M., 'The subject and power', in Dreyfous, H. and Rabinow, P.M., eds, *Foucault: Beyond Structuralism and Hermeneutics*. Harvester, Hemel Hempstead 1982, pp.208–26.

Foucault, M., 'Nietzsche, genealogy and history', in Bouchard, D.F., ed., *Language, Counter-Memory, Practice*. Cornell University Press, Ithaca 1980, pp.139–64.

Frazer, E. and Lacey, N., *The Politics of Community: A Feminist Critique of the Liberal-Communitarian Debate*. Harvester Wheatsheaf, Hemel Hempstead 1993.

Friesen, A., *Thomas Muentzer, a Destroyer of the Godless*. University of California Press, Berkeley 1990.

Gaius, *Institutes*, Gordon W.M. and Robinson, O.F. (trans). Duckworth, London 1988.

Gaismair, M., 'Territorial Constitution for Tyrol', in Baylor, M., ed., *The Radical Reformation*. Cambridge University Press, Cambridge 1526/1991, pp.254–60.

Gierke, O., *Theories of the Middle Age*. Cambridge University Press, Cambridge 1938.

Gilbert, N.W., 'The concept of will in early Latin philosophy', *Journal of the History of Philosophy*, 1, 1963, pp.17–35.

Gill, C., *Personality in Greek Epic, Tragedy, and Philosophy*. Clarendon Press, Oxford 1998.

Gilson, E., *The Christian Philosophy of St Thomas Aquinas*. University of Notre Dame Press, Notre Dame 2002.

Gordley, J., *The Philosophical Origins of Modern Contract Doctrine*. Clarendon Press, Oxford 1992.

Gottel, L., 'Risky women and Canadian sexual assaults law', paper presented at the Annual Meeting of the Law and Society Association, Berlin, July 2007.

Gough, J.W., *The Social Contract*. Clarendon Press, Oxford 1963.

Gould, J.B., 'The Stoic concept of fate', *Journal of the History of Ideas*, 35, 1974, pp.17–32.

Grebel, C., 'Letter to Thomas Müntzer', in Baylor, M., ed., *The Radical Reformation*. Cambridge University Press, Cambridge 1524/1991, pp.36–48.

Gritsch, E.W., *Thomas Müntzer: A Tragedy of Errors*. Fortress Press, Minneapolis 1989.

Grotius, H., *Commentary on the Law of Prize and Booty*, Williams, G. (trans). Clarendon Press, Oxford 1604/1950.

Grotius, H., *Prolegomena to the Law of the War and Peace*. Bobbs Merril, London 1625/1957.

Hampton, J., 'Two faces of contractarian thought', in Vallentyne, P., ed., *Contractarianism and Rational Choice*. Cambridge University Press, Cambridge 1991, pp.31–55.

Hampton, J., 'Feminist contractarianism', in Antony, L. and Witt, C., eds, *A Mind of One's Own: Feminist Essays on Reason and Objectivity*. Westview Press, Boulder 1993, pp.227–56.

Hekman, S.J., *Moral Voices, Moral Selves*. Polity Press, Oxford 1995.

Hergot, H., 'On the new transformation of the Christian life', in Baylor, M., ed., *The Radical Reformation*. Cambridge University Press, Cambridge 1527/1991, pp.210–25.

Hillerbrand, H.J., *Christendom Divided*. Hutchinson, London 1971.

Hostetler, J.A., *Hutterite Society*. Johns Hopkins University Press, Baltimore 1974.

Hobbes, T., *The Elements of Law Natural and Politic*. Frank Cass & Co, London 1889/1969.

Hobbes, T., *On the Citizen*, Tuck, R. and Silverthorne, M., eds Cambridge University Press, Cambridge 1642/1998.

Hobbes, T., *Leviathan*, Tuck, R., ed. Cambridge University Press, Cambridge 1651/1991.

Hochstrasser, T. and Schröder, P., *Early Modern Natural Law Theories*. Kluwer Academic Publications, Dordrecht 2003.

Hubmaier, B., 'On free will', in Williams, G.H. and Mergal, A., eds, *Spiritual and Anabaptist Writers: Documents Illustrative of the Radical Reformation*. The Westminster Press, Philadelphia 1527/1957, pp.114–35.

Hubmaier, B., 'On the Sword', in Baylor, M., ed., *The Radical Reformation*. Cambridge University Press, Cambridge 1527/1991, pp.181–209.

Huizinga, S., *The Waning of the Middle Ages*. Penguin, Harmondsworth 1955.

Hunter, I., *Rival Enlightenments*. Cambridge University Press, Cambridge 2001.

Hunter, I. and Saunders, D., *Natural Law and Civil Sovereignty*. Palgrave, London 2002.

Hut, H., 'On the mystery of baptism', in Baylor, M., ed., *The Radical Reformation*. Cambridge University Press, Cambridge 1520–27/1991, pp.152–71.

Inwood, B., *Ethics and Human Action in Early Stoicism*. Clarendon Press, Oxford 1987.

Jaggar, A., 'Taking consent seriously: feminist practical ethics and actual moral dialogue', in Winkler, E. and Coombs, J., eds, *Applied Ethics: A Reader*. Basil Blackwell, Cambridge 1993, pp.69–86.

Jones, R.M., *Spiritual Reformers in the 16th and 17th Centuries* Macmillan, London 1914.

Kahn, C.H., 'Discovering the will: from Aristotle to Augustine', in Dillon, J.M. and Long, A.A., eds, *The Question of 'Eclecticism': Studies in Later Greek Philosophy*. University of California Press, Berkeley 1988, pp.234–59.

Karlstadt, A., 'Whether one should proceed slowly', in Baylor, M., ed., *The Radical Reformation*. Cambridge University Press, Cambridge 1524/1991, pp.49–73.

Kaye, M., 'Equity's treatment of sexually transmitted debt', *Feminist Legal Studies*, 5, 1997, pp.35–55.

Kern, F., *Kingship and Law in the Middle Ages*. Basil Blackwell, Oxford 1948.

Kingdon, R.M., 'Calvinism and resistance theory 1550–1580', in Burns, J.H., ed., *The Cambridge History of Political Thought 1450–1700*. Cambridge University Press, Cambridge 1994, pp.193–218.

Laslett, P., 'Introduction', in Locke, J., *Two Treatises of Government*, Laslett, P., ed. Cambridge University Press, Cambridge 1698/1989, pp.3–123.

Levy, E., 'Natural law in Roman thought', *Studia et Documenta Historiae Iuris*, 15, 1949, pp.1–23.

Lilburne, J., 'Free-man's freedom vindicated', in Woodhouse, A., ed., *Puritanism and Liberty*. Dent, London 1646/1938, pp.317–18

Lilburne, J., 'The legal fundamental liberties of the people of England', in Haller, W. and Davies, G., eds, *The Levellers Tracts 1647–1653*. Peter Smith, Gloucester MA 1649/1964, pp.399–449.

Lilburne, J., 'The just defence of John Lilburne', in Haller, W. and Davies, G., eds, *The Levellers Tracts 1647–1653*. Peter Smith, Gloucester MA 1647/1964, pp.450–64.

Lilburne, J., 'England's birth-right justified', in Haller, W., ed., *Tracts on Liberty 1638–1647*. Octagon Books, New York 1645/1965, pp.258–307

Lim, H., 'Messages from a rarely visited island: duress and lack of consent in marriage', *Feminist Legal Studies*, 4, 1996, pp.195–220.

Locher, G.W., *Zwingli's Thought: New Perspectives*. E.J. Brill, Leiden 1981.

Locke, J., 'Man before and after the fall', in Goldie, M., ed., *Political Essays*. Cambridge University Press, Cambridge 1693/1997, pp.320–21.

Locke, J., *Two Treatises of Government*. Laslett, P., ed., Cambridge University Press, Cambridge 1698/1989.

Locke, J., 'Toleration, A, B, C, D', in Goldie, M., ed., *Political Essays*. Cambridge University Press, Cambridge 1675–1679/1997, pp.230–35, 246–48, 269, 276–77.

Locke, J., 'Essays on the Law of Nature', in Goldie, M., ed., *Political Essays*. Cambridge University Press, Cambridge 1663–64/1997 pp.79–133.

Long, A.A., *Problems of Stoicism*. Cambridge University Press, Cambridge 1971.

Long, A.A., 'Soul and body in Stoicism', *Phronesis*, 27, 1982, pp.34–57.

Long, A.A., 'Representation and the self in Stoicism', in Everson, S., ed., *Psychology*. Cambridge University Press, Cambridge 1991, pp.102–20.

Long, A.A., 'Greek ethics after Macintyre and the Stoic community of reason', in Long, A.A., ed., *Stoic Studies*. Cambridge University Press, Cambridge 2000, pp./156–78.

Long, A.A., and Sedley, D.N., *The Hellenistic Philosophers*. Cambridge University Press, Cambridge 1987.

Lovejoy, A.O., *The Great Chain of Being*. Harvard University Press, Cambridge MA 1936.

Luther, M., *The Bondage of the Will*, Parker, J.I. and Johnston, O.R., eds James Clarke & Co, London 1525/1957.

Luther, M., 'On secular authority', in Höpfl, H., ed., *Luther and Calvin on Secular Authority*. Cambridge University Press, Cambridge 1526/1991, pp.3–43.

MacIntyre, A., *A Short History of Ethics*. Routledge, London 1987.

MacKinnon, C., 'Feminism, marxism, method and the state: an agenda for theory', *Signs*, 7, 1982, pp.515–44.

MacKinnon, C., 'Feminism, Marxism, method and the state: toward feminist juris-prudence', *Signs*, 8, 1983, pp.635–58.

MacKinnon, C., *Toward a Feminist Theory of the State*. Harvard University Press, Cambridge MA 1989.

MacKinnon, C., *Women's Lives – Men's Laws*. The Belknap Press, Cambridge, MA 2005.

Macpherson, C., *The Political Theory of Possessive Individualism: Hobbes to Locke*. Oxford University Press, Oxford 1962.

Maffi, A., 'Family and property law', in Gagarin, M. and Cohen, D., eds, *Cambridge Companion to Ancient Greek Law*. Cambridge University Press, Cambridge 2005, pp.254–66.

Manz, F., 'Protest and defence', in Baylor, M.G., ed., *The Radical Reformation*. Cambridge University Press, Cambridge 1525/1991, pp.95–100.

Marcus Aurelius Antoninus, *Meditations*. Oxford University Press, Oxford 1989.

Mornay, P., 'Vindiciae contra tyrannos', in Franklin, J.H., ed., *Constitutionalism and Resistance in the Sixteenth Century*. Pegasus, New York 1579/1969, pp.141–99.

Müntzer, T., 'Sermon to princes', in Baylor, M., ed., *The Radical Reformation*. Cambridge University Press, Cambridge 1524/1991, pp.11–35.

Naffine, N., 'Possession: erotic love in rape', *Modern Law Review*, 57, 1994, pp.10–37.

Nedelsky, J., 'Reconceiving autonomy: sources, thoughts and possibilities', *Yale Journal of Law & Feminism*, 1, 1989, pp.7–36.

Nussbaum, M.C., *Sex and Social Justice*. Oxford University Press, Oxford 1999.

Oakley, F., 'Natural law, the Corpus Mysticum and consent in Conciliar thought from John of Paris to Mathias Ugonius', *Speculum*, 56, 1981, pp.786–810.

Oakley, F., 'Legitimation by consent: the question of medieval roots', *Viator*, 14, 1983, pp.303–35.

Okin, S.M., *Justice, Gender, and the Family*. Basic Books, New York 1989.

Oestreich, G., *Neostoicism and the Early Modern State*. Cambridge University Press, Cambridge 1982.

Overton, R., *An Arrow Against All Tyrants*. The Rota, Exeter 1646/1976.

Ozment, S.E., Exeter 1969, *Homo Spiritualis*. E.J. Brill, Leiden 1969.

Πανταξόπουλος, Ν.Ι., *Ρωμαϊκόν Δίκαιον εν Διαλεκτική Συναρτήσει προς το Ελληνικόν*. Αφοι Σάκκουλα, Θεσσαλονίκη 1968.

Pateman, C., 'Women and consent', *Political Theory*, 8, 1980, pp.149–68.

Pateman, C., *The Sexual Contract*. Polity Press, Cambridge 1988.

Pateman, C., 'Feminism and democracy', in *The Disorder of Women*. Polity Press, Cambridge 1989, pp.210–25.

Pateman, C., 'Beyond the sexual contract?', in Dench, G., ed., *Rewriting the Sexual Contract*. Institute of Community Studies, London 1997, pp.1–9.

Pateman, C., 'Self-ownership and property in person: democratization and a tale of two concepts', *The Journal of Political Philosophy*, 10, 2002, pp.20–53.

Pater, C.A., *Karlstadt as the Father of the Baptist Movements*. University of Toronto Press, Toronto 1984.

Pennock, R. and Chapman J.W., eds, *Coercion Nomos XIV: Yearbook of the American Society for Political and Legal Philosophy*. Aldine, Chicago 1972.

Popkin, R., *The History of Scepticism from Erasmus to Spinoza*. University of California Press, Berkeley 1979.

Pufendorf, S., *On the Law of Nature and Nations*. J. Walthoe et al., London 1672/1729.

Pufendorf, S., *On the Duty of Man and Citizen*, Tully, J., ed. Cambridge University Press, Cambridge 1673/1991.

Reynolds, P.L., *Marriage in the Western Church*. E.J. Brill, Leiden 1994.

Richardson, M., 'Protecting women who provide security for a husband's, partner's or child's debts: the value and limits of an economic perspective', *Legal Studies*, 13, 1996, pp.368–86.

Riedemannn, P., 'Account of our religion', in Hillerbrand, H.J., ed., *The Protestant Reformation*. Macmillan, London 1545/1968, pp.143–46.

Riley, P., *Will and Political Legitimacy*. Harvard University Press, Cambridge MA 1982.

Rist, J.M., *Stoic Philosophy*. Cambridge University Press, Cambridge 1969.

Rupprecht, H.A., 'Greek law in foreign surroundings: continuity and development', in Gagarin, M. and Cohen, D., eds, *Cambridge Companion to Ancient Greek Law*. Cambridge University Press, Cambridge 2005, pp.328–42.

Saller, R.P., 'The social dynamics of consent to marriage and sexual relations: the evidence of Roman comedy', in Laiou, A., ed., *Consent and Coercion to Sex and Marriage in Ancient and Medieval Societies*. Dumbarton Oaks Research Library Collection, Washington 1993.

Salmon, J.H., 'Catholic resistance theory, Ultramontanism, and the Royalist response, 1580–1620', in Burns J.H., ed., *The Cambridge History of Political Thought 1450–1700*. Cambridge University Press, Cambridge 1994, pp.219–53.

Sandbach, F.H., *The Stoics*. Duckworth, London 1994.

Sattler, M., 'The Schleitheim confession of faith', in Hillerbrand, H.J., ed., *The Protestant Reformation*. Macmillan, London 1527/1968, pp.129–36.

Scattola, M., 'Before and after natural law: models of natural law in ancient and modern times', in Hochstrasser, T. and Schröder, P., eds, *Early Modern Natural Law Theories*. Kluwer Academic Publications, Dordrecht 2003, pp.1–23.

Schulz, F., *Classical Roman Law*. Clarendon Press, Oxford 1951.

Sealey, R., *Women and Law in Classical Greece*. University of North Carolina Press, Chapel Hill 1990.

Selden, J., *Table-Talk of John Selden*. Quaritch, London 1689/1927.

Seneca, 'On the happy life', in *Moral Essays*. Harvard University Press, Loeb Classical Library, Cambridge MA 1932.

Seneca, 'On anger', in *Moral and Political Essays*, Cooper, J.M. and Procopé, J.F., eds Cambridge University Press, Cambridge 1995.

Sevenhuijsen, S., 'Justice, moral reasoning and the politics of child custody', in Meehan, W. and Sevenhuijsen, S., eds, *Equality Politics and Gender*. Sage, London 1991, pp.88–103.

Sevenhuijsen, S., *Citizenship and the Ethics of Care*. Routledge, London 1998.

Sider, R.J., *Andreas Bodenstein von Karlstadt*. E.J. Brill, Leiden 1974.

Shanley, M.L., 'Marriage contract and social contract in seventeenth century English political thought', in Elshtain, J.B., ed., *The Family in Political Thought*. Harvester, Brighton 1982, pp.80–95.

Skinner, Q., *The Foundations of Modern Political Thought 2*. Cambridge University Press, Cambridge 2000.

Sohm, R., *The Institutes*. Clarendon Press, Oxford 1907.

Spencer, W.W., 'St Augustine and the influence of religion in philosophy', *International Journal of Ethics*, 41, 1931, pp.461–79.

Stayer, J.M., *Anabaptists and the Sword*. Coronado Press, Lawrence 1976.

Sullivan, B., 'Trafficking in women, feminism and new international law', *International Feminist Journal of Politics*, 5, 2003, pp.67–91.

Sullivan, B., 'Prostitution and consent: beyond the liberal dichotomy of "free or forced" ', in Cowling, M. and Reynolds, P., eds, *Making Sense of Sexual Consent*. Ashgate, Aldershot 2004.

Syme, R., 'Dynastic marriages in the Roman aristocracy', *Diogenes*, 135, 1986 pp.1–10.

Taylor, C., *Sources of the Self: The Making of the Modern Identity*. Cambridge University Press, Cambridge 1989.

Tierney, B., *Religion, Law, and the Growth of Constitutional Thought 1150–1650*. Cambridge University Press, Cambridge 1982.

Treggiari, S., *Roman Marriage*. Clarendon Press, Oxford 1991.

Troeltsch, E., *The Social Teaching of the Christian Churches, vol II*. George Allen & Unwin Ltd, London 1956.

Tuck, R., *Natural Rights*. Cambridge University Press, Cambridge 1979.

Tuck, R., 'The "modern" school of natural law', in Pagden, A., ed., *The Languages of Political Theory in Early Modern Europe*. Cambridge University Press, Cambridge 1987, pp.99–122.

Tuck, R., 'Introduction' in Hobbes, T., *Leviathan*, Tuck, R., ed. Cambridge University Press, Cambridge 1651/1991.

Tuck, R., *Philosophy and Government 1572–1651*. Cambridge University Press, Cambridge 1993.

Tully, J., *A Discourse on Property: John Locke and his Adversaries*. Cambridge University Press, Cambridge 1982.

Tully, J., 'Introduction', in Pufendorf, S., *On the Duty of Man and Citizen*. Tully, J., ed. Cambridge University Press, Cambridge 1991 pp.xiv–xxxvi.

Tully, J., *An Approach to Political Philosophy: Locke in Contexts*. Cambridge University Press, Cambridge 1993.

Watanabe, M., 'Authority and consent in church government: Panormitanus, Aeneas Sylvius, Cusanus', *Journal of the History of Ideas*, 33, 1972, pp.217–36.

White, R.S., *Natural Law in English Renaissance Literature*. Cambridge University Press, Cambridge 1996.

Williams, G.H., *The Radical Reformation*. The Westminster Press, Philadelphia 1962.

Williams, G.H. and Mergal, A., *Spiritual and Anabaptist Writers: Documents Illustrative of the Radical Reformation*. The Westminster Press, Philadelphia 1957.

Ullmann, W., *Law and Politics in the Middle Ages*. The Sources of History Ltd, London 1975.

Vega, J., 'Coercion and consent: classical liberal concepts in texts on sexual violence', *International Journal of the Sociology of Law*, 16, 1988, pp.75–89.

Zwingli, U., *Commentary on True and False Religion*. The Labyrinth Press, Durham 1525/1981.

Part II

Theorising choice
and consent

Chapter 2

Woman as the subject of (family) law

Anél Boshoff

FAMILY LAW AND THE FEMALE SUBJECT

Family law, those rules defining and regulating the most intimate sphere of our lives, has traditionally occupied a unique and rather ambiguous position within the greater ideological system of the law. At least two aspects seemed to underlie our perception of family law. First, more than any other branch of the legal system, family law is perceived as belonging to the realm of the subjective, the personal and the concrete, somehow resisting the law's pull towards the objective, the principled and the abstract. It has an unruly character, emotional, irrational and mundane, but somehow dangerous. The second aspect, obviously related to the first, is family law's close connection with women or rather the female side of the gender dualism. Relating to the private sphere of the home and the family – the traditional domain of women – yet regulated by the legal rules of the state – men's territory – it is seen as perching uncomfortably on the two chairs of the public and the private.

In the past few years, South African family law has, in line with international developments, undergone a period of rapid and far-reaching change that seems to strike at the above basic assumptions that underlie marriage and family law. With the advent of South Africa's constitutional order, long-established gender inequality, at least in its formal guise, has been all but eradicated. The patriarchal powers once vested by the common law in the husband, his so-called 'marital power' over his property, his wife and his children, has been abolished in favour of a system of 'equal control'. According to the provisions of the Matrimonial Property Act, husband and wife now have identical powers over the administration of their joint estate and spouses must obtain each other's *mutual consent* for performing certain important juristic acts.[1] This results in both spouses having their capacity to act in the commercial world restricted. Likewise, the Guardianship Act[2] states that the sole guardianship that a father

---

1 Act 88 of 1984, sections 14 and 15.
2 Act 192 of 1993.

used to exercise over his intra-marital children (even after the court had awarded custody to the mother) is now shared equally with the mother. Both parents' consent is necessary for the child to enter into marriage, be adopted or for the alienation or encumbrance of the child's immovable property.[3]

In ruling upon the validity of same-sex marriages, the Supreme Court of Appeal in South Africa has recently stated that, but for one small technical exception, it is no longer necessary to be able to even distinguish between the 'husband' and the 'wife' when applying the rules of our matrimonial law.[4] The words 'husband' and 'wife' as they appear in the Marriage Act can, without any serious legal consequences, simply be replaced by the word 'spouse'.

Woman, now regarded as the gender-neutral 'spouse' and 'parent', rather than the gendered 'wife' and 'mother' of the past, seems to be successfully freed from the liberal notion of a sexualised dualism. The opposing male/female pair with its built-in hierarchical order, which favours the rational male side, no longer motivates the family law regime. With the effective integration of women into the formerly male-dominated system, there no longer seems to be a distinction between family law, as a 'soft/feminine/irrational' branch of the law, and the other 'hard/male/rational' areas of the law.[5] Women are free to give or withhold their consent, in the family as in the marketplace. They are equal 'subjects before the law', bearers of individual rights and the responsibilities of citizenship.

However, this buoyant view of women's 'emancipation' from inequality and their successful attainment of subjectivity, at least in the area of the family, needs to be problematised on at least two different but related levels. First, there is a serious question concerning the general concept of the free, autonomous and rational individual, the subject as a completely self-contained being. This image of subjectivity (formerly reserved for men, now extended to women), associated with the Enlightenment and the liberal political tradition, seems to be indispensable to the institutions and processes that justify the way modern social and political systems operate. To be a 'subject before the law', to be a participant in the legal debate and to freely give or withhold legal consent, we must be seen as subjects in this *politico-legal* sense of the word. Through the eyes of the law our interaction within the world can only be seen in terms of a consistent, self-identical and coherent entity called 'the subject'. Those theories

---

3   Sections 1(1) and 1(2).

4   *Fourie and Another v Minister of Home Affairs and Others* 2005 (3) SA 429 (SCA) *per* Judge of Appeal Farlam. According to the court the only common-law rule which makes it necessary to be able to identify the husband and which still forms part of our matrimonial law is the rule which provides that the proprietary consequences of a marriage are determined, where prospective spouses have different domiciles, by the law of the domicile of the husband at the time of marriage. All other rules apply equally to spouses.

5   Carrying the scheme further, there is also no need for the dichotomous view of the world whereby our affective lives are structured by the family and our productive lives by the market.

of equal personal choice and individual responsibility underlying our courts' jurisprudence on gender and the family are inextricably linked to a particular and (according to many) outdated sense of individual selfhood.

The fact that 'our', and maybe one can say women's in particular, experience of the legal system, the family, and their own role in it, does not correspond to the rosy picture painted by the courts and that our daily lives do not reflect the freedom and responsibility of choice, stem, I think, from this stunted perception of human and/or female subjectivity. The fiction of the *politico-legal* subject must be supplemented by the complexities of the *philosophical* subject: asking not only 'How does the world/the law see me?', but also 'How do I see/ know the world?' However, looking 'from the inside out', the subject appears more fragile than stable, more provisional than permanent. In a more complex construct of the subject the rational and the irrational are inextricably bound up with one another, and the idea of the fully conscious mind is threatened by the inevitable force of the unconscious.

This brings me to the second difficulty, namely that an emphasis on this more nuanced and more plausible view of subjectivity, which I termed *philosophical subjectivity*, one that corresponds better with our subjective experiences, may lead to women finding themselves again banished to the realm of the irrational, the subjective and the emotional – a (maybe in some areas privileged) place outside of the legal and symbolic order. The problem, in my view, is that women get caught within a kind of Manichean bind, where there are only two obvious options available: first, integrating themselves into the formerly Enlightenment or male-only territory of identity – an option that in the past has led to considerable political and social advances for women. Second, rejecting the simplistic and misleading notion of the free and autonomous Cartesian subject or *legal* subject, but facing the danger that women might remain, perpetually, on the borders of the existing system – philosophically undermining or deconstructing it, yet unable to initiate a political revolt against the disadvantages it might hold for them.

In this chapter I want to map out this second problem: what the consequences for subjectivity would be, should we reject the Cartesian view of the autonomous subject. I want to loosely structure the argument around two main groups of theories. On the one hand there are those who attempt to present a model of the nature of the individual subject, including a model on how subjectivity is formed. I shall use psychoanalysis, and particularly Lacan's version of structural linguistics, as a prime example of this approach – mainly because of the intense and diverse reaction his theory has produced among feminist writers. The second approach, what Mansfield terms an 'anti-subjective theory of the subject' (Mansfield, 2000: 8), is closely related to the work of Foucault. The basic tenet is that subjectivity is an illusion invented by dominant systems of social organisation in order to control and manage us. Subjectivity is not the way that we think about ourselves, but rather the way that we are *made* to think about ourselves; it is a historically contingent phenomenon.

In the concluding part of the chapter I turn to Derrida and consider the consequences for woman if dialogue (including legal dialogue) is no longer blocked by the gender hierarchy inherent in the Lacanian Law-of-the-Father and subjectivity has successfully been dislocated. Does the deconstruction of male subjectivity create the possibility for women to be subjects before the law? The question is whether it is possible to speak about post-deconstructive subjectivity that would still maintain the possibility of consent/dissent without inevitably creating new essentialist categories?

THE LAW-OF-THE-FATHER

I chose the work of Jacques Lacan, and specifically his view of gendered subjectivity, as the basis for an analysis of the female subject within the family for two reasons: the first is that Lacan repeats the Freudian schema, albeit with major variations, whereby gender and the family supply the core imagery for the development of the subject. In Lacan, the drama of the creation of stable identities and structures is displaced from anatomy to language (no longer the biological penis as marker of authority, but the symbolic phallus as transcendental signifier), yet the subject is still primarily constructed according to family relations. The second reason for using Lacan as a starting place is the varied and far-reaching responses, especially from feminist theorists, that his work has educed. Lacanianism thus presents an opportunity for feminist theorising, even though the theories are almost exclusively built around critiques of Lacan. What becomes clear in this process, however, is that the gender inequality that women experience could not be viewed solely as a matter of restrictive social roles and limited political opportunities, nor is it simply legal and educational institutions that produce masculine-dominated gender power structures. Systematic gender domination can be detected at the very heart, the most basic level, of human interaction – a level that according to Lacan has language as its basis.

The first important aspect, especially with reference to our participation in the legal system, is Lacan's conclusion that the unconscious is structured as a language (see in general Lacan, 1979). In order to take up a place in the human world, to be a subject before the law, we must locate ourselves in the symbolic field of language. However, language, far from being a tool that the human subject can utilise and manipulate for his or her own purposes, is rather something which precedes our subjectivity; it is the always already established background to our emerging selves (in the light of this our courts replacing the traditional gendered terms of 'husband' and 'wife' with the neutral word 'spouse' is indeed significant). Mansfield explains that in this linguistic system, Lacan's symbolic order, 'things appear to make sense, hierarchies of meaning are established, and society functions in a tense but efficient manner' (2000: 45). The essence of the symbolic (and the legal system can be seen as a prime example of this) is the fiction that language makes sense, that *a la* Saussure, there is a signified for every signifier (Saussure, 1983). This has the further implication that our selfhood cannot be established in isolation, but is completely reliant on our relationship with the other – and the ground for the establishment of each relationship is language.[6] One can say that what the law *calls* us, would be what we become.

The question is how do we become part of this symbolic order that is the necessary condition for rational human interaction? Lacan's answer, as was the case with Freud, relies heavily, even exclusively, on gender relations and a rather dramatic gender inequality. For Lacan, subjectivity can only become stable by entering the *masculine* domain of the symbolic. The Name-of-the-Father (*le nom-de-père*), or the phallus as signifier of the father, has replaced the father's penis (as it appears in Freud's work) as the basis of all social law. However, despite this linguistic turn, identity, order, meaning, reason and truth are still firmly on the side of the masculine, as they were for Freud. The symbolic order remains a *phallocentric* order.

What then is the position of women in a system defined first and foremost in masculine terms? To give an answer, albeit an overly simplistic one for the moment, one has to look at Lacan's concept of the Real. It must be remembered that the subject, for Lacan as for Freud, is not the same as the biological entity we call the human being. Only upon the successful completion of a complicated and dangerous psychological process, the Oedipal stage, is subjectivity attained. This process, a delicate interplay between the biological body and the emerging subject, takes place in the shared autonomous field of language. The body, however, is not something that can simply be 'operated' by the subject, it is not the metaphorical 'ghost in the machine'; it rather represents the limit of that which can be reached by the symbolic system – a sort of 'inert outside that language cannot reach' (Mansfield, 2000: 44). If the symbolic is male, one can say that the Real, that which remains separate from language and hence unsignifiable, is female. Ragland-Sullivan explains: 'But beyond language qua *logos*, Lacan postulates a positivized negative – the Woman' (1991: 61). The law, the moral law, grounds itself through an always, already established radical foreclosure of Woman, or rather a foreclosure of the 'positive' symbolisation of Woman.

In examining some of the arguments for and against retaining Lacan's basic schema, I shall try to maintain, as far as possible and well-aware of the internal inconsistencies, the original split between those committed to a construction of the subject and those dismissing the project in its entirety.

---

6   In classical Roman-Dutch theory, which forms the basis of all South African private law, the subject is reliant on a subject-subject relationship: in other words, the subject only has a right to something if there is another subject against whom he can have the right.

IRIGARAY AND THE FEMALE IMAGINARY

The issues of feminine identity and sexuality in psychoanalytical theory, led Irigaray, a trained Lacanian analyst, to sever her alliance with the Lacanian movement. Her work, maybe more than that of any other feminist, represents the construction of an alternative female subjectivity, separate from the purely masculine determinants and descriptions above.

Irigaray claims, quite correctly, I think, that feminine sexuality has never been theorised on its own terms. The most glaring and well-known example is Freud who, even when the evidence before him involved female patients, translated their experiences onto a masculine template. Female sexuality was seen as a (faint) echo or an inferior version of masculine sexuality. Irigaray writes:

> Woman and her pleasure are not mentioned in this conception of the sexual relationship. Her fate is one of 'lack', 'atrophy' (of her genitals), and 'penis envy', since the penis is the only recognized sex organ of any worth.
>
> (Irigaray, 1980: 99)

The significance of this subordination of female sexuality that saturates Western culture goes far beyond sexual practices – it permeates the very essence of our philosophical reflection and political practices (including that of the law). Masculine culture, with its orthodoxy that idealises formal structural qualities above all others,[7] seeks unity, stability, consistency and completion as its highest values. These values are in stark contrast to what she calls 'feminine culture' where things may have a dynamically changing or inconsistent identity, even have contradiction as their very essence – an idea that Irigaray describes as monstrous and abominable to a phallomorphic culture.

Irigaray's critique is not only directed at Freud's emphasis on the anatomy of the male genitals, but also targets Lacan's perception of language. In her early essay, 'This sex which is not one', Irigaray states that locating the essence of language in an obsession about 'the proper name, [and] the literal meaning', as Lacan does, has nothing to do with the necessary reality of language itself, but rather provides insight into a peculiarly masculine anxiety about the phallus and its privileges (1980: 102).

Irigaray's aspiration of establishing an alternative construction of the subject leads her to the definition of a 'female imaginary'. Following Freud's example, she structures the subject around the genitals, except this time it is the female genitals instead of the penis. The male obsession with unity, totality and purpose (flowing from the visibility of the penis) is provided with an alternative,

---

7   The symbolism of the phallic culture emphasises, according to Irigaray, the visual, or an aesthetic orthodoxy of stability and order. Female genitals represent 'the horror of having nothing to see' (1980: 101).

namely a female preoccupation with the plural and dynamic.[8] The implications of this shift in focus for cultural perceptions are profound. The traditional/male priority given to unity and consistency of meaning and identity in Western culture is replaced by a much more complex feminine culture built around an implicit difference from itself. In describing the typically feminine, she writes: ' "She" is indefinitely other in herself' (1980: 102). The strict dividing line between self and outside/other is blurred and the other is somehow included in the subject herself. This inclusion represents a challenge to autonomous identity, as we traditionally understand it, and leads to a process whereby difference is endlessly renewable. Likewise, feminine language represents a challenge to the idealised stabilities of the symbolic order. Feminine language, reflecting the difference implicit to female being, represents an internal difference and ambiguity. Irigaray writes:

> 'she' goes off in all directions . . . in which 'he' is unable to discern the coherence of any meaning. Contradictory words seem a little crazy to the logic of reason, and inaudible for him who listens with ready-made grids, a code prepared in advance.
>
> (Irigaray, 1980: 103)

> The alternative 'female imaginary' of Irigaray has often been criticised, usually because of its perceived essentialist nature. Although Irigaray denies postulating some naturally occurring essence of the female and insists on the open-endedness and fluidity of the feminine, the suspicion remains that gender identity and meaning have, like in Lacan, petrified into fixed and predictable categories.
>
> (Ragland-Sullivan, 1991: 54)

Even if these philosophical objections can be overlooked, it remains clear that the alternative (female) cultural values proposed by Irigaray are, at least at face value, irreconcilable with (male) values such as rationality, objectivity and certainty that currently underlie our modernist legal system. The 'pervasive maleness' of the law cannot be denied (Polan, 1982: 294). The political question of how to overcome this gender hegemony, at its very core, without abandoning itself to that which it seeks to criticise, remains largely unanswered by Irigaray. To use Adorno's phrase, how can we avoid the 'critique recoiling upon the critic' (Adorno, 1967: 34). Even so, Irigaray's bold utopian move created wholly new possibilities within the theoretical framework of psychoanalysis. Furthermore, the influence of such a framework, as we know from history, should not be underrated.

---

8   Because the female genitals are a variety of surfaces constantly in contact with each other, they cannot be reduced or compared to the straightforward and singular logic of the masculine (Mansfield, 2000: 71).

KRISTEVA AND THE SUBJECT-IN-PROCESS

Julia Kristeva, although she can also be classified as a post-Lacanian feminist theorist, reacted very differently from Irigaray to the atrophied patriarchy of Lacan's masculine symbolic order. Whereas Irigaray proposes to match the masculine transcendental signifier with a rival and equally powerful 'female imaginary', Kristeva suggests a much more ambiguous route of revolt. While remaining within Lacan's overall structure, she uses the weak, ambivalent and unresolved (one can even say 'dark') areas of his theory − where the unconscious 'by accident' breaks through in dreams, neurotic symptoms and slips of the tongue, to subvert and ultimately gain freedom from masculine dominance. After a brief synopsis of her thoughts on abjection, ambiguity and the subject-in-process, I shall turn to the implications this might have for female subjectivity in the realm of law and the family.

Both Freud and Lacan admitted that in order for the subject to reach a stable state, a state where there is a meaningful and predictable dividing line between the proper rational concerns of the social and the private remnants of our irrational unconscious, the subject must suffer some form of loss. In Lacan, a specific type of insatiable nostalgia called desire inevitably remains and is the price we must pay for repressing the unconscious and maintaining the stable model of the symbolic. Kristeva, however, suggests that this repression of the unconscious is never as complete as our psychoanalytical fathers would like us to believe. In *Powers of Horror: An Essay on Abjection* (1982), she refers to this incomplete repression as the 'process of abjection'. She explains that:

> [t]he 'unconscious' contents remain here *excluded* but in strange fashion: not radically enough for a secure differentiation between subject and object, and yet clearly enough for a defensive *position* to be established.
>
> (Kristeva, 1982: 7)

Far from experiencing our subjectivity as stable, knowable and ordered − safely barricaded from the unconscious − we, men and women, rather experience the unconscious material forever pressing in on and threatening the conscious, resulting in an intense feeling of ambivalence.

Kristeva directly links this hesitant experience of subjectivity to our equally hesitant experience of our individual bodies and our physical presence. The physical body can be seen as a reflection of the continuous drama of subjectivity and abjection. The fantasy of autonomous selfhood requires a strictly demarcated and unique individual body; a physical presence that would be a final validation of who we are, what Kristeva terms *le corps propre* (the clean and proper body) (Kristeva, 1982: 3). The problem is that the borders of our 'clean and proper body' are forever being perforated by our physical flows: sweat, urine, faeces, tears, vomit, blood (especially menstrual blood) (Mansfield, 2000: 83). That which flows from our bodies contaminates us, threatens the hygiene and firm borders of our physical presence, resulting in our own shame and disgust at what our bodies produce. In the process the 'defensive position' becomes all we have, the sum total of our subjectivity.

The meaning of abjection is, however, also entangled in the abstract and general sphere of truth and power. What is at stake here is not first and foremost the subject's relation to the body as such, but rather the 'clean and proper body' as an example of all systems of order, meaning, truth and law. Kristeva writes:

> It is thus not lack of cleanliness or health that causes abjection but what disturbs identity, system, order. What does not respect borders, positions, rules. The in-between, the ambiguous, the composite. The traitor, the liar, the criminal with a good conscience, the shameless rapist, the killer who claims he is a saviour.
>
> (Kristeva, 1982: 4)

Referring back to Lacan, Kristeva's conclusion is that the stability of both the symbolic and the dominant political order is dependent on our commitment to *le corps propre*. Abjection thus represents the internal ambiguity and uncertainty that logical systems must suppress or disguise. It represents a certain plurality that is always threatening to tear the system apart.

What is significant for the concerns of this chapter is that the political connection of abjection is specifically located within the gender politics of psychoanalysis. According to Kristeva the subject's entering into the stable realm of the masculine symbolic is never complete. The subject, in an endless struggle against his or her own inherent instability and plurality, remains fragile and vulnerable – s/he remains forever in-process. However, the two poles of this process, the stable symbolic order, on the one hand, and the indefiniteness of the abject impulse, on the other, are not gender neutral. Lacan made it clear that the symbolic is connected with the masculine and the patriarchal order. According to Kristeva, the abject, conversely, is inalienably connected with the feminine, especially the maternal. The masculine subject and the feminine abject in each person can, however, not be seen separately from each other. The longing to construct stable and limited laws and systems goes hand-in-hand with the longing to break them down – the latter is also a functionally indistinguishable part of the very operation of the symbolic order. According to Kristeva there is no commitment to masculine subjectivity without a simultaneous subversion of that subjectivity's wholeness and completion by an impulse to fragmentation, ambiguity and ambivalence that is connected with the maternal (1982: 6).

The question is whether Kristeva's gendered politics of abjection, framed as a continual struggle between the subject and the abject, can move women forward in a political quest for identity. From a feminist perspective she has been criticised for doing too little – from Irigaray's point of view Kristeva's understanding of the feminine as the subversive undershadow of the male symbolic order only frustrates attempts at constructing an autonomous female imaginary. Conversely, from Butler's point of view Kristeva is doing too much – Kristeva's effort at formulating a definition of the feminine merely denies the system's political manipulation of our so-called 'gender roles'. Kelly Oliver has condemned Kristeva's apparent reduction of the feminine to the maternal. According to Oliver this seems to be little different from the patriarchal understandings of the female 'role' that feminists have from the very outset fought against (1993: 48).

Yet for many women there seems to be, I think, a familiarity about what Kristeva describes; an intuition, if you like, that Kristeva's insights are 'closer to home' than the more utopian idea of Irigaray's 'female imaginary'. The strategy of subverting male subjectivity through its own weaknesses rather than confronting it with a radical alternative is to many women not completely foreign. We recognise the way in which the maternal *can* represent a certain sort of freedom from the burdening meaningfulness of formal symbolic and political orders. However, we recognise that at the heart of this freedom there is the horror and foreboding of the complete fragmentation and demise of these systems. We also experience that there is no conscious choice, as liberal politics would make us believe, between the subject (fully integrated into the symbolic order) and the abject. We do not experience them as discrete practical options and we never willingly choose either 'side'. Kristeva accepts the Lacanian insight that the impulse of the subject is always to accept the terms of the symbolic order, to 'obey the law' (just as our impulse is always to keep the body as 'clean and proper' as possible). Yet, as Mansfield describes it, this acceptance is always 'fringed around, harassed, sometimes even overwhelmed by the abjection which permanently accompanies it' (2000: 89). In the process it provides us with a kind of respite from the effort of 'being a subject'.

BUTLER AND THE (FEMALE) NON-SUBJECT

Judith Butler's radical Foucauldian critique of any formulation of 'female subjectivity', even a formulation as oblique and provisional as that of Kristeva, can be traced to Butler's inversion or rather deconstruction of the sex/gender distinction that underlies much of feminist theory. De Beauvoir famously claimed that there is no automatic relationship between the biological body with which you are born and the masculine or feminine cultural identity you attain – for instance that of 'mother' or 'father' (de Beauvoir, 1952: 35). The way our male or female bodies are interpreted and the roles and meanings ascribed to them are *politically and culturally determined* and not, as conservative family politics would have it, 'natural' consequences of our genitals, hormones and genes. In *Gender Trouble: Feminism and the Subversion of Identity* (1990), Butler argues that the situation may indeed be the opposite: the starting point is not biology, but culture. Whenever we start to theorise about nature, or our 'natural gendered bodies', we are already submersed within the cultural gender system within which we find ourselves. Nature and so-called 'natural categories', such as male and female, do not exist independent of and prior to the systems that theorise them.

What is more, this system, according to Butler, colonises every possible aspect of social life and, looking at our everyday lives, the 'tyranny' of gender over social behaviour can hardly be overstated. The insidious influence of 'gender' in the inscription of our very humanity is evident in the horror we experience at the use of the word 'it', rather than the conventional gendered 'he' or 'she'. The unease we have with the court's use of the gender-neutral word 'spouse', replacing 'husband' and 'wife' – the way that we feel that this does not represent the reality of our lives – would, according to Butler, be a symptom of the dominant system trapping us within its carefully maintained illusions.

Cultures, and we can include the law, require the division of gendered behaviour into two compulsory and clearly defined categories – masculine and feminine. Although these definitions are, in Butler's view, nothing more than political constructs, it is compulsory that they appear natural and inevitable – we must believe that they are 'true', and hence display a correct repetition of behaviours. The crucial point for me, however, is Butler's insight that although we are all subject to these deeply entrenched norms, we also cannot stop ourselves from violating them. It is impossible for the system to safeguard itself against our continuous (and often unplanned) resistance to and subversion of the norms of gender.

In order to establish whether psychoanalysis underlies or even supports a conservative and reactionary ideology or whether it is possible to build a progressive feminist politics on psychoanalytic grounds, one needs to look at the crucial issues of norms and normativity. Butler regards the symbolic structure as normative or regulative, because it implies a certain 'positive' law of what counts as kinship. For her, Lacan's notion of the symbolic is another word for normative, but in a way that remains hidden, thus qualifying as ideology, as Derrida says (Butler, 2000: 20).

However, from a different perspective one can say that Lacan's notion of the symbolic is not an authoritative system, but that it is radically empty. According to Sjöholm the very function of the symbolic in its most minimalist version is to stand for a prohibition *tout court*. This prohibition does not subjugate the subject, but rather constitutes a remedy for submission to authoritative systems. She argues that the symbolic does not prescribe norms, it is detached from normative content, but rather it limits the scope of any normative system. It is the enforcement of a gap between a normative order of values and codes, of practices and habits that we need to incorporate in our normal lives (the law), and the function of desire (which we then might call the ethical or justice).

The unintelligible limits of culture (or we can say the limit of the symbolic or of the law) are important, the fact that there is an outside or margin to culture/

law – that there is a point where it is foreclosed. There is a limit or impossibility in the structure of a subject, something that cannot be integrated into a symbolic order – an excess, in Derrida's terms. There is a part of the subject that would not be submitted to the normative order. On this point the argument is based on the (political) claim that normativity and ethics (or law and justice) can and should be separated.

On this point the argument comes very close to that of Derrida's necessary distinction between law and justice – and the positioning of woman on the side of justice; forever disrupting law's closure (Derrida, 1992: 15). In Lacan's reading this point of foreclosure would be death, incest, *jouissance*, feminine desire, and so forth (in other words, the Real). Derrida, of course, formulates differently. For him Woman and justice both play a role in the undoing of the law, deconstructing the Law-of-the-Father.

Sjöholm's reading of Lacan (as being compatible with Derrida) may, in my view, be overly optimistic. Lacan's system of foreclosure is more in the nature of what Lévi-Strauss would call founding cultural prohibitions (see in general Lévi-Strauss, 1969), firmly entrenching the patriarchal symbolic. It leaves no possibility for alternative or contingent prohibitions. Lacan himself was well aware of the 'subjective dead end' to which women have been condemned in a phallocentric system and in a patriarchal society. However, according to him, this was just the price to pay for civilisation. In 1951, commenting on the famous case of Dora, he insisted on the necessity for women to 'accept themselves as objects of man's desire', which leads to the painful necessity of abandoning any position as a subject (Marini, 1992: 80).

DECONSTRUCTING (AND RE-CONSTRUCTING) SUBJECTIVITY

Returning to the formal provisions of the South African family law regime, one can say that this is at present a system where gender-neutral 'spouses' grant each other consent to enter into legal transactions and where gender-neutral 'parents' consent to their children's juristic acts. However, this official or paper-law version of reality depends on two basic suppositions regarding subjectivity. The first is an acceptance of a stymied and unrealistic account of human self-hood as unitary, self-sufficient and transparent. The politico-legal subject, the bearer of individual rights, exercising free choice based on the rational promotion of his (or her) own interests is a superficial illusion that does not correspond to the way either men or women experience their being-in-the-world.

The psychoanalytical idea of the split subject – a self divided between the socially integrated processes of the conscious mind and the threatening and uncontrollable impulses of the unconscious – has irrevocably altered the way we think about ourselves and about the world. 'Legal subjects' are not free from the relentless inner struggle between the subject and the abject (in Kristeva's terms) and we experience our choice of either giving or withholding legal 'consent' as far less free and rational, far more driven by unconscious, irrational, dangerous and repressed desire, than the legal system can ever admit. Seen like this the version of family law that we now regard as 'outdated' – representing the dark and emotional pull of the private and the irrational – might be a more accurate representation of our true experience of the system and the world.

The second and related assumption is that in an effort to embrace gender neutrality, the category of male subjectivity, which has hitherto completely and exclusively occupied the landscape of the law, has now, unproblematically, opened up to also include the female subject. This process of becoming 'gender neutral' has also, surprisingly, not altered the basic tenets or fundamental structure of the legal subject. The unitary masculine principles that form the basis of the legal system – objectivity, order and stability – are now regarded as the neutral, inevitable and necessary parts of our, all of our, pragmatic human dealing with the material world. However, many feminists argue that masculine dominance of the system, far from being over and done with, is operating more effectively when concealed by a pseudo inclusiveness – when it simultaneously 'advances and generalises its priorities while concealing them' (Mansfield, 2000: 96).

If we reject the concept of the *politico-legal* subject and its core assumptions in favour of a more complex and I think more truthful account of the *philosophical* subject, a number of difficulties arise for theorists of female subjectivity. It is clear that the most influential modern constructs of the philosophical subject, loosely linked to Lacanian or post-Lacanian theories, take an emphatic line on the centrality of the masculine in the construction of subjectivity and, following from that, on the masculine dominance over the symbolic. Feminist theorists are faced with the alternative to either reject the entire idea of 'subjectivity' as an irredeemable male construct, irrevocably linked to an outdated metaphysical concept of the (male) one, or, alternatively, to accept the concept of the 'subject', but to deny that it is inevitably and exclusively linked to the masculine. For me both of these responses resonate with some aspect of our experience.

The more radical option of rejecting (or deconstructing) subjectivity, in line with the Foucauldian ideas of Butler, confirms our suspicions that women have been and are manipulated by an insidious ideological system (including the law), forcing us into preconceived gender roles. However, the utopian idea of gender-neutral androgynous 'spouses' and 'parents' does not fit our political, legal, emotional or intuitive experiences as 'wives' and 'mothers'. The nagging feeling remains that the 'multiplicity' would never be truly neutral and, even if it is, that we cannot and maybe also do not want to be truly neutral 'gendered' beings.

The other option, namely constructing an alternative and separate female subjectivity, is fraught with danger: either being too bold and doing too much (Irigaray) or being too tentative and doing too little (Kristeva). Staying within this debate, but slightly changing the angle, I want to conclude by referring to a conversation between Jacques Derrida and Jean-Luc Nancy on the possible 'reconstruction' of the subject. It seems to me that Derrida, whilst attempting to dislocate (male) subjectivity, still keeps open the possibility, albeit tentatively, of reconstructing the self 'differently'. The result is a mixture of *boldness* in the rejection of what he regards as ideological and unethical male dominance, and *caution* in reconstructing subjectivity, 'maintaining a kind of infinite vigilance or modesty that would always and at the same time denounce *any attempt at a new determination* of the subject' (Critchley, 1999: 73).

In a conversation with Jean-Luc Nancy, and in answer to the question: 'What, or rather who, is the subject?', Derrida makes the following remark:

> 'To be brief, I would say that it is in the relation to the "yes" or to the *Zusage* presupposed in every question that one must seek a new (post-deconstructive) determination of the responsibility of the "subject".'
>
> (Cadava et al, 1991: 105)

However, showing his discomfort with the word 'subject', he immediately goes on to say: '[I]t always seems to me to be more worthwhile, once this path has been laid down, to forget the word to some extent' (Cadava et al, 1991: 105). His uneasiness with reconstituting the category of subjectivity is shared by many theorists, including feminists, who believe that searching for a 'new concept' – one that would include women – is an essentialising gesture that reduces the aporetic status of woman and returns women to the dialectic logic of identity. It represents a trap whereby phallocentrism appears as feminism. Caputo asks:

> But, if there is a truth of woman, if woman is a proper, identifiable name, would that not constitute another violence, the violence of classification, categorization, constriction, and even caricature, of typing and stereotyping, the violence of an essentialism that binds?
>
> (Caputo, 1997: 142)

It is nonetheless clear that Derrida seeks a new determination of the subject. Still speaking to Nancy, he says:

> In order to recast, if not rigorously refound a discourse on the 'subject' . . . one has to go through the experience of a deconstruction. This deconstruction is neither negative nor nihilistic . . . A concept of responsibility comes at this price. We have not finished paying for it. I am talking about a responsibility that is not deaf to the injunctions of thinking. As you said one day, there is a duty in deconstruction. There has to be, if there is such a thing as duty. The subject, if subject there must be, is to come *after* this.
>
> (Cadava et al, 1991: 107–108)

Derrida provides us with a glimpse of the possible renewal of the 'subject' that seems to be consonant with a Levinasian responsibility to the other, 'an affirmative openness to the other prior to questioning' (Critchley, 1999: 71). Two aspects of this so-called *ethical* subjectivity deserve mention, albeit cursory. First: the ethical subject is an embodied being of flesh and blood – 'only a being that eats can be for the other' (Levinas, 1981: 74). Critchley explains that for Levinas:

> . . . ethics is *lived* in the sensibility of a corporeal obligation to the other. It is because the self is sensible, that is to say, vulnerable, passive, open to wounding, outrage and pain, but also open to the movement of the erotic, that it is capable or worthy of ethics.
>
> (Critchley, 1999: 64)

Second: the subjectivity of the subject is without identity, or rather, the identity of the subject is denied to consciousness, or to reflection, and is structured intersubjectively. This means that the subject can never be grasped essentially, in its being. Thus, the subject is never an instance of some general concept or genus of the human being: an ego, self-consciousness, or thinking thing (Critchley, 1999: 64).[9] The abstract and universal 'I' is reduced to 'me'. The subject is *me* and nobody else – myself as the one who undergoes the eternal demand of the other, who bears responsibility prior to my freedom (Critchley 1999: 66). Derrida speaks about a subject:

> . . . that would no longer include the figure of mastery of self, of adequation to self, center and origin of the world . . . but which would define the subject rather as the finite experience of non-identity to self, as the underivable interpellation inasmuch as it comes from the other, from the trace of the other.
>
> (Cadava et al, 1991: 103)

Seductive as Derrida's new account of subjectivity might be to women (and even to men), to speak about a *post*-deconstructive subjectivity remains highly problematic – as if deconstruction is a singular event with a distinct *before* and *after*. There is also the danger that woman's function (or burden) of displacing, or at least destabilising, essential masculine subjectivity, still casts her in the role of valued commodity. She is a useful 'lever' in dislocating the male subject (Rawlinson, 1997: 69), but men still philosophise through her, never allowing her to escape the bondage of metaphorical function (always providing the gap between the symbolic and the real in Sjöholm's words).

What is finally important, I think, is not to try and provide a definitive 'answer' to women's ability to give or withhold their consent, and, by implication, to define 'women's subjectivity'. What is important is that women

---

9   Taken from Dostoevsky (1972: 123).

continuously move between the perceived political need for stability and the intuitive desire for fluidity. This process should be characterised by the *bold* rejection of a historical, male-dominated version of human subjectivity and the *cautious* reformulation of an ethical alternative. In this way women will become and remain first-person participants, ethical *subjects* if you like, in this highly-charged and fragile debate.

BIBLIOGRAPHY

Adorno, T.W., *Prisms*, Weber, S. (trans). Neville Spearman, London 1967.

Butler, J., *Gender Trouble: Feminism and the Subversion of Identity*. Routledge, New York 1990.

Butler, J., *Antigone's Claim: Kinship Between Life and Death*. Columbia University Press, New York 2000.

Cadava, E., Connor, P. and Nancy, J.-L., eds, *Who Comes After the Subject?* Routledge, London 1991.

Caputo, J.D., 'Dreaming the innumerable', in Feder, E.K., Rawlingson, M.C. and Zakin, E., eds, *Derrida and Feminism: Recasting the Question of Woman*. Routledge, New York 1997, pp.141–60.

Cornell, D., 'Where love begins: sexual difference and the limit of the masculine symbolic', in Feder, E.K., Rawlingson, M.C. and Zakin, E., eds, *Derrida and Feminism: Recasting the Question of Woman*. Routledge, New York 1997, pp.161–206.

Critchley, S., *Ethics, Politics, Subjectivity*. Verso Press, London 1999.

Cronjé, D.S.P. and Heaton, J., *South African Family Law*. LexisNexis Butterworths, Durban 2004.

de Beauvoir, S., *The Second Sex*, Parshley, H.M. (trans). Bantam, New York 1952.

Derrida, J., 'The "mystical foundation of authority" ', in Cornell, D., Rosenfeld, M. and Carlson, D.G., eds, *Deconstruction and the Possibility of Justice*. Routledge, New York 1992, pp.3–67.

Dostoevsky, F., *Notes from Underground*. Penguin, Harmondsworth 1972.

Feder, E.K., Rawlingson, M.C. and Zakin, E., eds, *Derrida and Feminism: Recasting the Question of Woman*. Routledge, New York 1997.

Freud, S., *On Sexuality*, Strachey, J. (trans). Penguin, Harmondsworth 1977.

Irigaray, L., 'This sex which is not one', in Marks, E. and de Courtivron, I., eds, *New French Feminisms: An Anthology*. University of Massachussets Press, Amherst 1980.

Kristeva, J., *Powers of Horror: An Essay on Abjection*, Roudiez, L.S. (trans). Columbia University Press, New York 1982.

Lacan, J., *The Four Fundamental Concepts of Psychoanalysis*, Sheridan, A. (trans). Penguin, Harmondsworth 1979.

Lévi-Strauss, C., *The Elementary Structures of Kinship*. Beacon Press, Boston 1969.

Levinas, E., *Otherwise Than Being or Beyond Essence*, Lingis, A. (trans). Nijhoff, The Hague 1981.

Mansfield, N., *Subjectivity. Theories of the Self from Freud to Haraway*. New York University Press, New York 2000.

Marini, M., *Jacques Lacan. The French Context*, Tomiche, A. (trans). Rutgers University Press, New Jersey 1992.

Oliver, K. *Reading Kristeva: Unraveling the Double-Bind.* Indiana University Press, Bloomington 1993.

Polan, D., 'Towards a theory of law and patriarchy', in Kairys, D., ed., *The Politics of Law.* Pantheon, New York 1982, pp.294–303.

Ragland-Sullivan, E., 'The sexual masquerade: a Lacanian theory of sexual difference', in Ragland-Sullivan, E. and Bracher M. eds, *Lacan and the Subject of Language.* Routledge, New York 1991, pp.49–83.

Rawlinson, M.C., 'Levers, signature and secrets', in Feder, E.K., Rawlinson, M.C. and Zakin, E., eds, *Derrida and Feminism: Recasting the Question of Women.* Routledge, New York 1997, pp.69–86.

Saussure, F., *Course in General Linguistics*, Harris, R. (trans). Duckworth, London 1983.

Sjöholm, C., *The Antigone Complex: Ethics and the Invention of Feminine Desire.* Stanford University Press, Stanford 2004.

Chapter 3

The conditions of consent

Louise du Toit

INTRODUCTION

I argue in this chapter that the phenomenon of rape broadly understood (including the law against rape and professional responses to the rape victim) *simultaneously assumes and undermines women's sexual subjectivity* or self-hood.[1] More specifically: rape law provides a good example of how, within the late modern western symbolic, women are held accountable and responsible in ways that are irreconcilable with the extent to which their most basic (in the sense of fundamental, transcendental, or necessary) freedoms are undermined. The necessary conditions for women's 'consent' to sexual intercourse as required by the application and interpretation of current rape law are not in place. Women's sexual subjectivity is undermined and subverted in and by a rape-prone[2] society, the event of rape itself and by the law against rape, to such an extent that women typically cannot function fully on the level of giving or withholding meaningful consent. The meaningful consent assumed as possible by rape law is associated with the traditional liberal notions of free will, contractualism, free negotiation, formal equality, assertiveness, competitiveness, and so on, and as such presupposes the *freedoms of the subject*. I argue here that we cannot take subjective freedoms for granted, and therefore need to consider more closely the level of becoming a subject, or the *freedom to be a subject*, when we confront the problems at the heart of current rape law.

In the first section I defend my claim that current prevalent formulations and applications of the standard law against rape constitute a performative contradiction in that they both assume or require and at the same time undermine the

---

1 I use the terms 'subjectivity' and 'selfhood' interchangeably in this chapter.

2 I use the concept of 'rape-prone' society as coined by Peggy Reeves Sanday. She defined a 'rape-prone society as one in which the incidence of rape is reported by observers to be high, or rape is excused as a ceremonial expression of masculinity, or rape is an act by which men are allowed to punish or threaten women'. Conversely, she defined a 'rape-free society as one in which the act of rape is either infrequent of does not occur', and in which 'sexual aggression is socially disapproved and punished severely' (Sanday, 1996: 192).

liberal version of women's consent in the context of heterosexual intercourse.[3] I do this through a critical close reading and analysis of the law as a text. Through this analysis I demonstrate that the common liberal assumption of the subject or self as a pre-existent and complete entity in itself prior to social engagements (Diprose, 1994: 10), coupled with the current formulation of rape law, results in a systemic, ideological misunderstanding of the *nature* of rape and a concomitant distortion of the *harms* resulting from rape. The way in which the law frames rape leads to a pernicious trivialisation and eroticisation of rape. In the second section of the chapter I use Lacanian theory as appropriated by Drucilla Cornell to present an alternative view of the subject as fragile, temporal and intersubjectively constituted. This dynamic and intersubjective view of the self, I argue, helps us to understand the severity of the damages caused by rape, and it also shows how rape and rape law undermine the conditions for women's sexual subjectivity and thus consent. The third section of my chapter is devoted to showing that my argument thus far implies that the legal domain should concern itself with protection of the material, symbolic and other conditions necessary for the individuation of all humans in their own sexuate being, i.e., for the formation and maintenance of the kind of subject presupposed by that domain, namely a free and responsible sexual agent. I argue that a more just rape law will have to address the level of becoming-a-sexual-self and will thus require a radical rethinking of the current definitions and their applications.

RAPE LAW SIMULTANEOUSLY REQUIRES AND UNDERMINES 'CONSENT'

The term 'consent' plays a key role in the formulation and application of rape law as it currently stands[4] in many western countries. Of course, 'consent' is not only present in rape law – it features at various other places in the legal system – but my focus here will be on its role and function in rape law. My main claim is that a critical analysis of the function of 'consent' in rape law shows that *it presupposes what it undermines*, namely *women's full-blown sexual agency*, which means that rape law contains a performative paradox or contradiction, which works to the detriment of women. In order to explain the nature of this paradox, we need to look closely at the formulation of the law itself. The South African legal definition of rape[5] states that 'a man commits rape when he

---

3   Mainly for the sake of simplicity I focus in this chapter on 'male on female' rape.
4   South African rape law has for some years been under discussion and revision by the South African Law Reform Commission, and the Sexual Offences Amendment Bill 2003 was finally accepted in June 2007. This was too late for its ramifications to be fully incorporated into my discussion here.
5   Sexual Offences Act 23 of 1957.

engages in intercourse with a woman;[6] by force or threat of force; against her will and without her consent'. This formulation implies that rape is 'normal heterosexual intercourse' gone wrong, where normality may be equated with a one-sided sexual act initiated and carried out by a man, and which involves a woman's body. Note that 'a man engaging in intercourse with a woman' (as a one-sided action, requiring no agency or subjectivity on the side of the woman) does not constitute rape in itself. It is rather when *three further* conditions are satisfied, that the 'normal' one-sided activity of something that men do to or with women's bodies turns into rape.

The first condition is that the man must use force or the threat of force when he 'engages in intercourse with' the woman. However, this in itself still does not constitute rape, because he may ostensibly be using force or threat of force to perform *his* action on and with *her* body *with* the woman's will and consent. Or so it would seem, according to the formulation. This apparent contradiction, i.e., the possibility that a man would 'engage in sexual intercourse' with a woman, using force or the threat of force to do so, even while she desires his actions, this unlikely and difficult to imagine scenario would then call for the further two conditions to be fulfilled. First, his actions must not only constitute sexual intercourse and must not only be done through force or threat of force, but must *additionally* be against her will, which would then be fulfilling the second condition. Furthermore in the third place, he must not only be forcing sexual intercourse against her will; he must additionally be doing this *without* her *consent*. This formulation of the law against rape thus implies that a man may be forcing sexual intercourse with a woman against her will but at the same time be doing this *with* her consent, which would presumably necessitate the third condition. This third condition leaves us with maybe the greatest puzzle, but I contend that we need to understand it historically, and view it through the lens of the late and reluctant acceptance of the idea of marital rape. The slow acceptance of marital rape as a legal possibility is a clear indication of the extent to which rape is still very often implicitly viewed as a kind of *property crime*, and sexual relations more generally as relations of male ownership of, and control over, women's sexuality. Before the acknowledgement of marital rape, if a man forced sex with his wife against her will, then it was still not regarded as rape, because the formal consent was deemed to have been given by way of the marriage contract, months or years ago, and was considered irreversible except through divorce. This would be a clear case of where her consent and her will clashed, because they existed in different time frames. If this is indeed the historical origin of the peculiar formulation of this law, then it is both easier to understand and more urgent that it be reformulated in accordance with the

6   In 1994 the addition here of '(not his wife)' was scrapped from the law-books; marital rape has since been a legal possibility in South African law, but very few cases made it to court. The Supreme Court of Appeal case *S v Mvambu* (2004) (3) 45 (SCA) was hailed by the press as a 'landmark ruling'.

fuller recognition of women's sexual agency that is expressed by the recent legal acknowledgement of the possibility of rape within marriage.

The net effect of the three conditions that need to be fulfilled before a man 'engaging in sexual intercourse' with a woman commits rape, is that the complainant in the rape case typically has a hard time proving that the sexual intercourse happened (1) through force or threat of force, (2) against her will *and* (3) without her consent. It is thus not enough that a man's one-sided action of sexual intercourse with a woman is performed through ('by') force or threat of force for it to be considered a crime. The two additional conditions of rape place the focus of the law squarely on the woman's response to this forceful and one-sided action of the man. By adding 'against her will and without her consent' as necessary conditions to the very definition of rape, the law turns the woman's deepest motives and feelings as well as her overt behaviour during the forced 'sex' into ostensibly objective *criteria for defining what happened to her.* We know the rest of the story very well: how often women's paralysis, reactions of shock, nausea, submission or fear are used to argue in court that the forced sex was either not (completely) against her will or not without her consent, however implicitly given. In no other crime does the response of the victim play such a large role in the very definition of the crime. Imagine that one's response to being robbed or hijacked during the very event could plausibly be considered a decisive factor in determining whether the crime has actually transpired. Why does rape law do this? In other words, why do we not simply define rape as 'forced sexual intercourse'?

At least part of the answer seems to me to lie in the way in which rape law encodes and reinforces a male-dominated, male-biased and one-sided view of ('normal, heterosexual') 'sex as such'. Criminal law, and rape law in particular, is the main tool with which we legally regulate the (sexual) relations between the sexes. This law embodies a paradoxical logic at work over a much broader spectrum, namely that women's full subjectivity and agency are systematically undermined even as they are upheld in other ways. We see this in the very formulation of rape law, which posits one-sided masculine sexual action upon the body of woman as normative, as the point of departure. In the first part of its formulation, then, rape law normalises male sexual agency as acquisitive, assertive, primary and active, and female sexual agency as secondary, derivative, passive and responsive. This one-sidedness, this asymmetry with regard to sexual agency and subjectivity, the law assures us, is not the problem. It is, on the contrary, natural, and the normative background against which the deviation of rape has to be gauged. If heterosexual intercourse is something *men do*, then the other side of the coin is that sex is something that *women* naturally, or normally, undergo, passively experience, and *consent to*. Rape law thus both presupposes and naturalises women's consent to sex − 'consent' is the manner in which women 'engage in' sex, 'have' sex, and have *a* sex. I have indicated above that the rape law as it stands allows for the possibility that women may even will and consent to *forced* sexual intercourse, since the law *does not* define rape as forced sex. It thereby naturalises not only one-sided, but forced, even *violent* masculine sexual actions, since it envisages that such actions may be desired and/or sanctioned by women. By implying that women are likely to want or at least consent to forced sex (clearly something of a contradiction in itself), the law radically undermines women's sexual agency. At the same time, and now we can see the full paradox of it, the law *demands* full-blown sexual agency in women by placing so much emphasis (two of the three conditions used for *defining* rape) on her *response* to the forced situation.

In summary, one can say that rape law practically erases women's sexual *freedom* and active *desire* (through the portrayal of women's normal sexual agency as essentially secondary and responsive), but at the same time demands a very high level of sexual *responsibility* in women. The law does not take women's sexual desire into consideration, and thus it does not ask whether the woman unambiguously intended, wanted or desired the sexual actions undergone, but rather whether she *allowed* them to take place, in a context which is already conceded to be one of power imbalance and one-sided initiative. The law thus frames and constructs 'normal' heterosexual intercourse as a male-driven, forceful and one-sided event involving woman's essentially passive sexualised body, but then in its tail, right at the end, it turns the woman's consent, her response, into a crucial axis for determining the very nature of the event. By formulating her response and responsibility in negative terms ('*against* her will and *without* her consent'), the law reinforces her essential passivity at the same time as it expects of her to act responsibly and autonomously, to accept responsibility for the event.

The exact formulation of the law thus provides many possible avenues for arguing that forced sex does not constitute rape – avenues which all ultimately run through the beleaguered *selfhood* of the complainant, dividing her actions against her will, her body against her mind, her fear or shock against her will and desire, holding her responsible for what transpires in a situation of domination. It is no wonder that, given the law as it stands, lawyers for the defence zoom in on the state of mind of the rape victim, since that provides a particularly vulnerable target: the ambiguous zone of female sexual subjectivity,[7] on which, moreover, the definition of rape largely pivots. By undermining, splitting or further fragmenting through their competitive performance the victim's selfhood, they continue quite literally the 'work' of the rapist. If they manage to undermine her selfhood enough, her breakdown as sexual subject serves to disqualify the event as rape by paradoxically and painfully doubling or repeating it in a legalised, public setting, and in the presence of the accused. Rape splits the victim into separate 'parts' and forces her in some sense or another to act against her self, to become an agent in her own undoing.[8]

---

7   Of course, my claim is not here that women's sexual subjectivity is inherently ambiguous, but that it is *constructed* as such, first and foremost by the law against rape itself.

8   Cf. Du Toit (2005). I return to this theme in section two of the chapter.

By 'breakdown as sexual subject' I simply mean here that, under cross-examination, rape complainants are often portrayed as internally inconsistent, as somehow less than full sexual subjects with sexual desires clear to themselves and to everyone else. The court drama which enacts and performs the breakdown of the complainant as sexual subject is simultaneously an uncanny repetition of her breakdown as subject during the rape itself and legal 'proof' that she is essentially 'unrapeable', since only full and responsible sexual agents can clearly dissent to or resist 'normal' male sexual advances. As long as this kind of strategy on the part of the defence is allowed, courts ignore the reality of overwhelming power imbalances both in rape and in the court itself, and they also reject and repress a view of the sexual self as dynamic and intersubjectively and temporally constituted – the view which I defend here. They ignore and reject these to the detriment of justice for women everywhere. I discuss these issues further in the second half of the chapter. By splitting her selfhood once again during cross-examination, in an attempt to prove the woman's inconsistency (e.g., between actions and feelings) during the rape, the lawyers for the defence ironically 'prove' that rape did not occur, by exploiting its most damaging effect. In other words, they use the core meaning, strategy and effect of rape – the desubjectification (or objectification) and self-betrayal of the woman – to argue that she did not act like a proper subject during the event, and that she was therefore never raped in the first place. This is the legal strategy suggested by the current formulation of the law – to show how 'forced' sex was 'consented' to.

The paradox or maybe impossibility of what is required, is legally 'satisfied' by re-presenting the woman's sexual subjectivity as the paradox, the impossibility, the enigma which satisfies the paradoxical requirements. By showing that this woman does not know what she sexually wants, and/or cannot communicate it unambiguously, that she is thus not a full and fully responsible sexual subject, lawyers for the defence prove to the court that this woman (and 'such' women) cannot be raped. In the infamous case of *S v Zuma*,[9] for example, Judge Van der Merwe presents the complainant as on the one hand 'a strong person well in control of herself knowing what she wants'.[10] On the other hand he says '(i)t is quite clear that the complainant has experienced previous trauma and it is quite possible that she perceives any sexual behaviour as threatening'[11] and 'the complainant is a sick person who needs help'.[12] The complainant is portrayed as deeply confused, an enigma even to herself, in order to answer the question of why anybody would risk her life (she received substantial death threats and had to leave the country ahead of the verdict) and reputation to make a false rape allegation against a popular politician and former vice-president of her country, knowing that around 6% of rape cases end in convic-

---

9 *S v Zuma* (2006) 2 SA (CR) 191 (W).
10 At 197d.
11 At 221g.
12 At 221e.

tion. The judge ignored the question about the kind of sexual responsibility that could reasonably be expected of someone like Jacob Zuma toward a person who is both sexually traumatised and 'sick'.

Clearly what is at stake here is how we (and the law) conceive of the female subject as a sexuate being, within a context of sexual difference and interaction. I propose that we drop the Lockean view of the self as stable over time, as distinct from the body, as owning property in the body, as possessing a self-contained identity prior to relations with others, and as establishing social relationships 'without affecting the respective identities of the different parties involved' (Diprose, 1994: 9–10). Instead, I propose that we adopt a view of the self as inherently fragile, intersubjective and socially constituted; in short, a more Lacanian view of the self, which I now elaborate.

THE 'WOUND OF FEMININITY'

Sexual subjectivity or selfhood is in itself a constant struggle, never finished, never completed or finally achieved. (Sexual) subjectivity is open-ended, contested, dynamic and changing, and intersubjectively constituted, and this is true for everyone. However, this is also why women's sexual subjectivity is systematically undermined in a rape-prone society which trivialises rape and its harms, and this impacts crucially upon every woman in that society, not just the direct victims of rape. The (rape) law as an important Lacanian Other moreover constructs women's sexuality as responsive, derivative and passive, as I have shown. Women's sexual subjectivity is furthermore systematically undermined by male-centred religions and the pornography industry that each in their own way conflates women's personhood with their sexuality and constructs women's sexuate being as *shamefully antithetical* to full personhood (Cornell, 1995: 19). Drucilla Cornell appropriates the Lacanian term 'the wound of femininity' to refer to the 'ripping of one's sex and sexual persona away from any affirmation of oneself as a person with power and creativity' (1995: 7). The symbolic split effected within western metaphysics between the female or feminine sex and full personhood, means that women encounter particular difficulties in their (human) quest to become selves, or to become 'individuated'. This split or wound between objective and subjective selves, between desire and social behaviour, also helps to explain why it is so difficult 'to affirm the feminine within sexual difference as other than the imposed masquerade' (Cornell, 1995: 7).[13]

In general one may thus say that women's sexual subjectivity, women's freedom to develop and express their sexuate being, is systematically undermined, and more specifically, that this already fragile sense of self (a self integrated

13 It should be noted that I draw here on a feminist reworking or interpretation of Lacanian concepts and thus on a reading of Lacan which is probably not loyal to his own original project and intentions.

with a sexuate body, desire and agency) is severely damaged in rape. To be raped radically undermines a woman's capacity to be and to function as a sexual subject in the first place. This is the case because rape is above all an injury to the psyche, to a woman's sense of herself. Rape explicitly destroys the necessary conditions for being a self and for giving or withholding consent in that it splits a woman off from herself as a sex object and forces her into a suicidal pact with the rapist. That is, rape forces a woman to comply with, and participate in, the reduction of her being to a brute materiality, and forces her sense of self into an imaginary space where she is *nothing but* a body, a sex, and a thing to be used and to be acted upon by another and *his* projection and imagination. Indeed, rape is akin to murder, it is a kind of spiritual murder, in that it undermines the victim's capacity to experience herself as an integrated, sexual and subjective whole, and to live a life of coherence. It constitutes a gross violation of human rights, because it effectively removes her capacity to project herself as whole and over time and to imagine herself as an effective presence in the world. This crucial loss of self is a constant threat to women in sexist and especially in rape-prone societies – a loss which is activated in the most direct way in rape and more indirectly in instances of sexual harassment, objectification, everyday sexist behaviour, cross-examination of alleged rape victims and so on.

Cornell takes over from Lacan his notion of the fragility and non-transparency of the self to itself. The sexual imago in particular is pre-conscious and too fundamental to one's identity that it can be understood as consciously assumed (Cornell, 1995: 8). Neither sexuality nor the body can be meaningfully separated from the self on this account. Sexuality is integral and fundamental to one's being and to deny any person the freedom to exist (as they are, in and through their sexual imago) is to deny them 'a fundamental part of their identity' (Cornell, 1995: 8). Cornell draws on John Rawls' (1971: 440) account of imposed shame, and one may also refer to Avishai Margalit's (1996) account of humiliation, both of which emphasise that people can paradoxically be deprived of (the primary good of) *self-respect* through the actions of others. However, unlike Rawls, Cornell argues that self-respect is not only something that we owe others as persons; it is rather to be thought of as 'fundamental to the very formation of what we think of as personhood' (Cornell, 1995: 9). This insistence is roughly based on a Lacanian understanding of the (always tentative) formation of the self. On Cornell's reading of Lacan, the self is socially and symbolically constituted, but never completed, and as such it remains dependent on the social and the symbolic.

The intense pleasure experienced by the infant during the 'mirror stage', when it sees its own image in a mirror, means for Lacan that the infant experiences the mirror image as an idealised self, a whole and coherent, unified self, which contradicts her subjective experience of herself as helpless, fragmented, and scattered (Cavallaro, 2003: 29). The mirror image thus 'functions both as a projection and an anticipation of what the infant might become but is not now' (Cornell, 1995: 39). This uneasy split or distance between our immediate embodiment and subjective states and feelings on the one hand and our anticipated or projected 'whole' self on the other, is a permanent feature of our lives as humans. Human identity is split (Cavallaro, 2003: 30) and based on mechanisms of alienation, fiction and misrecognition (Cavallaro, 2003: 29). In the mirror phase the self is divided into the 'I' that watches and the 'I' that is being watched, and the subject constructs an image of itself by identifying with something other than itself, namely the fiction, the fleeting apparition of an image (Cavallaro, 2003: 29). The infant is completely dependent on others to provide her with a mirror image (especially of course on her primary care-giver/s), and she transfers the function of mirror to other people and the way they look at her, speak with her and treat her. Through their gaze and actions, others confirm her projected identity and bodily integrity (Cornell, 1995: 39).

This other, 'both appears as whole and confirms the infant in its projected and anticipated coherence by mirroring him or her as a self', and thus becomes 'the matrix of a sense of continuity and coherence which the child's present state of bodily disorganisation would belie' (Cornell, 1995: 39). The whole, intact, clearly demarcated and stable self which is taken for granted in much liberal theory is thus a fiction, a mirage, but nevertheless an absolutely *necessary fiction* or mirage, other to and crucially different from the reality of bodily disorganisa-tion and emotional confusion. It is the fiction that we need in order to be(come) individuated and to be in a position where we can *start* to act autonomously, consistently and responsibly. This fiction is thus a necessary condition for the logic of consent; it is a necessary condition for achieving (always tentatively and by the grace of others who bestow and confirm this fictive identity) the degree of selfhood that the law requires of us. Selfhood is thus not basically separate from the body as the Platonic tradition would have us believe; reflected and anticipated *bodily integrity* is rather central and fundamental to our ongoing experience of ourselves as subjects. The stability of the image which confirms this fiction of us for us is what gives both spatial and temporal, both diachronic and synchronic coherence to our existence, and what makes a meaningful, narratable (symbolic) life possible (cf. Cavarero, 2000).

Since the adult's sense of self 'continues to involve the projection of bodily integrity and its recognition by others' (Cornell, 1995: 40), our bodies never properly 'belong' to us. Such a full belonging, based on the possibility of a completed subjectivisation, is a fiction or a fantasy which imagines as com-pleted that which can never be completed. Yet, it is a necessary fiction – I need to have confirmed by everyone I meet that I am *not* my body, reducible to it, but rather that I own my body, transcend it, that I am a subject and a person, an ongoing and coherent project, projected into the future by myself rather than an object or a thing merely undergoing my life. The distance between the lived body and the objectified body and the affirmation of that distance by others is thus crucial for our projection of ourselves as subjects, as whole and autono-mous. This is why Cornell can say that 'to reduce the self to just "some body" is to rob it of [its] future anterior' (1995: 40) and this is also why we never complete the mirror stage once and for all. It is rather a place or stage that we routinely revisit, and which makes us forever vulnerable to the person or symbolic system that refuses to acknowledge or confirm the difference or distance between our lived experience and our projected wholeness. Shame or humiliation is caused by the exposure of my fictitious self, my ideal and integrated self *as* a fiction. Shame happens when I am thrown back onto my raw, objective bodiliness and reduced to it, or when my personhood is denied on the basis of my body, my 'thingness', when personhood as such is defined as antithetical to *my* sexuate being.[14] Elaine Scarry (1985: 47) provides a vivid account of how this process of dehumanising through the silencing of the voice and the presencing of the body in pain is carefully orchestrated in torture. She points out that victims of torture experience an acute sense of *self*-betrayal. Margalit (1996) also refers to this same phenomenon in describing the paradox at the heart of humiliation: one cannot be humiliated without one's complicity, because humiliation is precisely to be deprived by someone else, paradoxically, of *the respect that one owes oneself.* The paradox is explained, I think, through Lacan's explanation of the extent to which self-respect is dependent on the recognition of others, as set out above.

Against this background one can make more sense of the term 'the wound of femininity' and its reference to the way in which women are split off from themselves as sex objects. During what Lacan refers to as 'the era of the ego' in the western world, women are chosen to perform the function of mirrors for the confirmation of masculine egos, but women are at the same time objectified as mirrors and functions and not allowed to 'ascend to the position of subjects' because then they would threaten the becoming-subjects of men (Cornell, 1995: 40). If women were recognised as an(other) subject, then women would be in a position to withhold affirmation and to destroy the necessary fiction of men as whole, intact and integrated beings. The price for masculine subjectivity being secured is paid by women who are kept outside of the position of full personhood and subjectivity. A similar logic of course plays itself out in Hegel's master–slave dialectic (Du Toit, 2005: 73 ff).

It is my contention that we cannot clearly think about rape (law) if we ignore the 'wound of femininity' as well as the inherent fragility of the sexual self. For a discussion of the implications of these insights for rape law, I turn to the next and last section.

---

14 I would argue that racism displays the same logic, where the racial(ised) body is equated with an existence that is somehow less than fully human or that is the opposite of personhood, or a detriment to it.

IMPLICATIONS FOR RAPE LAW

Drawing on these Lacanian-Hegelian insights, one can understand the need to move away from a basically contractual understanding of heterosexual encounters, because that model presupposes but at the same time veils the process of becoming a person and a full sexual subject. That model, as I have explained, presumes that the self remains essentially intact over time and throughout contract-like encounters with other people. According to the alternative model I sketched out above, however, sexual subjectivity and bodily integrity are necessary fictions and forever dependent on intersubjective affirmation. Moreover, *women's* sexual subjectivity carries the 'wound' or 'scar' inflicted by the western symbolic (including religions, pornography, rape law and romantic movies) in terms of which their sexual subjectivity is constructed as particularly dubious, fragile and unstable. It is thus not enough to reform rape law by insisting that the court makes sure that what looked like 'consent' in the context was indeed consent. It may of course help in any particular case that the court scrutinises the context for traces of external pressure which led to an apparent but not an actual consent on the side of the complainant-force or threat of force being the most obvious kind of example.

However, as long as we retain the concept of 'consent', we remain stuck in the symbolic representation of women's sexuality as fundamentally responsive and secondary, and thus detract from women's status as full sexual subjects. We do this by retaining a basic asymmetry (based on the active–passive hierarchial dichotomy) at the heart of what is regarded as 'normal' heterosexual encounters. Even if we change our reading of 'consent' from associations with submission and acquiescence to associations with freedom and active desire or clear intent, the presumption of consent as given unless proven otherwise remains within the context of criminal law, which entrenches the asymmetry on a deeper level. Moreover, as long as we conceive of rape as 'sex without consent' we normalise and naturalise (background, framing) masculine models of unilateral, acquisitive sexual agency and repress other models of sexual agency that would be more appropriate to women's sexual agency and that might conceivably be less acquisitive and assertive and more communicative and reciprocal. There is thus a tendency in rape law (and its reform) to 'normalise' and 'universalise' men's lives, experiences and sexualities, at the expense of 'an equivalent evaluation of the feminine within our system of sexual difference', as Cornell (1995: 19) calls it. What is lost from view is the fact that the dominant forms of masculine identity and sexuality that we tend to universalise and normalise are in fact forms of identity and sexuality which are structurally dependent upon and thus parasitic on the de-humanisation of its 'other', namely of feminine identity and sexuality. Also, through their universalising tendency, certain liberal attempts at reform may erase femininity and its specificities, the real differences between the sexes and their placement in the world, by postulating 'the subject' as sexless, or as 'above sex' (Cornell, 1995: 33–34).

'Consent' is furthermore often read in this context as permission to use a woman's sexuality where that sexuality is seen as static, thing-like and similar to a piece of property, desired by one party but possessed by another. The recognition of marital rape is a recent and still contested milestone in our fight against the notion of rape as a property crime. Women's sexuality and reproductive capacities have for millennia been understood as men's property, and Levi-Strauss (1969) has shown how kinship relations worldwide are regulated by the circulation of women as 'goods'. Some liberal feminists have taken over the notion of sexuality as 'property in the body' while challenging the idea that *men* own women's sexual property in the body. The logical development was then to insist that *women own their own sexual body property*, and may dispose of it as they wish. Rosalyn Diprose (1994: 12) has argued convincingly, employing a phenomenological model of the body-subject, that this model is particularly inadequate for female embodiment, and especially for female-specific forms of embodiment such as pregnancy and surrogacy.

I would argue along the same lines that the property model of sexuality is woefully inadequate for expressing the injustice of rape. The property model assumes that the 'self' is essentially separate from the body and 'rules' over it, or 'uses' it for its own purposes. According to such a model, the 'self' as such remains intact during rape, even if the sexual 'body' is violated. To be raped means within this legal framework to have one's sexual property in the body used without permission. From this follows an undue and misplaced focus on the physical harms sustained by the victim – harms that are then taken as the measure of over-all damage sustained. By imagining that the woman's self is fully present throughout the event of rape and only hampered in her expression of her sexual wishes through external circumstances such as force and threat, one cannot do justice to the particular nature of the damage of rape which needs to be understood as an *undoing of the self*, and an undoing, moreover, in which the self is necessarily complicit. If rape is fundamentally about not getting what one wants sexually, or rather, getting what one doesn't want sexually, then the far-reaching damage of rape is baffling. Why do rape victims present with Post-Traumatic Stress Disorder (cf. Brison, 2002)? The contractual model applied to rape denies or hides most of the deep and enduring psychic damage sustained by rape victims, so that when it comes to sentencing, there are no clearly articulated harms to juxtapose to the richly presented context of the rapist's life and background.

In order to make a more radical break with contractual, property and consent models that hide the true nature of rape, I want to follow Cornell (1995: 4), who argues that the law needs much rather to protect *the minimum conditions of individuation* of every person, i.e., the conditions of becoming a person of every person. These include for her the protection of (1) bodily integrity, (2) access to symbolic forms sufficient to achieve linguistic skills permitting the differentiation of oneself from others and (3) the protection of the 'imaginary domain' itself, which is the psychic space in which we imagine and re-imagine ourselves and from where we project who we wish to be and to become. This protective function of the law would presumably include restrictions on the law itself, in the sense of the law limiting itself in that it is not allowed to shame or humiliate anyone by translating anyone's sexuate being into an unworthiness of full personhood. The law may neither implicitly nor explicitly shatter or unmask the projected personal wholeness of any person or any group of persons. In the same breath, however, Cornell cautions that the law as such is an instrument of force and therefore has inherent limitations. Feminists should not rely on the law for changing everything that is wrong. The fundamental asymmetry between the sexes is deeply entrenched in the symbolic order of the west and in the symbolic orders of all three of the monotheistic, scripture-based world religions. It therefore needs to be challenged on many levels and in different domains of life, and not only within the legal domain. It also implies that a feminist program of legal reform has to be accompanied by 'the re-imagining and the resymbolisation of the feminine within sexual difference which takes back "ourselves" from the masculine imaginary' (Cornell, 1995: 50).

However, staying within concerns about the law, clearly, from what I have argued so far, one of the most decisive resymbolisations needed in the context of rape law is of feminine sexuality as inappropriable, inviolable. Moreover, such a resymbolisation needs to be undertaken with the full acknowledgement of our tendency to universalise masculine sexual identities, and thus with great sensitivity towards lived sexual differences. Our sexed bodies are very differently structured and they thus mediate phenomenologically very different worlds to us, female and male respectively. We experience, live and project our sexual being differently from one another; there is no single sexual subjectivity. For Luce Irigaray (2001: 6), we need to crucially abandon the traditional model of the subject, 'not in order to add a little bit here or a little bit there, but so that we can abandon the model of a single and singular subject altogether'. For her then, a prerequisite for a proper ethical relation between the sexes is the basic recognition of *the subject as two*,[15] and along with this, the acknowledgement that sexual difference is 'the most radical limit opposed to the totalizing will of the subject' (Irigaray, 2001: 6).

It is therefore imperative that rape law, if it is to aspire towards justice for women, acknowledge sexual difference and the impossibility of a 'view from nowhere'. It should thus incorporate overt caution about the court's tendency to replicate the perspective and actions of the alleged rapist. Something like an inverse of the old 'cautionary' rule is needed: no longer should judges and juries be reminded that women tend to lie about rape, but they should rather be

15 By this Irigaray means that any particular 'human subject' is at the same time fully human and only one sexually particular aspect or part (one half) of what it means to be human. 'Humanity' cannot be generalised from one (type of) human being alone, since at its most basic level, humanity consists of two kinds or types, namely women and men. Every human being is either a woman or a man, and no one is neither or both.

reminded about the unlikelihood of false rape accusations in light of, among other things, the low conviction rate. They should also be reminded about the 'wound of femininity' and the odds against which women struggle to establish and maintain sexual agency in an antagonistic symbolic order. Judges and juries should be cautioned to make sure they understand the radical nature of rape damage, of how rape tends to 'undo' the selfhood and undermine the dignity of the victim and they should caution themselves to thoroughly humanise the complainant rather than to either demonise her or cast her in the stereotype of the victim. By 'humanise' I mean here that they should contemplate the dynamic, open-ended, intersubjective and fragile nature of the human ego (a condition in which we all share) and take that into consideration when they consider the case before them. Judges and juries will under these new conditions also no longer be able to escape their own sexual specificity – each, whether female or male, will have to take her own sexuate perspective into account, make it a part of the overall picture. They should also be vigilant about focusing on either accused or complainant to the exclusion of the other; they need to see how every heterosexual encounter is partly a making (an affirmation) and partly an unmaking (objectification, de-subjectification) of the other sex. These kinds of considerations will work against the tendency to reduce, objectify and functionalise female sexuality and to split it off from the woman's personhood.

These acknowledgements are moreover needed to break down the pernicious and tenacious view of female sexuality as property and function. A renunciation of the desire to possess and use the other sex is the necessary condition for recognising the sexual other as other, for acknowledging them in their sexuate being, and thus for granting them (or bestowing upon them) the possibility or gift of individuation and, only in the end, also for sexual decision making and agency. The 'problem' with rape law and consent is that democracy has not yet dawned for women, but that the law assumes that it has. We thus need laws and civil codes that protect the dignity of women *as women*, that proactively protect and promote women's imagined bodily integrity as female sexuate beings, and that protect women's access to symbolic forms (including religion and law, and the inner chambers where these are continuously created and re-created) so that we may freely imagine and reimagine our identities as female human beings (Irigaray, 2001: 38–39, 71–72). Without this kind of protection, women remain imprisoned in a masculine imaginary, which means that, at the most crucial (transformative, constitutive and vulnerable) moments, such as in rape verdicts, women have their bodies 'turned over to the minds of men' (Cornell, 1995: 47), as we South Africans have once again seen happen during the Zuma rape case in 2006.

In 2003, the South African Parliament's portfolio committee on justice and constitutional development started work on the first draft of the Criminal Law (Sexual Offences) Amendment Bill, prepared by the South African Law Reform Commission. Among other things, the Commission:

> ... removed the term 'consent' from the definition of rape, replacing it with the notion of sexual penetration in 'coercive circumstances'; set sharply defined limits on circumstances in which victims could be questioned about their sexual history ... and provided for support personnel to assist survivors in court.
>
> (Dawes, 2006: 4)

In line with my argument about the right to be a subject above, it also:

> ... declared all complainants in rape cases 'vulnerable witnesses' and required prosecutors to inform them of protective measures available to them, such as ordering the public to leave the court, testifying via closed circuit camera and prohibiting the publication of certain details.
>
> (Dawes, 2006: 4)

All of these measures would potentially help much to protect the imaginary domain of the complainant and to protect the conditions of her subjectivity or selfhood. However, as Cornell cautions, the law is a weak instrument in itself and always partly dependent on political processes. This Bill was for four years not brought before Parliament; and every draft since the first one has weakened the complainant's position; both the term 'consent' and the derogatory 'cautionary rule' were left intact by the portfolio committee. However, even in this watered-down version, 'consent' is still importantly defined as 'free agreement', with the implication that the use of force, threats, the abuse of authority and fraudulent claims would all constitute circumstances where 'consent' would be considered to have been absent, even if 'the complainant offered no obvious verbal or physical resistance' (Dawes, 2006: 4). The watered-down Bill was recently passed through Parliament, but up until now, South African women have had to endure a scandalous repetition of the undoing of the sexuate self at the hands of our courts.[16] It is indeed true: democracy has not yet dawned for women living in the youngest democracy in the world.

BIBLIOGRAPHY

Brison, S.J., *Aftermath: Violence and the Remaking of a Self*. Princeton University Press, Princeton 2002.
Cavallaro, D., *French Feminist Theory: An Introduction*. Continuum, London 2003.
Cavarero, A., *Relating Narratives: Storytelling and Selfhood*. Routledge, London 2000.
Cornell, D., *The Imaginary Domain: Abortion, Pornography and Sexual Harassment*. Routledge, New York 1995.

16 This article is written in response to and in condemnation of the court's treatment of the woman, nicknamed 'Kwesi', who accused Jacob Zuma, South Africa's ex-vice-president, of raping her, and lost the case.

Dawes, N., 'The law that could have stumped Kemp', *Mail & Guardian*, 17–23 March 2006, p.4.

De Beauvoir, S., *The Second Sex*, Parshley, H.M. (trans). Vintage, London 1997.

Diprose, R., *The Bodies of Women: Ethics, Embodiment and Sexual Difference.* Routledge, London 1994.

Du Toit, L., 'A phenomenology of rape: forging a new vocabulary for action', in Gouws, A., ed., *Unthinking Citizenship: Feminist Debates in Contemporary South Africa.* Ashgate, Aldershot 2005, pp.253–74.

Du Toit, L., *The Making and Unmaking of the Feminine Self*, unpublished thesis. University of Johannesburg 2005.

Hegel, G.W.F. *Phenomenology of Spirit*, Miller, A.V. (trans). Oxford University Press, Oxford 1979.

Irigaray, L., *Speculum of the Other Woman*, Gill, G.C. (trans). Cornell University Press, Ithaca, New York 1985.

Irigaray, L., *Democracy Begins Between Two*, Anderson, K. (trans). Routledge, New York 2001.

Lévi-Strauss C., *The Elementary Structures of Kinship.* Beacon Press, Boston 1969.

Margalit, A., *The Decent Society*, Goldblum, N. (trans). Harvard University Press, Cambridge, Massachusetts 1996.

Rawls, J., *A Theory of Justice.* The Belknap Press, Cambridge MA 1971.

Sanday, P.R., 'Rape-prone versus rape-free campus cultures', *Violence Against Women,* 2, 1996, pp. 191–208.

Scarry, E., *The Body in Pain: The Making and Unmaking of the World*, Oxford University Press, Oxford 1985.

Chapter 4

The politics of consent, friendship and sovereignty

Karin van Marle

Against the humility of friendship stands the logic of sovereignty.

(Bergowitz and Cornell, 2005: 331)

INTRODUCTION

I want to address the theme of consent by looking at its relation with politics. The broad contention is that the prevalent understanding of politics influences approaches to and ultimately the working of consent and of course also dissent and refusal. Central to my reflection is the distinction between politics and the political as drawn by Claude Lefort (Lefort, 1988: 9–20), Philippe Lacoue-Labarthe and Jean-Luc Nancy (Lacoue-Labarthe and Nancy, 1997: 107–21; see also Van der Walt, 2005: 6–7). For these thinkers 'politics' refers to the actual exercise of power within a society, whereas 'the political' is the fundamental form and constitutive principles of a society. The relationship between politics and the political is paradoxical – politics aims to simultaneously open and close a space for the political (Lacoue-Labarthe and Nancy, 1997: 110). Chantal Mouffe, in reaction to a rationalist, universalist and individualist understanding of politics, insists on an understanding of the political that 'cannot be restricted to a certain type of institution, or envisaged as constituting a specific sphere or level of society' (Mouffe, 1993: 3). She conceives of the political as 'a dimension that is inherent to every human society and that determines our ontological condition' (1993: 3). Mouffe calls for the return of the political in the face of liberalism's incapacity to appreciate and understand the political (1993: 4). I elaborate on Mouffe's notion of radical democracy, which allows antagonisms, below.

We should recall also Lacoue-Labarthe and Nancy's notion of the 'withholding or withdrawal of the political' (1997: 112). Following Lefort they view the political as an expression of the foundations of Western philosophical thought. However, the political is also a retreat from these foundational principles. The withholding or withdrawal of the political allows for certain expressions to become accepted with the effect that others are excluded. They state:

In speaking of the retreat, we meant that something draws back into (or from) . . . The retreat appears . . . as the retreat of transcendence or alterity. What draws back would be, then, the political itself as a specific dimension or as the dimension of a specific alterity.

(Lacoue-Labarthe and Nancy, 1997: 129–30)

Van der Walt explains:

The political also consists in the withdrawal of otherness. Their [Lacoue-Labarthe and Nancy's] concern with the political is a concern to retrieve the political or the alterity of the political from this retreat from present manifestations of the political.

(Van der Walt, 2005: 7)

The reflections on politics and consent in this chapter are guided by the notions of the political that I have referred to above. I consider how, as observed by these theorists, the fundamental forms and principles of a society and the retreat from them, by allowing the exclusion of difference and the withdrawal of otherness, affect the possibilities of consent by affirming a certain masculine normativity.[1]

How we understand politics, the political and consequently democracy affects our understanding of law and rights, which in turn affects our regard of the political and legal subject, who ultimately gives or withholds consent. For consent to have any value the actual consent should not merely refer to an agreement to certain terms – all parties concerned should be part of the actual drafting of the terms. In our evaluation of consent we should heed the withdrawal that allows the privileging of certain expressions to the exclusion of other possibilities. I argue that consent should entail more than agreement towards already established terms – the notion of consent as well as that to which we consent must be radically rethought and opened. As already alluded to I want to reiterate a point that may be obvious but that to my mind is not always given sufficient emphasis: thinking about consent should encompass a simultaneous reflection on dissent and possibilities for difference and being different. Consent can only have meaning within a context where dissent and refusal are real possibilities – in other words where the withdrawal of otherness that precludes dissent is illuminated.

---

1   This was illustrated in the rape case of Jacob Zuma (ex-deputy president of South Africa), in which Judge Willem Van der Merwe decided to allow testimony about the history of the complainant. Zuma in his testimony relied on what he referred to as 'Zulu culture' to explain how he could infer consent from the conduct of the complainant. Many people have remarked that the culture he relied on was not really 'Zulu culture', but rather 'Zuma culture', a male culture. Lisa Vetten, in a talk at the University of Pretoria on 19 May 2006, observed that the legal culture that Van der Merwe relied on and 'Zuma culture' is the same – the prevailing culture is one of maleness and masculinity.

Framing my argument within the notions of friendship and sovereignty, I consider whether the former might allow space for dissent, refusal and consent, whereas the latter, because of its own logic, might not. However, taking into account Derrida's (1997) reflections on friendship, I also question the possibilities of friendship. Drucilla Cornell's and Roger Bergowitz's (2005) reflection on Clint Eastwood's film *Mystic River*, in which they explicitly focus on the theme of revenge and masculinity, provides the starting point for the theme of friendship and sovereignty that I find suggestive for a feminist political thinking of consent, i.e., a politics of consent that is alert to the exclusion and othering of difference in assessing the possibilities of social relations and interactions. Even a trite distinction between a liberal, a deliberative and a critical (communicative or agonistic) model of politics and democracy already illustrates different implications for consent. Added to these distinctions, reflections on recognition/acknowledgement, unpredictability, sovereignty and friendship could contribute to a feminist political thinking about consent.

The chapter below unfolds as follows: I start with a discussion of Bergowitz and Cornell, and the introduction of friendship and sovereignty to a politics of consent. I then briefly recall the well-known distinctions between liberal, deliberative and communicative or agonistic models of politics and democracy, their relation to the notion of sovereignty and consent and the implications for consent. Next, an argument by Patchen Markell (2003) for a politics of acknowledgement as alternative to a politics of recognition and its relation with friendship and sovereignty will be put forward. Of interest to me in his argument is the reliance on Hannah Arendt's (1958) notions of action and speech, unpredictability and 'welcoming'. Following from that, Adriana Cavarero's (2005) employment of Arendt in her thinking on narrative politics comes into play. Markell, Arendt and Cavarero reiterate the necessity for multiple possibilities of social relations, interactions and being in contrast to the exclusion of liberal politics. In light of this, I briefly refer to a South African constitutional court decision where the court, by following a very limited view of female sexuality, confirmed the criminalisation of sex work. Towards the end I problematise my own reliance on friendship by recalling Derrida's reflections on the politics of friendship, his exposure of friendship always becoming exclusive and his notion of a 'democracy to come' that promises another friendship.

FRIENDSHIP AND SOVEREIGNTY IN *MYSTIC RIVER*

Bergowitz and Cornell analyse the Clint Eastwood film *Mystic River* in terms of the themes of revenge and masculinity (2005: 316–32). The three main male characters of the film each undergo trauma in their lives and react to this trauma in three distinctive ways. Of interest to the theme of consent is the connection to sovereignty and friendship in their reactions. The story starts when the three men are young boys playing street hockey in their old neighbourhood. The cycle of traumatic events is put in motion when one of the boys – Dave – is kid-napped and thereafter sodomised by two men. The film continues years later when the three boys are grown-up men struggling with continued trauma. Dave lives with his wife and son in the old neighbourhood. Jimmy, with a daughter from a first marriage, his second wife and two more daughters, is also still in the old neighbourhood, trying to live a life within the law after having been in jail for a while. At the beginning of the film, Jimmy's eldest daughter is brutally murdered. Sean is a detective and the only one of the three childhood friends who moved out of the old neighbourhood. The murder of Jimmy's daughter brings him back to the neighbourhood and into contact with Dave and Jimmy, whom he hasn't seen for years.

Cornell and Bergowitz are interested in the film's exploration of revenge as a response to trauma and loss and its connection to violence and masculinity. They follow an argument of Karen Horney in which she distinguishes between two alternatives to revenge. Revenge is described as a 'fantasy of control' (by Bergowitz and Cornell) and a 'value of vindictiveness' (by Horney) (Bergowitz and Cornell, 2005: 316). Two alternatives to revenge are 'neurosis' and 'becoming more human' (2005: 317). Bergowitz and Cornell follow these three possible responses to trauma – revenge, neurosis, and becoming more human – in order to analyse the three main characters, Dave Boyle, Jimmy Markham and Sean Devine.

Dave, who was raped as a young boy, can respond to his trauma only by neurosis/collapse (2005: 317). He survived the trauma, 'but not as himself . . . whoever got out of the basement was not Dave Boyle' (2005: 321). Later in the film Dave encounters a man raping a young boy and he reacts by killing the man. He is incapable of relating these events first to his wife, and later again when confronted by Jimmy, who suspects him to be the killer of his daughter. Jimmy and Sean and their responses relate directly to notions of sovereignty and friendship. Jimmy 'refuses to admit his vulnerability to trauma' (2005: 317). He seeks to regain control of his life and accordingly his own finitude (2005: 317). Living out this notion of self-sovereignty, Jimmy acts in revenge. He takes justice into his own hands and kills in an act of revenge. However, he kills the wrong person, Dave, instead of his daughter's real killer. Sean is traumatised by the event of his wife leaving him while she was pregnant with their child. As the film progresses Sean, in contrast to Jimmy, slowly accepts his own limits and finitude.

The authors describe Sean's choice of becoming more human as 'a powerful counterweight to Jimmy's more traditional masculine heroism' (2005: 317). Of significance is Jimmy's portrayal as being a 'king', a sovereign (2005: 323). His wrongful killing of Dave is seen as some kind of a royal prerogative grounded in love for his family (2005: 324). His kingship (sovereignty) is seen as something natural and the right to revenge flows from that. As the authors put it, 'Jimmy's claim to kingship and his arrogation of the right of revenge is grounded in nothing but his elemental and orgasmic fertility. It is a right he has as the man he is' (2005: 328). This notion of masculine sovereignty reaches beyond the confines of *Mystic River* as 'a tale of revenge'. Man's sovereignty and its effect on everyday life are illuminated by the portrayal of Jimmy. What makes this more disturbing is Jimmy's wife, Annabeth's complicity in protecting his kingship. In contrast to the wives of Dave and Sean, Annabeth is a perfect example of the 'dutiful and adoring' wife (2005: 324). Dave's wife, Celeste, does not manage to comprehend his trauma and after suspecting him of killing Jimmy's daughter tells Jimmy. Laura, Sean's wife, leaves him in order to show him that she demands to be treated as his equal. What does man's illusion of his encompassing and ever-spreading sovereignty mean for the politics of consent? And more than that woman's reliance on and support of it?

Sean's response to his wife's demand to be treated as an equal is seen by the authors as a sign of 'some hope for the end of the cycle of violence unleashed by the traumatic event caught in the kidnapping of Dave Boyle' (2005: 331). In contrast to Jimmy, Sean does not aspire to live outside the law, he is not a king, a sovereign living a fantasy of infinitude. Sean responds to the trauma of his marriage by 'becoming more human'. He acknowledges his own vulnerability and by doing that opens himself up to regard his wife as his equal. Bergowitz and Cornell comment on the theme of fidelity in the film, a theme also taken up by Eastwood in another film, *Unforgiven* (2005: 329). They interpret the 'promise of fidelity as a way in which the masculine persona resists the notion of the exchangeability of women' and regard Sean's fidelity as 'one way a man can take the necessary first steps in creating an actual space to articulate a masculinity that does not have to define itself upon treating women as exchangeable objects' (2005: 329). This notion of fidelity connected to friendship is suggestive for a kind of politics of consent where women and men can contest and discuss the terms and meanings of consent.

As indicated in the introduction my contention is that for consent to make any real sense we need to be aware of the withdrawal of the political that enables society to exclude all forms of difference and dissent from masculine normativity and culture. The promise of fidelity as developed by Eastwood and taken further by Bergowitz and Cornell could be one way of challenging the privileging of masculine normativity and culture that presently precludes all other possibilities of social interaction and ultimately for consent. Following a Freudian analysis the authors show how Sean manages to shift from seeing Laura as a fetishised object to seeing her as a person (2005: 329–30). Laura resists his reduction of her own understanding of herself by first leaving, but later by responding to him in silence waiting for him to speak to her. The authors understand Sean's fidelity to her as a woman – even one that he fails to see as a whole woman because of the repressed fear of what the female body represents, castration – as opening a first step for the possibility of transformation (2005: 330).

The theme of sovereignty and the fear of castration are represented by the rape and kidnapping of Dave Boyle. Both Sean and Jimmy realise the possibility that they can be penetrated, a threat to the male fantasy of sovereignty and control, but ultimately respond in two different ways (2005: 330). Jimmy asserts his masculinity by acting out his kingship and sovereignty. Sean accepts his own frailty, finitude and humanity and attempts to open a space of friendship where he and his wife can meet (2005: 331; see also Frank, 2004). The theme of friendship is central to the kind of politics that I think could provide a framework for consent other than the known examples ranging from forced consent to a mere going along, i.e., for consent where dissent and refusal could be real options, where masculine culture does not prevail by preventing all forms of difference. Patchen Markell (2003) describes the struggle for sovereignty as central to the modern masculine ideology of identity. I will return to his discussion of the struggle for sovereignty within the context of recognition and acknowledgement after briefly recounting the distinction between liberal, deliberative and critical (communicative and agonistic) models of politics and democracy and the implications for consent.

LIBERAL, DELIBERATIVE AND CRITICAL POLITICS

Liberal politics

Authors employ various terms to capture the meaning and application of a liberal approach to democracy and politics, amongst others strategic, procedural, aggregative and interest-based. The crux of this conception is an understanding of democracy and politics as nothing more than a process through which individual preferences and demands can be expressed by voting for leaders, rules or policies (Young, 1996: 120). A strict private/public divide is central to the liberal conception – because of value pluralism, neutrality must be guarded in the public sphere. We find no conception of the 'common good' in this model, merely individuals seeking to protect their self-interest. Rights in this conception are seen as natural, or pre-political, with the effect that no collective deliberation is needed to decide on the minimum requirements for a just society. Viewing the notion of consent from this model, we can argue that the liberal model does not take account of power imbalances and inequalities in society. A traditional understanding of the sovereign state, as well as of the sovereign self, accompany the liberal model. It assumes that all individuals have similar and equal opportunities for bargaining, agreeing and disagreeing. Women's exclusion from politics and their according lack of power to give or withhold consent are impossible to raise within this conception. One fails to see an opening for a space of friendship where people can be regarded and respected on their own terms here. Rights, because they are taken as prepolitical, are never part of a process of deliberation; balancing rights is seen as a process of trumping where some people win and others lose, in contrast with, for example, a notion of rights as relationships where it is acknowledged that the individuals involved and the rights in question are always already embedded within relationships. Consent in this model means nothing more than agreeing to already established norms. The masculine social contract is accepted as the only possible proposal.

Deliberative politics

Deliberative democracy is the most popular conception posed as an alternative to the classical liberal conception. According to this conception democracy is a process where citizens meet in order to discuss issues of collective concern, for example rights and values. In contrast to the strategic/interest-based concern of the classical liberal model, in deliberative democracy citizens would transform their preferences to public-minded ends through a process of rational deliberation (Young, 1996: 121). One of the claims of deliberative democracy is that it could reconcile the tension between individual interests and collective concerns by way of a process of rational deliberation. Chantal Mouffe notes that models of deliberative democracy attempt to offer an alternative to classical liberal models (strategic, interest-based) by promoting a form of normative rationality (Mouffe 2000: 115). However, she contends that it is important to realise that deliberative democrats are still supporters of liberal democracy and attempt to reconcile the idea of popular sovereignty with the defense of liberal institutions. In other words, they do not aim to reject liberalism, but rather aim to restore its moral dimension. They strive towards reconnecting liberal values with democracy. Deliberative democrats believe that by providing for adequate procedures, agreement between liberal rights and popular sovereignty can be reached.

We can see that this notion, although maybe slightly better than pure liberalism, ultimately fails to include fully the hitherto excluded, for example women. The issue of consent might even be more problematic here because of the assumption of open and free dialogue and participation.

Critical politics

Iris Marion Young raises two points of critique concerning deliberative democracy. The first point of critique emphasises exclusionary implications of deliberative democracy (1996: 122). She explains that deliberative democrats assume that if political and economic equality is achieved all speakers will have an equal chance to speak. However, she notes that one's 'internalized sense of the right one has to speak' must also be recognised (1996: 122). The assumed neutrality of deliberation must be challenged. The Western, (white) male and competitive nature of deliberation must be noted. Further, deliberation's privileging of formal and general speech as well as its privileging of dispassionate and disembodied speech are of an exclusionary nature. The second point of critique is that the deliberative model assumes unity. A central feature of

deliberative democracy is that people's personal preferences can be transformed from subjective desires to objective claims, in other words that self-
transcendence can take place. Some theorists of deliberative democracy appeal
to a prior sense of unity. Young objects to this because in contemporary plural-
ist society such unity cannot be assumed. It also obviates the need for self-
transcendence central to deliberative democracy. Some deliberative democrats
regard unity not as a starting point, but as an end goal. Young argues that this is
also problematic – some participants, because they already feel excluded from
the deliberation, might feel that their experience is less important with the effect
that unity is forced upon them (Young 1996: 126).

Young argues for a broader conception of deliberation, namely communicative democracy. Communicative democracy includes three additional elements
which are excluded from the deliberative model, namely greeting, rhetoric and
storytelling. According to Young these elements recognise embodiment and
particularity and assist in establishing and maintaining plurality. More than
that, these elements could accommodate cultural differences in the absence of
shared understandings (1996: 129). A model of communicative democracy goes
beyond deliberative democracy to accommodate a plurality of perspectives
and speaking styles. It ultimately addresses the reality of unshared meanings.
This approach might be able to open a space for friendship from whence a
transformation of politics that would ultimately affect consent could start.

Chantal Mouffe puts forward a conception of 'agonistic' democracy as an
alternative to both aggregative (liberal) and deliberative models of democracy.
She argues for a model able to grasp the 'nature of the political' by placing
power and antagonism at its centre (2000: 124). In contrast to deliberative
democracy, which holds that a democratic society will be able to escape power
in its social relations, agonistic democracy focuses on how to 'constitute forms
of power more compatible with democratic values' (Mouffe, 2000: 125). Agonistic democracy allows claims to 'legitimate power', in other words a link
between legitimacy and power in contrast to deliberative democracy that
seeks to eliminate power by means of rational argumentation. The distinction
between politics and the political stands central to agonistic democracy:

> By 'the political', I refer to the dimension of antagonism inherent in human
> relations, antagonism that can take many forms and emerge in different
> types of social relations. 'Politics', on the other hand, indicates the
> ensemble of practices, discourses and institutions which seek to establish a
> certain order and organize human coexistence in conditions that are always
> potentially conflictual because they are affected by the dimension of 'the
> political'.
>
> (Mouffe, 2000: 126)

In an agonistic model of democracy the central question for democracy is not
how to arrive at a rational consensus, but rather how to create a unity in a

context of conflict and diversity: 'The uniqueness of democratic politics does not consist in overcoming this us/them opposition – that is impossible – but in the different way in which it is established' (Mouffe, 2000: 126). The aim of democratic politics is not to eradicate the 'them', but to find a way in which the 'them' can be respected despite their differences. The enemy is reconceptualised as adversary, antagonism reconceptualised as agonism (Mouffe, 2000: 126). An important feature of agonistic democracy is that in contrast to deliberative democracy it allows passion, passions are mobilised 'towards democratic designs' (Mouffe, 2000: 127). Agonistic democracy like deliberative democracy requires a certain form of consensus, a consensus about what Mouffe calls the 'ethico-political' principles. However, agonistic democracy acknowledges that such a consensus would itself be limited by 'conflictual consensus' because the ethico-political principles would be open to different interpretations (Mouffe, 2000: 127). An agonistic model, by accepting the presence of agonism, conflict and passion is more open to human finitude and the risk of failure. Like the communicative model, this could open a space for another kind of politics where friendships could be explored, the fantasy of sovereignty at least blurred.

A POLITICS OF ACKNOWLEDGEMENT, HUMAN ACTION AND STORYTELLING

Patchen Markell in a work, *Bound by Recognition* (2003; see also Cocks, 2006), develops a politics of acknowledgement as an alternative to a politics of recognition that has become central to certain forms of identity politics, but also to democracy and justice in general. Suggestive for my investigation of consent is his argument that recognition assumes a notion of the self that asserts a kind of sovereignty in contrast to friendship. In the discussion above I have followed the distinction drawn between sovereignty and friendship by Bergowitz and Cornell in their analysis of the main characters of *Mystic River*. As I understand Markell, acknowledgement would be closer to a relation based on friendship, rather than sovereignty.

He argues that misrecogntion has come to be seen as synonymous with injustice and questions this approach where democracy is equated with mutual transparency, a world without alienation where people seem to be confident of their invulnerability to powers beyond their control (2003: 3). Following Arendt's (1958) notion of human unpredictability and her warning against over-ambitious attempts to rescue social and political life from its own fragility, he asks whether mutual recognition ever could be possible. He argues that the relation between human agency and specific identity in the notion of recognition could blind us to aspects in our own situation (2003: 4). For Markell, mutual recognition is an impossible and incoherent objective because of human finitude, the openness and unpredictability of the future. He follows Arendt's notion of the 'non-sovereign character of human action' (Arendt, 1958: 179; Markell, 2003:

5). Misrecognition in her understanding would mean the misrecognition of one's own fundamental circumstances. Markell offers the following definition of misrecognition, namely 'ways of patterning and arranging the world that allow some people and groups to enjoy sovereign agency at other's expense' (2003: 5). For him there lies a certain irony in the ideal of recognition in that the desire for sovereign agency itself sustains forms of injustice (2003: 5). Acknowledgement could offer a better alternative than recognition because it does not demand that all people be known and respected as who they really are and would accordingly not be reduced to a specific sense of sovereignty or invulnerability.

Acknowledgement in his view amounts to the following: it is self rather than other directed; the object is not one's own identity, but rather one's own basic ontological condition; finitude that is central to acknowledgement is understood as the practical limits in the face of unpredictability and contingency rather than the impossibility of knowing others; and finally, it is understood as accepting the risk of conflict, hostility and misunderstanding (2003: 38). The politics of recognition is always characterised by a certain important misrecognition of the self, for example the failure to acknowledge one's own basic ontological conditions (2003: 10). He explains this by stating that the pursuit of recognition goes hand in hand with an aspiration to sovereignty. Although recent calls for recognition by certain groups, for example, display a shift from an atomistic idea of self to socially and historically situated subjects, there is a clear assumption of the nature of one's identity or the group's identity. For Arendt identity comes into being through public deeds and words, in action and in speech – agents do not have control over their own identities, who we are is rather the outcome of our interactions and engagements (friendships) with other people. Arendt claimed that 'nobody could be the author or producer of his own life story' (Arendt, 1958: 13). Identity can only be observed in retrospect by a storyteller of one's life.

Adriana Cavarero follows Hannah Arendt's and Karen Blixen's insistence on storytelling as a way of putting forward a new way of politics (Cavarero, 2000; see also Cavarero, 2005). Central to her argument is the uniqueness of every person so often negated by traditional philosophy, or to connect with Markell by fixing a particular identity. Cavarero recalls the following story told by Karen Blixen:

> A man, who lived by a pond, was awakened one night by a great noise. He went out into the night and headed for the pond, but in the darkness, running up and down, back and forth, guided only by the noise, he stumbled and fell repeatedly. At last, he found a leak in the dike, from which water and fish were escaping. He set to work plugging the leak and only when he had finished went back to bed. The next morning, looking out of the window, he saw with surprise that his footprints had traced the figure of a stork on the ground.
>
> (Cavarero, 2000: 1)

Blixen responds to this story by asking: 'when the design of my life is complete, will I see, or will others see a stork?' (Cavarero, 2000: 1). Cavarero continues and asks if 'the course of every life allows itself to be looked upon in the end like a design that has a meaning?' (2000: 1). However, she adds an important aspect – the design in question cannot be foreseen, projected or controlled. The man in the story did not intend anything more than to fulfill the purpose of finding the cause of the noise and then fixing the dike. The significance of this story is the end result – the 'figural unity of the design' that simply happened without any preconceived plan, design or project.

Following Arendt and Blixen, Cavarero's argument rests on the notion that a person's uniqueness, *who* someone is, can only be revealed by stories. She contrasts this to philosophy's tendency to define and to generalise, to focus merely on *what* someone is. One could add not only law's tendency to define and generalise, but also the failure of all attempts of legal reform and policy (gender mainstreaming for example) to address the uniqueness of a person's life. I understand Cavarero's concern with the *who* in terms of friendship and the *what* in terms of sovereignty. A person's life story as said above cannot be designed or planned. It is also temporal and fragile – the stork that appeared was not only unintentional but also fleeting, momentary. In Cavarero's words: 'it is the fleeting mark of a unity that is only glimpsed. It is the gift of a moment in the mirage of desire' (2000: 2). For Cavarero, philosophy, law and policy cannot capture who someone is because who someone is lies outside language and also because of each person's uniqueness and singularity. She draws an important relation between the story, the revelation who someone is and what she regards as a new approach to and understanding of politics. Following Arendt, Cavarero sees in storytelling an alternative approach to politics that captures the uniqueness of each person as well as the interaction between people. Central to this sense of politics is that each person's life story can be told – the potential of narrability of one's life is prior to the content – and the interaction that takes place between people. Storytelling is political because it is relational. Storytelling as a political act invokes the struggle of a collective subjectivity, but also emphasises the fragility of the unique. Of significance is Cavarero's notion of another kind of subjectivity – not claiming the all and ever presence of mastery, but narrability.

As already alluded to above, the knowledge of the life story, what the life story says, is not what is important, but rather the fact that each person has a life story – the narratable self. This sense of the self, the who, revealed by stories defies and stands in resistance to present discourses of unity and generalisation.

Markell's uneasiness with identity politics, following Arendt, resonates with Cavarero's argument about the who that can only be disclosed through action and speech, storytelling. For Markell, the aspiration to achieve sovereign agency is contradictory to the very condition of plurality. The tradition of Western philosophy is to escape the condition of non-sovereignty by either abstention from human affairs or by recasting human affairs as matters of making rather than acting. Markell refers to modern politics and its affinity with rule-boundedness, the acceptance to be subject to sovereign governance. He relates the wish for recognition with Western philosophy's wish for the security and preoccupation with death (2003: 14) that Arendt refused by making natality and new beginning central to her theory of political action. Recognition in all forms, like death, will always be a reduction of someone 'as such and such, that is as something which we fundamentally are not' (Markell, 2003: 14). He refers to Arendt's use of 'welcoming' instead of 'to be recognized' (2003: 180). Welcoming is seen as something that cannot be earned or deserved, but rather the risky inclusion of another in a shared activity without reference to her identity, character or merit.[2]

Following Markell's argument, acknowledgement starts from the self, from a dismantlement of one's own privilege before including. This is also illustrated by Sean's action in *Mystic River* – only after accepting his own finitude can he engage with his wife in a meaningful way, in friendship. According to Markell the assertion of identity and the claim for recognition based on that identity assumes an impossible knowledge and a claim of sovereignty that can only end in a reduction of what someone is. Friendship and narrative politics could create a space for difference, for not knowing, and challenge masculine normativity that excludes difference and alterity. It could accordingly open more possibilities for consent, dissent and refusal.

One of the problems of a politics of recognition based on a restricted recognition has been illustrated in a recent South African case, which I discuss below.

A POLITICS OF CONSTITUTIONAL RECOGNITION IN *JORDAN*

In a case note on the South African case of *S v Jordan*,[3] a case in which the constitutional court confirmed the validity of the criminalisation of sex work, Wessel le Roux laments the path taken by the court of addressing the plight of the respondents within the framework of the 'politics of constitutional recognition', thereby neglecting the framing of sex work as an economic issue (2003: 453). Le Roux goes to great lengths to make an argument as to why the court's reasoning that the case had to be decided under the interim constitution, whose section protecting the right to economic activity differed significantly from that of the final constitution, is flawed. Of more interest here is his argument that the

---

2   See also Gillian Rose's discussion of risk in relation to Hannah Arendt, Rahel Varnhagen and Rosa Luxembourg, in *The Broken Middle* (1992).
3   *S v Jordan*, 2002 (6) SA 642 (CC).

court's choice of a politics of recognition instead of a politics of distribution is reflective of present constitutional politics (2003: 462). He notes that as with the gay liberation struggle, the sex workers in *Jordan* fought for more than mere liberal toleration, but for 'cultural recognition and diversity' in their struggle to legalise sex work (2003: 464). In *National Coalition for Gay and Lesbian Equality v Minister of Justice*,[4] the case where the court had to decide on the constitutionality of the rule that criminalised gay sex, the right to equality was put forward as the central focal point of the case. As Le Roux notes, political (and public) recognition for gay relationships was central to the case. The constitutional court responded by giving constitutional recognition to gay relationships, in particular in order to protect the 'intimate and nurturing' nature of these relationships.

Consequent to this line of argument, the court in *Jordan* could not legalise sex work for the reason that sex workers, or as the court preferred to name them, prostitutes, are not involved in 'intimate and nurturing relationships' (2003: 463). Le Roux, following an argument by Margaret Radin, describes the court's approach to female sexuality as 'a precarious dream of true female love' (2003: 463). This resonates with the judgment in *President of the Republic of South Africa v Hugo*,[5] a case where a prisoner who was a single father challenged a presidential pardon which released single mothers from prison. In *Hugo*, although it might be argued that the court was closer to recognising the economic issues at hand, the court followed a similar approach towards women by stereotyping them as the primary caretakers of young children. The credo of intimate and caring relationships was again the underlying reasoning for legalising gay marriages recently in the case of *Minister of Home Affairs v Fourie*.[6]

Recalling the three wives of the three main male characters in *Mystic River*, Jimmy's wife Annabeth symbolises the court's dream of the loving, caring, faithful wife, the woman who will stand by her man and convince him of his kingship, his infinity if needs be. The precarious relationship between sovereignty and friendship arises again – the ideal relationship that fulfils the court's dream of the faithful wife (or partner) is one in the realm of sovereignty and not friendship. The sex worker escapes a fixed identity – she lives in what Rose (1992) calls the broken middle, a life of equivocation and risk. Not only does the sex worker escape the constitutional dream of the caring and faithful wife, she also escapes the identity of the prostitute, the stereotypical bad woman. It is the ordinariness, the everydayness of the sex worker, engaging in economic activity to provide for herself and the people that she cares about, that the court fails to recognise. The impossibility of the sex worker to be placed within a specific identity is symbolic of life in general. No one's identity can be fixed once and for all. Returning to the Arendtian notion of natality or Cavarero's

---

4 *National Coalition for Gay and Lesbian Equality v Minister of Justice*, 1999 (1) SA 6 (CC).
5 *President of the Republic of South Africa v Hugo*, 1997 (4) SA 1 (CC).
6 *Minister of Home Affairs v Fourie*, 2005 (3) SA 429 (CC).

distinction between the who and the what, because of plurality and difference, who someone is will always escape fixed definition. The logic of sovereignty cannot allow a politics of friendship that is open to plurality and difference.

The argument that I've been making from the outset of this chapter is that the kind of politics that would allow consent to be more than mere coercion must be one based on friendship and not sovereignty. To what extent could Markell's notion of acknowledgement escape the flaws of recognition? In relation to the sovereignty/friendship line of argument, one could agree that acknowledgement might be closer to a kind of politics that allows difference and plurality – isn't friendship the space where we could acknowledge our own finitude, where spaces for true consensual relations could be disclosed?

CONSENT, FRIENDSHIP, SOVEREIGNTY

> The human being who has lost his place in a community, his political status in the struggle of time, and the legal personality which makes his actions and part of his destiny a consistent whole, is left with those qualities which usually can become articulate only in the sphere of private life and must remain unqualified, mere existence in all matters of public concern. This mere existence . . . can be adequately dealt with only by the unpredictable hazards of friendship and sympathy, or by the great and incalculable grace of love, which says with Augustine, '*Volo ut sis* (I want you to be),' without being able to give any particular reason for such supreme and unsurpassable affirmation.
>
> (Arendt, 1951: 301)

> There is no friendship without this knowledge of finitude.
>
> (Derrida, 1986: 29; Thomson, 2005a: 20)

So far I have reflected on the relation between consent, politics and the political. I have argued for a feminist politics of consent that would aim to disclose and disrupt masculine normativity so that possibilities for multiple social interactions, relations and ways of being can be considered. I have followed a distinction between friendship and sovereignty that regards friendship as a relation that respects equality, difference and fidelity and sovereignty as a relation of control, self-assertion and violence. I have considered whether liberal and deliberative conceptions of politics and a politics of recognition play along with a politics of sovereignty that privileges and excludes and whether communicative (Young) and agonistic (Mouffe) politics and a politics of acknowledgement (Markell), human action and new beginning (Arendt) and storytelling (Cavarero) reflect a politics of friendship. In light of the observations on the withdrawal of the political (Lacoue-Labarthe and Nancy), a relation of sovereignty is made possible because of the withdrawal and consequent exclusion of difference that privilege one way of sociality. In this concluding section I reveal some caution with respect to this reliance on friendship with reference to Derrida's notion of friendship.

In *The Politics of Friendship* (1997), Derrida is concerned with an understanding of democracy that is different from other kinds of political associations based on hierarchy and inequality. He turns to friendship as a possible form of democratic equality, but exposes the paradox of friendship, namely that the desire to have friends betrays the possibility of friendship. Derrida illustrates how all forms of friendship become fraternity by preferring certain friends, thereby excluding others. Friendship should entail the 'possibility of befriending just anyone' (Thomson, 2005a: 10; Derrida, 1997: 22). However, fraternity is already 'an established relation with friends' (Thomson, 2005a: 10; Derrida, 1997: 22–23). Not only is friendship in terms of fraternity based on a logic of preference, it is presented as something natural. Yet again we see the withdrawal of the political that allows one social interaction to become the norm to the exclusion of others. If all friendships become brotherhood could friendship be followed as a possible relation that could allow for multiple socialities and accordingly spaces for consent, dissent and refusal?

A crucial issue in *The Politics of Friendship* is the question of the 'sister' (1997: 271–306). If all friendships become fraternity – a brotherhood amongst men – what about the friendship amongst women and between men and women? All relations and social interactions are based on a masculine politics that allows no real consent, dissent and refusal. Women face a double exclusion – they are excluded by a hegemonic discourse that recognises only the same; when recognised they are instantly neutralised, generalised, humanised. Where does this leave women? Derrida names two options: one, we could admit that the political is in fact part of this phallogocentrism and decide to displace politics altogether – we could consider what would replace politics as such; two, we could keep the name of politics but analyse the logic and disrupt it from within (1997: 158; see also Thomson, 2005a, 2005b). And of course for Derrida there is no choice. As in other examples he holds on to a double strategy.

> If there were a single thesis to this essay, it would posit that there could be no choice: the decision would once again consist in deciding without excluding, in the invention of other names and other concepts, in moving out *beyond this* politics without ceasing to intervene therein to transform it.
>
> (Derrida, 1997: 158–59)

Thomson explains Derrida's notion of 'aimance' as an experience of friendship between active and passive, a relation without distinction and without exclusion (2005a: 15). He identifies two contradictory moments of friendship, the one being the possibility of having many friends with whom I am in no relation active or passive yet; the other one being the moment where I betray the possibility of having many friends by preferring certain friends and excluding others (2005a: 16).

The logic of fraternisation for Derrida is the necessity of betrayal and exclusion. Thomson turns here to responsibility. For Derrida one acts only responsibly if one acts beyond mere calculability and concludes that fraternity is nothing but 'the becoming irresponsible of friendship' (Thomson, 2005a: 16; see also Thomson, 2005b). If friendship could provide a better politics and create more space for consent, it will have to be a responsible friendship, which heeds sovereign masculinity that appears to be natural and is enforced by mere calculability. As in other works Derrida hopes for the day that friendship could be thought of as something that could include also the sister – that could move beyond friendship as fraternity.

> For democracy remains to come . . . Is it possible to open up to the 'come' of a certain democracy which is no longer an insult to the friendship we have striven to think beyond the homo-fraternal and phallogocentric schema?
>
> (Derrida, 1997: 306)

In this chapter I have argued for a feminist politics of consent that would expose masculine normativity and insist on friendship in the face of sovereignty. Derrida's caution on the understanding and working of friendship as nothing but a natural bond amongst men and his call for another kind of friendship must be heard.

> When will we be ready for an experience of freedom and equality that is capable of respectfully experiencing that friendship, which would at least be just, just beyond the law, and measured up against its measurelessness?
>
> (Derrida, 1997: 306)

BIBLIOGRAPHY

Arendt, H., *The Origins of Totalitarianism*. Harcourt, Brace & Co, New York 1951.

Arendt, H., *The Human Condition*. University of Chicago Press, Chicago 1958.

Bergowitz, R. and Cornell, D., 'Parables of revenge and masculinity in Clint Eastwood's *Mystic River*', *Law, Culture and Humanities*, 1, 2005, pp.316–32.

Blixen, K., *Out of Africa*. Random House, New York 1938.

Cavarero, A., *Relating Narratives, Storytelling and Selfhood*. Routledge, London 2000.

Cavarero, A., *For More than One Voice: Toward a Philosophy of Vocal Expression*. Stanford University Press, Stanford 2005.

Cocks, J., 'Sovereignty, identity, and insecurity: a commentary on Patchen Markell's *Bound by Recognition*', *Polity*, 38, 2006, pp.13–19.

Derrida, J., *Memoires for Paul de Man*. Columbia University Press, New York 1986.

Derrida, J., *The Politics of Friendship*. Verso, London 1997.

Derrida, J., *Rogues: Two Essays on Reason*. Stanford University Press, Stanford 2005.

Frank, J., *A Democracy of Distinction*. University of Chicago Press, Chicago 2004.

Lacoue-Labarthe, P. and Nancy, J.-L., eds, *Retreating the Political*. Routledge, New York 1997.

Lefort, C., *Democracy and Political Theory*, Macey, D. (trans). Blackwell, Oxford 1988.

Le Roux, W.B., 'Sex work, the right to occupational freedom and the constitutional politics of recognition', *South African Law Journal*, *120*, 2003, pp.452–65.

Markell, P., *Bound by Recognition*. Princeton University Press, Princeton 2003.

Mouffe, C., *The Return of the Political*. Verso, London 1993.

Mouffe, C., 'For an agonistic model of democracy', in O'Sullivan, N., ed., *Political Theory in Transition*. Routledge, London 2000, pp.113–30.

Rose, G., *The Broken Middle*. Blackwell, Oxford 1992.

Thomson, A., 'What's to become of "democracy to come"?', *Postmodern Culture*, *15.3*, 2005a, pp.1–26.

Thomson, A., *Deconstruction and Democracy*. Continuum, London 2005b.

Van der Walt, J.W.G., *Law and Sacrifice*. Birkbeck Law Press, London 2005.

Young, I.M., 'Communication and the other: beyond deliberative democracy', in Benhabib, S., ed., *Democracy and Difference: Contesting the Boundaries of the Political*. Princeton University Press, Princeton 1996, pp.120–35.

Chapter 5

Choosing freely: theoretically reframing the concept of consent

Sharon Cowan

INTRODUCTION*

Many feminists critics have taken to task the traditions of Western science and philosophy for their reliance upon hierarchical dichotomies such as male/female, mind/body, rational/emotional, objective/subjective, science/nature and the ways in which woman came to represent the supposedly weaker side of each dualism (body, emotion, nature, etc). These hierarchical divisions have been highlighted by feminists and other critical scholars in many disciplines, for example: in science by critics such as Sandra Harding (1991), in ecology by Vandana Shiva (1989), in law by Catharine MacKinnon (1989), in psychology by Carol Gilligan (1982) and in language by Luce Irigaray (1985). Such feminist analytical work has in the main been spawned by radical feminist critique, but it has recently been extended through post-modern scholarship to focus not only on the designation of Woman as 'other' and inferior, but also on the very distinction itself – to what extent can we really separate nature from science, or mind from body?

In this chapter I explore the way in which rape laws have evolved in the shadow of a particular dualism, resulting in consistently unsatisfactory and ineffective protections for women against sexual assault. Rape has, at various points in time in different jurisdictions, been defined either as a crime of property, a crime of violence, or more recently, as a violation of autonomy. These debates over the definition of rape have been set against the backdrop of the mind/body dichotomy. Nicola Lacey, for example, has suggested that rape law is 'caught . . . between two equally unsatisfactory poles generated by the mind body dualism' (1998: 115). At the same time, it is evident that the boundary between mind and body itself is inherently unstable and is undermined by the

---

* Presentation of the original conference paper on which this chapter is based was made possible by means of a British Academy Overseas Travel Grant for which the author is most grateful. Thanks also to Gillian Calder and Victor Tadros for comments on an earlier draft, and to Rosemary Hunter for invaluable editorial assistance and comments.

very application of law itself; since it is impossible to see inside the mind in order to ascertain people's intentions and beliefs, criminal law infers the mental state of its subjects from actions performed through the body. This is especially problematic in rape where intentions, desires and consent itself, in particular that of the complainant in a rape trial, have historically been inferred from dress, behaviour, intoxication and previous sexual history.

I will argue here that even as rape law evolves, there is a recurring under-lying tension as to which aspect – body or mind – should be the focal point in defining and determining the harm done through sexual assault. In my view rape laws must attempt to avoid the conflation of body with mind, but must also preclude a dichotomised either/or focus on mind/body. It should be possible to acknowledge within rape laws the *convergence* of body and mind, in order to promote respect for and protection of both the embodied and the attitudinal aspects of sexual intimacy. This chapter begins with a discussion of the general question of whether consent is something that must be performed through the body, or whether consent is rather a state of mind. I will then examine how this dichotomy has historically played out as rape law has evolved from an offence of violence to an infringement of autonomy. Finally, I will examine suggestions for reformulating rape laws in a way that allows body *and* mind, not as separate entities but in their convergence in a sense of self, to be encompassed within the definition of the harm of sexual assault.

CONSENT – CAUGHT BETWEEN BODY AND MIND

It is often said that the presence of consent alters the rights and obligations of parties (Hurd, 1996: 123–24) so that where there is consent to a particular action such as touching, the consenter gives up their right not to be touched, and the toucher gains the right to touch without behaving wrongfully. However, this analysis does not in itself answer the question of what constitutes consent. Can consent properly be said to be a state of mind? Or, in order for it to change the rights and obligations of parties involved, must that state of mind be performed, as act or word, through the body, before we can say it constitutes *consent*? In the philosophical canon, there are competing views on this question.

The polarised positions taken in this debate are represented briefly here in summaries of the work of philosophers Heidi Hurd (1996) and Nathan Brett (1998), who have both written on this subject in the context of sexual assault. In her paper 'The moral magic of consent', Hurd perceives consent as attitudinal. She argues that 'a person does all that she needs to do in order to alter the moral rights or obligations of another simply by entertaining the *mens rea* of consent' – that is, consent is an attitude, formed in the *mind* of the consenter (1996: 122). If there is no meaningful choice made by the consenter, because of lack of capacity or opportunity to choose an alternative, consent is not present. Her argument relies on the general claim that the criteria by which we should assess consent mirror those by which we assess criminal liability. Therefore, it is the mental state that is the crucial determining factor of what counts as consent. Without it, an action that looks like consent just *isn't*. It is not enough to say that the consenter desires the other's action. Rather consent is akin to a more purposive state of mind, i.e. intention. Only if the consenter intends to consent to (allow, enable) another's actions will that amount to valid consent (1996: 125, 130). Moreover, the action of the other must match the consenter's description of it (134). Hurd rejects the suggestion that consent is a combination of intention and an action, since an action can only ever be evidence of mental state, and therefore cannot replace intention as being of primary moral relevance. In this way, those who have lost their physical autonomy, perhaps through physical disability, can be protected against sexual assault (136–37).

Nathan Brett, on the other hand, perceives consent as a performative action. For him, the change in rights and obligations of parties is brought about by the giving of permission, and this is achieved by speaking or doing consent (1998: 69). He highlights the fact that consent in a medical law context could not properly be said to be purely a state of mind (70). Consent is 'not an attitude at all. It is to act in a way that has conventional significance in communicating permission' (73). The degree to which something is desired is irrelevant – thus his conception of consent would properly include those who give in to sex for reasons of a 'desire for silence rather than sex' (71–72). The relevant thing is the giving of consent, the action, and not the mental state regarding it (76). Consent as constituted by a mental state does not work in the context of sex because we are often ambivalent in our attitudes about sex. Therefore, the matter turns on what we do or say to give the other party permission to act (80). Brett dismisses the critique that performative models do not capture cases of fraud or force where a person performs consent but the consent is not valid, by saying that the performance under such circumstances does not have the power to change the moral rights and duties of the parties involved (80).

These summaries of the complex debate exemplified in the work of Hurd and Brett give a flavour of the often conflicted nature of discussions about what counts as consent (see also Malm, 1996). However, both positions pose problems for feminist reforms of rape. To say that consent is only a mental attitude does not address the question of ambivalent mental states, and how parties are to discern consent. However, to maintain that consent is purely performative is to minimise the contextual importance of substantive conditions that drive consent, and is perhaps over-inclusive. Both positions are evident in the history of rape law; the debate over what counts as consent in rape laws takes place against this backdrop of whether mind or body can properly be said to be the locus of consent.

Since consent continues to be, philosophically and practically, the focal point in sexual assault, theorising a concept of consent that problematises the body/mind dualism is a central challenge for feminist critiques of rape law. In the next two sections I discuss the process of evolution of rape laws, ostensibly moving away from the body and towards the mind of the victim of rape. Yet the body of the rape complainant returns to centre stage in the rape trial. Throughout this process, mind and body are perceived as two separable and distinct entities, although one is often 'read off' from the other.

CONSENT AND RAPE – THE JOURNEY FROM BODY TO MIND AND BACK AGAIN

Historically, many rape laws did not refer to consent as such, but instead required that the defendant must have used force against the body of the woman, and the woman must have shown physical resistance. It would not have been sufficient for a woman to claim that in her mind she did not want to have sexual intercourse with the defendant. That the offence required the use of physical force is particularly paradoxical where rape laws define rape as sexual intercourse 'against the will' of the victim. This is a common formulation of the offence of rape, as explored in Susan Brownmiller's groundbreaking work *Against Our Will* (1975). In Scotland, for example, the definition of rape until 2002 was sexual intercourse with a woman 'against her will'.[1] Although the term 'will' is associated with questions about one's intentions, desires, purpose and so on, i.e. issues relating to the *mind*, laws on rape which rely on the 'against the will' formulation have in practice grounded the definition of rape in an inquiry as to the amount of force used against, and the level of physical resistance expressed through, the victim's *body*. Prior to the 2002 change in the law, it was not rape in Scotland to have sexual intercourse with an unconscious or sleeping woman for the reason that she had not refused consent.[2] Furthermore, definitions of rape in many American states have remained rooted in the idea that an element of force must be used, even if the requirement that a woman must physically resist has been abandoned (see Note, 2004: 2347–48).

Because of this problematic focus on force and resistance as evidenced through the body of the raped woman, which occluded the specific question of whether or not the sex was wanted, feminists pressed for a shift in emphasis from body to mind, in the form of legal acknowledgment that the wrong of rape is grounded in the infringement of the right to choose for one's self whether and how to be sexually intimate. Consequently, some jurisdictions have moved away from a definition which explicitly focuses on the body as the locus of speculation regarding whether or not there was consent. Rather, rape is

---

1   The case of *Lord Advocate's Reference No.1 of 2001* [2002] SLT 466 redefined rape in Scotland as sexual intercourse without the consent of the victim.

2   In these cases the charge instead would be one of clandestine injury, an offence which was taken much less seriously by the courts as evidenced by a recent case, *Paton v HMA* [2002] SCCR 57.

defined in terms of a violation of sexual autonomy and choice, that is, a lack of consent. The reasoning behind this shift was to show that 'real rape' was not confined only to cases where violence was used.[3] In other words the question, at least in the criminal justice systems which have shifted towards a 'lack of consent' definition of rape, is ostensibly one of whether or not the sex was wanted by the complainant, and whether or not the accused person appreciated this. Under a lack of consent test, submission through silence is not enough to establish consent and a lack of verbal or bodily expression of non-consent will not in theory impede a conviction for rape, at least in England and Wales.[4] In effect, action is not required to show lack of consent; either some sort of expression of consent, or at least a genuine belief in such, is required to indicate that sexual intercourse is wanted. However, the rule that silence does not equal consent does not engage with the question of what *does* constitute consent, and this question poses some problems which I will address below.

The distinction between what was going on in the woman's mind as to whether the sex was wanted, and what the defendant thought was going on in the woman's mind, is expressed in criminal law through the terms *actus reus* and *mens rea*. In Canadian criminal law, for example, the *actus reus* of rape is established if it can be demonstrated that the woman had no will or desire to have sex with the defendant. However, that is clearly not sufficient, since the criminal law demands that the defendant must have some *mens rea* or blameworthy mental state with regard to the act, without which, even if the sex was for the woman unwanted, there can be no finding of rape.

Whether or not a lack of consent was appreciated almost always comes down to whether such non-consent was expressed rather than felt by the victim. The legal gaze thus always returns to the body of the woman when asking the central question which is determinative of liability, in order to assess the defendant's claim that she really did consent, or that he genuinely believed her to be consenting. His basis for either claim is inevitably bound up with the woman's body. Where he claims that she was consenting, an examination of the woman's body will be one central piece of evidence regarding consent (was there, for example, evidence of force or resistance that would indicate a lack of consent?). Where he claims that he mistakenly believed her to be consenting, his belief will usually be based on what the complainant did or said (or failed to do or say), and his perception that she expressed through her body her real, inner desire for sex. While it is common in criminal law to look to a defendant's actions to infer

---

3   However, two potential implications here are that where no actual violent force is used by the defendant, sex without consent is not in itself seen as a form of violence; and that criminal justice agents and juries may continue to cling to stereotypical beliefs about what rape *really* is when discriminating between stranger violence cases and intimate partner or acquaintance 'lack of consent' cases.

4   See *R v Olugboga* [1982] QB 320 – consent can be 'reluctant acquiescence', but is not equal to mere submission.

his mental state, here we are focusing on the body of the raped woman in order to assess the mental state of the man who raped her. In this respect there seems to be no escape from the opposition of mind/body (even while mental states and physical actions are conflated), or the association of women with body, men with the mind.

In contemporary law reform strategies, many jurisdictions have moved towards a focus on autonomy as a way of understanding consent. In the next section I explore arguments that sexual autonomy helps us to capture the wrong of non-consensual sexual intimacy. However, I will argue that it is doubtful that reliance on the concept of autonomy can help to prevent rape law's continual vacillation between body and mind. Indeed, emphasising autonomy can serve to perpetuate rather than undermine the body/mind distinction.

CONSENT AND SEXUAL AUTONOMY

> Society is committed to protecting the personal integrity, both physical and psychological, of every individual. Having control over who touches one's body, and how, lies at the core of human dignity and autonomy.[5]

Contemporary rape law in many jurisdictions is grounded in the protection of individual autonomy to make choices as to one's sexual relationships and contacts. This has been expressed by the Scottish Law Commission recently in the following terms:

> In trying to locate the wrongs involved in certain forms of sexual conduct the most fundamental principle is respect for a person's sexual autonomy. Autonomy is a complex idea but in the context of legal regulation of sexual conduct it involves placing emphasis on a person freely choosing to engage in sexual activity . . . Where a person participates in a sexual act in respect of which she has not freely chosen to be involved, that person's autonomy has been infringed, and a wrong has been done to her.
>
> (Scottish Law Commission, 2006: para.2.3)

Part of this liberal emphasis on rights and responsibilities is an understanding of autonomy as individualised, i.e. not relational, or in terms of the context and substance of interconnecting subjectivities. Thus, while it has been widely used as a way of understanding the wrong of sexual assault, the concept of autonomy has been the subject of much feminist critique (Weait, 2005).[6]

---

5   Major J, *R v Ewanchuk* [1999] 1 SCR at para.28.
6   On the concept of 'relational' autonomy and on valuing dependency, see e.g. Fineman (2003); Friedman (2003).

Because of this connection between autonomy and liberal notions of the bounded self, and because of the centrality of mental capacity (i.e. free will) rather than the embodied self (Lacey, 1998: 111; see also Nedelsky, 1989), Nicola Lacey problematises autonomy and consent as individualistic and removed from any social context. She asserts:

> In focusing on an individualised notion of consent, rather than the conditions under which choices can be meaningful, the prevailing idea of sexual autonomy assumes the mind to be dominant and controlling, irrespective of material circumstances.
>
> (Lacey, 1998: 117)

Part of Lacey's argument is that a particular understanding of autonomy lies at the heart of what the criminal law sees as the wrong of rape – i.e. the violation of *free will*, or the freely made choice to engage in sexual intimacy. To that extent, the way in which rape laws are expressed reflects a concern with the mind rather than the body: 'Nothing in criminal law doctrine invites any expression of the corporeal dimension of this violation of choice' (Lacey, 1998: 112). The other wrong of rape, obscured by a focus on a free will-based notion of autonomy, is what she calls the *affective* dimension, which, although it is taken into account at the sentencing stage, is not a core part of the definitional wrong as stated by the criminal law in its current liberal framework (1998: 115). Rape laws should acknowledge that rape is an offence against the self, and the sense of self, that is, that both the mind and body of a victim are engaged when unwanted sexual intercourse occurs. A focus on a liberal notion of autonomy obscures not just the bodily harm, but the extent to which body and mind converge.

Lacey prefers the more contextualised notion of sexual integrity, which, she argues, better demonstrates that part of the harm centres on the victim's inability to integrate psychic and bodily experiences (1998: 118). She believes that the idea of autonomy is too closely related to its history of the abstract choosing subject and so is always going to lean towards concealment of the body (119). Referring to Cornell, Lacey maintains that the project of personhood requires a more active, positive and embodied view of the sexual self than autonomy has traditionally allowed (120; see also Childs, 2001: 311). Ideally then, we should both conceptualise and operationalise consent in the context of sexual assault and rape in a way that demonstrates respect for what we might call 'embodied autonomy' or what Lacey would call sexual integrity. The aim, then, of any rape law should be promotion of sexual contact as mutual, communicative and as a positive aspect or reflection of sexual integrity/autonomy.

EMBODIED AUTONOMY, OR REUNITING BODY AND MIND

In conceptualising consent, Monica Cowart argues that we should have one view of consent for the purposes of all human activity, and define consent in an 'unbiased, systematic manner that can be theoretically applied' (2004: 496). Her argument is based on the view of genuine consent as necessarily being preceded by a number of conditions which must exist in order for the act of consent to be performed, and that it is the speaker's intention, alongside the essential characteristics of the act of consent, that gives rise to real consent. So, for Cowart, consent is a combination of what the speaker intended, and the characteristics of the exchange between the parties, as long as these fulfil her minimum necessary conditions, as described below. So, 'for an act of consent to occur, the appropriate intention must always correspond with the core principle that defines that act' (2004: 524). Thus she aims to bring together intention, or mind, with bodily expressions of that intention, managing to avoid the absolute mind versus body approach adopted by philosophers such as Hurd and Brett. According to Cowart, only where the will and the action are positively present and converge is consent really present.

The conditions she refers to include minimum standards of communication, and a mutual understanding of the thing being consented to (X not Y). In this regard, the mental states of both parties have to be taken into account. This clearly accounts for cases where A tells B that he is performing some kind of medical or other therapeutic treatment, which she consents to, but he then goes on to sexually assault her.[7] In addition, a range of real choices is a minimum necessary condition for consent to exist – Cowart explains that 'if the individual is limited to only one option (i.e. forced to either grant or refuse) then an act of consent cannot occur since the nature of a request implies that the respondent will be able to grant or deny it' (2004: 511). She recognises, therefore, as does for example medico-legal discourse, that a right to consent is only meaningful if accompanied by a corresponding right to refuse, and this question of available options should be assessed from the individual's own point of view (514). Further, incorporating the speaker's intention into the equation deals with cases of coerced consent – if B says yes to sex with A because she has been coerced, her real intention is not to have sex but to avoid the harm threatened, therefore there is no consent, even if she said yes. That consent is given of a person's own free will and not coerced is also one of her minimum necessary conditions for consent to exist in the first place – 'acts of consent should occur when an individual's will is in compliance with an action that is proposed by another' (513). Again, only where intention and action converge will consent be said to exist. Thus Cowart's approach more accurately reflects the substance of

---

7   As in the cases of *R v Flattery* (1877) 2 QBD 410; *R v Williams* [1923] 1 KB 240.

the agreement or lack thereof between the parties than the position taken in much legal discourse, where consent is taken to subsist until vitiated by certain circumstances (Cowan, 2007).

The next question, then, is whether we can escape rape law's vacillation between mind and body in practice. Here I will examine the issue of whether sexual contact was wanted, within a framework of analysis that combines intention with action. I will argue that we can capture within law the spirit of Cowart's attempt to converge body and mind, by highlighting the process and context of communication and negotiation between partners to sexual intimacy. In doing so, we can also bring attention back to the defendant in a rape trial, and avoid a primary focus on the bodily expressions of consent that may or may not have been made by the complainant.

CONSENT, COMMUNICATION AND NEGOTIATION

Michelle Anderson (2005) characterises existing consent models in rape law as either 'No Models' or 'Yes Models'. Under the No Model, which is used in many US states, the complainant must have communicated 'no' in order for consent to be absent and for there to be a finding of rape. This does not require that the defendant has used force, only that he acted without the consent of the complainant. Nor does it require the physical resistance of the woman concerned, only that she should have verbally refused. However, this is clearly problematic; it requires the woman to signal non-consent, without which consent is presumed. The feminist critiques of this approach are longstanding (see, e.g. MacKinnon, 1989).

Many jurisdictions that have relied on the No Model have since moved towards what Anderson would call the Yes Model of consent, which requires affirmative consent and recognises that silence does not equal consent. The Yes Model, however, is only marginally better than the No Model according to Anderson. This is for two reasons. First, conceptually, the model still relies on consent, a concept which cannot practically do all the work in the context of rape. A single term which is rooted in notions of the liberal atomistic self, and has traditionally been drawn narrowly in rape law, is ill equipped to capture the wrongs of rape which arise in a variety of different contexts − rape through coercion, through drugging, through threats, through fraud and so on. Victor Tadros (2006) makes a similar point.

Second, on a practical level, the objection focuses on the expression of consent − that a yes can be inferred through the body, from non-verbal behaviour. Many contemporary commentators who believe that consent to sex can be established through communication suggest that this can occur non-verbally (see, e.g. Schulhofer, 1998; Wertheimer, 2003; Husak and Thomas, 2001). In some American states, 'positive co-operation' in sexual contact is needed in order for that contact to be lawful, but actual words are not required, and consent can be communicated by 'overt action' (Note, 2004: 2350–51).

There are many problems with this reading of what can constitute consent in a Yes Model, not least of which is the evidence from empirical observations of responses to rape, showing that some rape victims react to sexual trauma through physical paralysis and mental dissociation (Anderson, 2005: 105). Under the Yes Model this could conceivably be interpreted as consent. There are also serious questions as to whether non-verbal signals should be able to constitute consent in every circumstance. Arguably, for example, two people in a long-term relationship who have developed good communication about their desires are differently placed from those on a first date who do not know each other at all. Partners who have established a pattern or custom of communications need not necessarily express consent verbally on every occasion (Anderson, 2005: 117). However, there are good reasons to think that where parties are unfamiliar with each other's body language, and have no background knowledge of the ways in which the other responds to intimate situations, it will often be the case that men will misinterpret women's 'signals'. Sociological research shows that men often infer consent (e.g. from flirting) where there is none (Anderson, 2005: 117).

In addition, both Yes and No Models place the onus on the responding party (usually the woman) to accept or refuse consent. Consent is perceived to be an enabling permission, given by one (the passive party) to another (the active party) who wants the right to lawfully engage in sexual intimacy. The same can be true of consent in other contexts, such as medicine, where a patient agrees to some procedure being carried out by a health care worker, or where permission is given by a suspect to a police officer to carry out a search of their person. Both of these examples show consent working in a primarily unilateral, and arguably gendered, sense. Especially in a sexual assault context, this view of consent supports the gendered depiction of the person asking for permission (by definition the man in rape cases) as the active party, and the respondent (usually the woman) as passively receptive (see also Lacey, 1998: 114).[8]

Of course on one level this is an accurate description of what has occurred, and for some it might be a necessary political evil to accept women as the 'passive' victim in return for an acknowledgement that this was sexual contact of an intimate nature that was not desired or authorised. However, and as Anderson says, in the real world, sexual contact is not usually a set of acts performed by an active party on a passively accepting recipient. It is not

---

8   This approach to female sexuality is still visible in contemporary legal discourse – where two under-age consenting adults have sex, both English and Scots law treat the young man as the perpetrator and the young woman as the victim, and this has been held not to be discriminatory. See *E v DPP*, *Times* 8 February 2005; and s.5(3) of the Criminal Law (Consolidation) (Scotland) Act 1995. See also Note (1999).

appropriate for contemporary rape law to support an understanding of women's sexuality as passive, or of women as completely lacking in agency in sexual intimacy, nor is it an appropriate way of describing the reality of many people's sexual experiences. Sexual acts usually happen as continuing acts that weave together over a period of time rather than as snapshot moments where we can discern fixed active/passive roles.[9]

Anderson suggests that if making consent the central element of the offence of rape can only offer us a choice of the Yes or the No Models of consent, we should abandon lack of consent as a definitional part of the offence. Rather, law should look to the substantive question of whether or not the acts were mutual, and more specifically, whether and how they were *negotiated*. Negotiation would be defined as 'an open discussion in which partners come to a free autonomous agreement about the act of penetration' (Anderson, 2005: 107). Agreement is also interpreted as something which is 'dynamic and active', and contextually and temporally sensitive (215). Negotiation involves 'reciprocal responsibilities between the parties' (123). One advantage of this approach is that it reflects the ongoing process involved rather than trying to capture yes/no snapshot moments in time. Furthermore, if the parties are engaging in sexual penetration for the first time, verbal negotiation would be required, both legally and ethically (131), thus requiring a *conversation* (138). By definition negotiation is verbal, unless the parties have a pre-existing context of knowledge, trust and communication. Anderson claims that this model would promote respect and humanity, 'maximize autonomy and equality and minimize coercion and subordination' (107).

Thus she manages to avoid a rigid rule that there must always be verbal communication, meeting the challenge of the critique that communication models are unworkable because 'real life' relationships do not always depend on verbal exchanges. At the same time she retains the main plank of positive communication models, in stating that unless there are good reasons to believe that a context of trust and knowledge exists between the parties, negotiation must be verbally expressed. The model is also gender neutral – the offence is sexual penetration without negotiation, and so women and men can be both perpetrators and victims. The model would not necessarily prevent rapes, but would signal, through the legal process, what sorts of interactions would be unlawful. Difficulties with proof would be no greater than those currently faced

---

9   That is not to say that parties cannot choose to behave in this way, and I do not propose to deal here with the subject of SM and negotiation of roles and boundaries in that context. It should also be noted that consent is not the only consideration in this problem area, and should not be the only target of feminist critique within rape law. The dichotomised and gendered active/passive approach to sexuality is also constructed by the very fact that rape is defined as an act of *penile* penetration, where sex is always already something that men do to women, and which women can either accept or refuse. Again, however, this essay cannot do justice to this complex debate (see, e.g. Gardner and Shute, 2000; Roberts and Mohr, 1994).

in the courtroom when people disagree about whether or not there was consent, or a genuine belief in consent.

This approach extends a communicative model of consent to require negotiation between parties rather than burdening one party (the woman) with the responsibility for communicating consent or its absence. While the model does not address questions of whether women can ever truly and freely negotiate as equals with men, especially on issues of sex, the power of this model becomes apparent by looking at the ways in which it has been recently critiqued.

Cowling criticises communicative models, mainly on three counts – they do not allow for women who want to be passive when engaging in sexual 'romance'; they take us too far away from the reality of most sexual encounters; and that a yes (however communicated) expressed under patriarchy is not enough to establish agreement (he calls this the Dworkin/MacKinnon objection) (2002/3: 52). With regard to the first criticism, it can be said that through negotiation parties could agree to take whatever roles they like in sexual intimacy, but there might be strong policy reasons for requiring that conversations be had between the parties before the defendant can rely on a defence of belief in consent that is grounded in a woman's passive acceptance. We gain more than we lose from this requirement. In answer to the second charge, it might be true to say that explicit consent is an unrealistic expectation, especially between long-term partners. However, a general communicative model does not have to follow the Antioch College Sexual Offences policy in requiring that all consent must be verbally agreed. Cowling paints a stereotypical picture of the communication model when he uses the Antioch example as representative of the model. As Anderson notes, there may be circumstances where a verbal conversation is not necessary, but these are questions of fact in every case.

As to the third criticism, David Archard critiques the 'MacKinnon/Dworkin' arguments against consent on the basis that they are universalist and do not take into account the complexities of the simultaneous operation of different axes of power such as race and class as well as gender (1998: 87–94). Consent, while often constrained, cannot be said to be totally impossible between all men and all women at all times. Conversely, however, clearly a communication of a 'yes' is not always sufficient, as for example fraud-rape cases demonstrate. Cowling is right in suggesting that a system based merely on question/response does not result in effective rape laws. However, the point of communicative sexuality is to look beyond even an explicit yes/no to the process by which the choice was made.

Cowling's scepticism comes from an unfortunately narrow reading of communicative sexuality as being solely about an explicit ask/respond model. On the contrary, real communication goes beyond the moment of question/response to make sure parties understand not just linguistic and physical conventions in communication, but that, as Cowart (2004) would have it, they understand each other's intentions. It is important to recognise that critiques such as Cowling's miss their target – they do not in fact go to the heart of the ideal of communication or negotiation per se, but rather to the limits of communication when it operates under the constraints inherent within the concept of consent itself.

This is one of the reasons that some writers in this area have rejected consent as a definitional part of the offence of rape and have focused instead on the circumstances in which the consent, communication or negotiation takes place (Tadros, 2006). Anderson's negotiation model does more to address the question of the knowledge of the parties with respect to the context surrounding the agreement, and in that sense a defendant could not rely on wilful blindness to claim that he thought there was consent to sex. A requirement for real and genuine communication through negotiation would allow for a charge of rape in fraud cases. For coercion cases to be included, however, it would be necessary to ensure that there was what Tadros (1999) calls 'fair opportunity to express your will', because 'negotiation' can, and often does, take place between two inherently unequal parties. A formal contract model (based on liberal, capitalist, masculinist ideals) does not work in this context. According to Tadros, if the defendant knew (or arguably should have known) that the other party did not have a fair opportunity to express her will, and 'negotiated' on that basis to reach a 'yes', he would be charged with rape.

Cowling is resistant to the 'wholesale changes to sexual customs' that moving to a communicative mode would bring (2002/3: 58), and the 'extreme ideas encapsulating communicative sexuality' (63). Yet wholesale changes have often been necessary in the arena of sexual assault. Just as we recognised in law the reality of wife rape, an extreme move for many commentators (e.g. Williams, 1991), we need to begin to talk about the promotion of sexual contact as mutual, communicative and as a positive aspect or reflection of sexual integrity/ autonomy.

CONCLUSION

Rape law is haunted by the spectre of women's bodies, even as it moves towards the ideal of protecting sexual autonomy. Rape laws in themselves do not prevent rape. No manner of theorising about consent will be even nearly sufficient to address questions of how to deal with the problem of rape (Kelly et al, 2005). However, it is necessary to try to define the wrong caused by sexual assault, and to try to refine the law so that it properly sets out the parameters of unlawful conduct and the kinds of behaviour that are expected in sexual matters. The process of engendering a change in the views impacting on the commission, reporting and treatment of rape is at least engaged by asking what we mean in practice by consent and choice, and whether our legal concepts can stand up to the job of protecting the vulnerable whilst allowing the positive development of sexual personhood. As Lacey (1998: 122) has stated: 'the most important conditions for sexual equality and integrity lie in cultural attitudes rather than coercive legal rules'. We need also, therefore, to change 'prevailing gender norms' (Jewkes and Abrahams, 2002: 1242) in order to ensure that rape laws are implemented and not circumvented.

I have argued that it is imperative that the wrong of rape is defined in a way that encompasses a violation of not only body and mind as separate entities, but a violation of the embodied autonomous self. This may not be possible within a legal framework that relies solely on consent as a crucial defining factor of the offence. Retaining consent may not allow us to move beyond the debates that dichotomise consent as either a state of mind or a bodily performance. While Monica Cowart relies on a permission model which does nothing to undermine the active/passive gendered roles in sexually intimate situations, her approach allows us a way of theorising about consent that does not divorce body from mind, or associate men and women to either side of the mind/body dichotomy. Both parties must intend and perform consent for sexual intercourse to be lawful. This analysis is useful for anti-consent critics who wish to formulate an offence of rape where the wrong is a violation of embodied autonomy. When read alongside Michelle Anderson's negotiation model, which stresses an active role for both parties, this might provide a way of envisaging a convergence of both mind and body, active and responsive roles, within a rape law that enhances sexual autonomy and respects the bodily and affective aspects of sexual intimacy.

BIBLIOGRAPHY

Anderson, M., 'Negotiating sex', *Southern California Law Review*, 78, 2005, pp.101–38.
Archard, D., *Sexual Consent*. Westview Press, Oxford 1998.
Brett, N., 'Sexual offenses and consent', *Canadian Journal of Law and Jurisprudence*, *11(1)*, 1998, pp.69–88.
Brownmiller, S., *Against Our Will*. Bantam Books, London 1975.
Childs, M., 'Sexual autonomy and law', *Modern Law Review*, 64, 2001, pp.309–23.
Cowan, S., 'Freedom and capacity to make a choice: a feminist analysis of consent in the criminal law', in Munro, V. and Stychin, C., eds, *Sexuality and the Law: Feminist Engagements*. Routledge–Cavendish, Abingdon, Oxford 2007, pp.51–71.
Cowart, M., 'Consent, speech act theory, and legal disputes', *Law and Philosophy*, 23, 2004, pp.495–525.
Cowling, M., 'Should communicative sexuality be written into English law on rape?', *Contemporary Issues in Law*, 2002/03, pp.47–63.
Fineman, M., *The Autonomy Myth: a Theory of Dependency*. The New Press, New York 2003.
Friedman, M., *Autonomy, Gender, Politics*. Oxford University Press, Oxford 2003.
Gardner, J. and Shute, S., 'The wrongness of rape', in Horder, J., ed., *Oxford Essays on Jurisprudence* (Fourth Series). Oxford University Press, Oxford 2000, pp.193–217.
Gilligan, C., *In a Different Voice: Psychological Theory and Women's Development*. Harvard University Press, Cambridge MA 1982.

Harding, S., *Whose Science? Whose Knowledge? Thinking from Women's Lives*. Open University Press, Milton Keynes 1991.

Husak, D. and Thomas, G., 'Rapes without rapists: consent and reasonable mistake', *Philosophical Issues*, 11, 2001, pp.86–117.

Hurd, H., 'The moral magic of consent', *Legal Theory*, 2, 1996, pp.121–46.

Irigaray, L., *This Sex Which is Not One*, Porter, C. with Burke, C. (trans). Cornell University Press, Ithaca 1985.

'I was sexually assaulted . . . and contracted HIV', *The Guardian*, 18 February 2006.

Jewkes, R. and Abrahams, N., 'The epidemiology of rape and sexual coercion in South Africa: an overview', *Social Science and Medicine*, 55, 2002, pp.1231–44.

Kelly, L., Lovett, J. and Regan, L., *A Gap or a Chasm? Attrition in Reported Rape Cases* (Home Office Research Study 293). HMSO, London 2005.

Lacey, N., *Unspeakable Subjects: Feminist Essays in Legal and Social Theory*. Hart, Oxford 1998.

MacKinnon, C., *Towards a Feminist Theory of the State*. Harvard University Press, Cambridge MA 1989.

Malm, H., 'The ontological status of consent and its implications for the law on rape', *Legal Theory*, 2, 1996, pp.147–64.

Nedelsky, J., 'Reconceiving autonomy: sources, thoughts, and possibilities', *Yale Journal of Law & Feminism*, 1, 1989, pp.7–36.

Note, 'Feminist legal analysis and sexual autonomy: using statutory rape laws as an illustration', *Harvard Law Review*, 112, 1999, pp.1064–81.

Note, 'Acquaintance rape and degrees of consent: "no" means "no" but what does "yes" mean?', *Harvard Law Review*, 117, 2004, pp.2341–64.

Roberts, J. and Mohr, R., eds, *Confronting Sexual Assault. A Decade of Social and Legal Change*. University of Toronto Press, Toronto 1994.

Schulhofer, S., *Unwanted Sex: The Culture of Intimidation and the Failure of Law*. Harvard University Press, Cambridge MA 1998.

Scottish Law Commission, *Rape and Other Sexual Offences* (Discussion Paper 131). The Stationery Office, Edinburgh 2006.

Shiva, V., *Staying Alive: Women Ecology and Development*. Zed Books, London 1989.

Tadros, V., 'No consent: a historical critique of the actus reus of rape', *Edinburgh Law Review*, 3, 1999, pp.317–40.

Tadros, V., 'Rape without consent', *Oxford Journal of Legal Studies*, 26, 2006 pp.515–43.

Weait, M., 'Criminal law and the sexual transmission of HIV: *R v Dica*', *Modern Law Review*, 68, 2005, pp.120–33.

Wertheimer, A., *Consent to Sexual Relations*. Cambridge University Press, New York 2003.

Williams, G., 'The problem of domestic rape', *New Law Journal*, 15 February 1991.

Part III

Operationalising choice and consent

Chapter 6

Stories of mistaken consent: still in the shadow of *Morgan*

Heather Douglas

INTRODUCTION

Over the past 20 years there have been significant changes to Australian sexual offences legislation with respect to the definition of consent. Most legislative definitions of consent in the context of rape now require that the victim has the capacity to consent and that the consent is 'free and voluntary' or the product of 'free agreement' (McSherry and Naylor, 2004: 210; Sheehy, 1996: 92). Such terminology reflects a communicative model of consent where parties should be in mutual agreement before they proceed (Chamallas, 1988: 853; Schulhofer, 1998: 85). Most legislative definitions also list a number of matters that vitiate consent, including force, threats and fraud.[1]

To the extent that legislation can provide a public message about socially acceptable behaviour, the various changes to the definition of consent are positive. In spite of these changes, prosecuting a rape continues to be a distressing undertaking for victims, with dubious rates of success. Research about the impact of legislative change is ambivalent. Heenan and McKelvie's research found that legislative changes to the definition of consent did not appear to have significantly increased the number of successful rape prosecutions (1997: 39). However, an earlier review of changes to rape legislation in New South Wales showed some positive improvements in relation to pleas of guilty, reductions in acquittals, increased sentences and increased police acceptance of rape reports, but these were rather slight (Brown, 2006: 730). It continues to be the case that pleas of guilty are far less likely in sexual assault matters than other crimes. Where generally about half of all defendants plead guilty, in contrast, about one-quarter of defendants plead guilty in rape matters (Office of Women's Policy, 2000: 214–15). In circumstances where complainants are asleep, intoxicated or intellectually disabled and have a doubtful level of cognitive capacity to consent,[2] defendants regularly plead not guilty, taking the matter to trial and

---

1   See, e.g. s.348 of the Criminal Code (Qld).
2   For examples, see: *R v Keevers, R v Filewood* [2004] QCA 207, 18 June 2004; *R v Blayney and Another* (2003) 140 A Crim R 249; *R v Mrzljak* (2004) 152 A Crim R 315.

often on to appeal (Office of Women's Policy, 2000: 215). For victims there is likely to be a long and distressing delay between the initial rape and the final outcome of a prosecution. Some commentators have noted that rapes that include additional evidence of physical violence are more likely to be successfully prosecuted (Larcombe, 2002: 140). However, even in situations that include additional physical violence, where women are bound and/or bashed as they are raped for example,[3] defendants have sometimes argued that the violence is part of the performance of consensual sex.

In order to address the perceived failings of rape law, some reformers and commentators have focused on reforms to the type of evidence that can be presented to the court and the manner in which such evidence can be presented (Victorian Law Reform Commission, 2004: 87–258). These changes have been designed to assist the victim to give her account of consent to the court and to undercut the risk of the inference of consent from the victim's behaviour (such as the victim's wearing of particular clothing or her intoxication) (McSherry and Naylor, 2004: 211–20; Young, 1998). Despite the various reforms, discussion within case law constantly (re)emphasises the question of how men who are charged with rape have perceived consent in the specific circumstances of the case. This approach suggests that the victim's perspective is ultimately immaterial and that the central focus is on how the perpetrator constructed consent rather than whether the victim consented (Rush and Young, 1997: 106).

Shifting the inquiry about consent from what the victim consented to, to whether the defendant believed there was consent, signals the defence of mistake. The defence of mistake supports an acquittal when the prosecution cannot prove beyond a reasonable doubt that the defendant was not mistaken about the victim's consent. Cornell has asked how it is that 'feminist legal reforms have been so difficult to sustain and why the conditions of women's inequality [are] continually restored' (Cornell, 1992: 68). Perhaps part of the answer to her question in this context lies in the role of mistake as a defence to a charge of rape, and its relationship to the construction of consent in those cases where the defendant argues that he mistakenly believed there was consent. In this chapter I re-investigate the *mens rea* of rape and show how the enduring focus on the defendant's subjective view of the event constantly diminishes the impact of reforms to the legislative definitions of consent.

Two recent decisions in the High Court of Australia (HCA), *DPP (NT) v WJI*[4] and *Banditt v R*,[5] suggest that the question of whether there is free agreement between the parties is still not the central concern in the courtroom. These two decisions suggest that in a rape trial the focus remains on whether or not the defendant believed there was consent. Historically, in the Australian

3   See, e.g. *R v Willersdorf* [2001] QCA 183, 15 May 2001.
4   *DPP (NT) v WJI* [2004] HCA 27, 6 October 2004.
5   *Banditt v R* [2005] HCA 80, 15 December 2005.

criminal code jurisdictions, the defence of mistake has required that the defendant honestly *and* reasonably believe that the victim is consenting to the sexual contact (Colvin et al, 2005: 122). In order to rebut this defence the prosecution has only been required to prove that the mistake was objectively unreasonable. Despite this history, in the recent *WJI* decision, the HCA defined the defence of mistake in relation to consent in the Northern Territory, a criminal code jurisdiction, as requiring that the mistake only needs to be honest and does not need to be reasonable. In 2005, in the aptly named case of *Banditt*, where the defendant broke into the victim's house and had sex with her as she slept, the HCA allowed special leave to appeal on questions relating to consent and the construction of honest mistake. Both of these cases constantly refer to the 1976 English case of *DPP v Morgan*[6] as an important authority for the positions stated.

As part of the examination of mistake about consent I will revisit the underlying principles of rape. This will include an examination of the case of *Morgan* and a consideration of the cases of *WJI* and *Banditt*. This examination suggests that in spite of legislative changes, a construction of consent that favours the accused continues to be the crucial concern in the courtroom. Unless there is a shift away from the focus on the defendant's perception of consent (Rush and Young, 1997: 100) and a rebalancing towards a consideration of what *both* the defendant and victim perceived, there will remain the problem of honest men and (un)raped women and therefore an endless failure of rape law.

UNDERLYING PRINCIPLES

The problem of successfully prosecuting the crime of rape relates to the question of how the role of the criminal law is understood. Although the understanding of what criminal law is supposed to do is not incapable of change, it appears to be fairly solidly entrenched (Brown, 2006: 2). In rape prosecutions, the idea that rape is an easy claim to make and difficult to refute also seems to be entrenched (Graycar and Morgan, 2002: 354). Generally, there has been some recognition of the need to balance the welfare of victims with procedural fairness for defendants. For example, most Australian jurisdictions now place a limit on the use that can be made of evidence about the victim's sexual history, the requirement for a recent complaint has been relaxed and screens may sometimes be used so that the defendant cannot make eye contact with the victim (Sheehy, 2002: 2). However, despite these changes in rape prosecutions, the court's attention inexorably returns to the accused's version of events.

Historically, the criminal law prohibits conduct because it is morally or

6   *DPP v Morgan* [1976] AC 182.

ethically wrong or because prohibitions assist in the general regulation of society. The reason for prohibition has depended on the type of conduct. Murder and stealing, for example, are crimes that are traditionally considered to be ethically or morally wrong (Colvin, 2004: 4). Rape, initially because it was conceptualised as a crime against property, is also considered to be a moral wrong (Rush, 1997: 78). Rape has retained this categorisation despite being considered in more recent times as a crime of violence or a crime against the person (Sheehy, 2002: 9). Crimes of moral wrongfulness have usually required that the actor possess a specific intention, for example for murder, an intention to kill or cause grievous bodily harm. Usually, whether the actor intended to carry out the prohibited act is a matter only he can reveal. Thus generally, at least for crimes based on moral wrongfulness, 'moral obligation has been determined not by the actual facts but by the actor's opinion regarding them' (O'Connor and Fairall, 1996: 31).

In Australia, different jurisdictions have taken different approaches to defining the crime of rape and this has impacted on the way the defence of mistake has been applied. The criminal code jurisdictions of Queensland, Western Australia, Tasmania and the Northern Territory take a distinctive approach to defining the crime of rape. A prerequisite for a successful prosecution of rape in these states is proof beyond reasonable doubt that the actor intended to have sexual intercourse with the victim, and the prosecution must also prove that the victim was not consenting (McSherry and Naylor, 2004: 210). For example, the Queensland provision states that 'a person rapes another person if . . . the person has carnal knowledge with or of the other person without the other person's consent.'[7] Generally, in the code jurisdictions, rape has been understood as a crime of general intent. That is, the *mens rea* of the crime does not extend beyond the act carried out and its consequences. Unlike common law jurisdictions, in most of the criminal code jurisdictions the defendant can raise a complete defence of honest and reasonable mistake of fact (the fact being the question of consent).[8] In the common law jurisdictions in Australia (Victoria, New South Wales, South Australia and the Australian Capital Territory) a successful prosecution of rape requires that the Crown prove beyond a reasonable doubt that the defendant had sex with the victim knowing that she was not consenting. For example, the relevant New South Wales provision states that '[a]ny person who has sexual intercourse with another person without the consent of the other person and who *knows* that the other person does not consent to the sexual intercourse is liable to imprisonment'.[9] Unlike the code

---

7   Criminal Code Act 1899 (Qld), s.349(2)(a). The equivalent provisions in the other code states are: Criminal Code 1913 (WA), s.325; Criminal Code Act 1924 (Tas), s.185; Criminal Code (NT), s.192.

8   Criminal Code (Qld), s.24; Criminal Code (WA), s.24; Criminal Code (Tas), s.14; Criminal Code (NT), s.32.

9   Crimes Act 1900 (NSW), s.611 (emphasis added).

jurisdictions, knowledge of lack of consent is an element of the offence and rape has been understood in these jurisdictions as a crime of specific intent. Similar to the code jurisdictions noted above, the defendant can raise a defence of mistake, but, following the case of *Morgan* (discussed below), the mistake is only required to be honest.[10] This explains, in part, how the evidence in a particular case may prove that the victim did not consent, but there may be no conviction as her 'no' may be 'honestly' interpreted as 'yes' by the defendant.

The Victorian Law Reform Commission (VLRC) recently recommended modification to the subjective position reflected in this version of the mistake defence for a number of reasons, including that the position undermines the communicative consent model and influences trial outcomes (VLRC, 2004: 406). This recommendation is in line with other jurisdictions. New Zealand, Canada and England have all shifted to a more objective standard which reflects the position in most of the Australian code jurisdictions.[11] The VLRC recommended that the test for mistake should include an objective element, arguing that it would encourage 'responsible sexual relations . . . protect sexual autonomy and make an important symbolic statement that the law no longer accepts outdated views on female subjectivity, seduction and sexual conquest' (VLRC, 2004: 417). The VLRC comments reflect the recurring problem of rape: that its construction constantly returns to the question of the state of mind of the defendant. MacKinnon has clearly articulated the problem. She notes that:

> . . . the injury of rape lies in the meaning of the act to its victims, but the standard for its criminality lies in the meaning of the same act to the assailants . . . the deeper problem is rape law's assumption that a single, objective state of affairs existed. When the reality is split . . . the law tends to conclude that a rape *did not happen*.
>
> (MacKinnon, 1983: 652)

The defence of mistake, especially where it is only required to be honest, assists in the conclusion that rape did not happen. In the next section I will revisit the case of *Morgan*, a case that continues to be the authority for the defence of honest mistake in rape. This is followed by an examination of the cases of *WJI*, an appeal from a criminal code jurisdiction, and *Banditt*, an appeal from a common law jurisdiction.

---

10 *DPP v Morgan* [1976] AC 182; Crimes Act 1958 (Vic), s.38; Crimes Act 1900 (NSW), s.611; Criminal Law Consolidation Act 1935 (SA), s.48; Crimes Act 1900 (ACT), s.54.
11 Crimes Act 1961 (NZ), s.128; Criminal Code 1985 (Canada), s.273; Sexual Offences Act 2003 (UK), s.1.

REVISITING *MORGAN* – HONEST MISTAKE AND INDIFFERENCE

The majority decisions in the case of *Morgan* have maintained a surprising level of significance in discussions about rape and consent in the common law jurisdictions in Australia. In the memorable facts of the case, a senior member of the Royal Air Force, Morgan, had invited three junior colleagues back to his home to have sex with his wife. Morgan had advised his colleagues that his wife would show some resistance, but that it was a pretence on her part that stimulated her enjoyment. Clearly this was a situation of male fantasy translated into reality. All three of the younger men were unknown to the victim and they held her down while their colleagues had sex with her in turn. The victim's husband then had sex with her. Initially all four were found guilty of rape at trial and all appealed, eventually to the House of Lords. At trial the judge had directed the jury that any mistake about consent must be honest and reasonable in order to provide a defence to rape and this direction was the central appeal point. There was significant discussion by the majority judges of the House of Lords of the state of mind required for rape.

The majority Law Lords accepted that rape imports at least indifference to the woman's consent. Lord Hailsham[12] pointed out that the prohibited act in rape is to have sexual intercourse with the victim without their consent. On his reasoning, the mens rea is the intention to do the prohibited act, with the qualification that recklessly 'and not caring' or proceeding 'willy nilly' whether the victim consents or not, is 'equivalent on ordinary principles' to intent.[13] Therefore, he reasoned, if the mental element is intent to have sexual intercourse with a women who is not consenting, it would be unacceptable to require that the mistake be honest *and* reasonable. Lord Hailsham argued that requiring that the mistake be reasonable would be inconsistent with the central element of intent because an honest belief in consent would negative the required intent. His interpretation meant that the burden of proof remained squarely with the prosecution (and in a de facto sense the victim) to prove the requisite state of mind of the defendant. Part of his reason for this approach related to the gravity of the crime. His analysis fits with traditional criminal law principles that intent in crimes of specific intent is a subjective question. Although the prosecution is required to prove it, the question is really one that only the defendant can answer.

In contrast, the dissenting Law Lords found that a mistake about consent would need to be both honest and reasonable to negative the charge of rape. Lord Edmund Davies' view was that he was constrained by precedent and that he was therefore obliged to accept the requirement that mistakes should

---

12 *DPP v Morgan* [1976] AC 182 at 204–15.
13 Above at 209.

be both honest and reasonable. He suggested that the legislature might deal with the problem. He commented, however, that in his view, 'honest belief, however foolishly formed ... seems ... incompatible with an intention to rape'.[14]

Lord Simon[15] provided the only real dissenting voice. He suggested that crimes are distinguished as either crimes of general or specific intent. He explained that crimes of general intent are those crimes that express or imply a necessary intention within their definition that does not go beyond the act. Generally, this encompasses criminal offences where the act corresponds with the intention. He gave the example of assault and explained that the act of assault is an act that causes another person to apprehend immediate and unlawful violence. His view was that the intention is proven when the prosecution can show that the defendant foresaw that his act would probably cause apprehension of immediate and unlawful violence or was reckless about causing such apprehension. He distinguished such crimes from crimes of specific intent such as murder. He noted that the act in murder is the killing, but the crime also requires that the defendant intended to kill or cause grievous bodily harm. Importantly, Lord Simon defines rape as a crime of general intent, like assault, rather than a crime of specific intent. On this analysis, in order to demonstrate mistake, the evidential burden shifts to the defence who must present evidence to negative the general intent. Both dissenting judges examined the development of the common law relating to crimes of general intent and concluded that a mistake must be both honest and reasonable in order to negative the state of mind associated with the act in crimes of general intent. Lord Simon noted that 'a respectable woman who has been ravished would hardly feel that she was vindicated by being told that her assailant must go unpunished because he believed, quite unreasonably, that she was consenting'.[16]

Rush and Young have developed an alternative version of rape which does not focus on consent, so that mistake of any sort is irrelevant; however, they suggest that if there is to be a defence of mistake it should be both honest and reasonable (Rush and Young, 1997: 131). Their arguments in support of this position reflect the arguments of the dissenting judgments in *Morgan*. It is, however, the majority judgment in *Morgan* that focuses on the defendant's view of consent, that continues to be highly influential on the Australian judiciary, despite years of legislative reform (Faulkner, 1991: 60). The decision in the recent *WJI* case also deferred to the authority of *Morgan*, despite dealing with a criminal code jurisdiction. This issue is discussed below.

14 Above at 226.
15 Above at 210.
16 Above at 221.

REIGNING IN THE GRIFFITH CODE

The Griffith Criminal Code was originally drafted in 1899 by Sir Samuel Griffith for the then colony of Queensland. It was based on the 19th century draft of the English Criminal Code (which never became law). The Griffith Code was highly influential and was later taken up in other jurisdictions in Australia, Africa and some Pacific Islands (Mackenzie, 2002: 59–60). In Australia, versions of the Griffith Criminal Code continue to operate in Queensland, Western Australian, Tasmania and the Northern Territory: these are described as the 'code jurisdictions'. In these jurisdictions the codes specifically provide for a defence of mistake. A mistake of fact will operate as a defence (to the extent of the mistake) where the mistake is both honest and reasonable.[17] The statutory provisions relating to the defence of mistake have been applied to mistakes about consent in rape trials and in Court of Appeal judgments in Queensland, Western Australia and Tasmania.[18] The application of the statutory mistake defence to consent in rape cases in these jurisdictions has never been tested in the High Court, however.

Recently, in the case of *WJI*, the Northern Territory Director of Public Prosecutions referred questions for consideration and opinion to the HCA, involving directions about intention and mistake that had been given during a rape trial. Section 192(3) of the Criminal Code (NT) sets out the crime of rape as follows: 'any person who has sexual intercourse with another person without the consent of the other person, is guilty of a crime and is liable for imprisonment for life.' The language of this provision is essentially mirrored in each of the other three codes.[19] In the *WJI* case, the trial judge had directed the jury that a mistaken belief did not have to be based on reasonable grounds.[20]

In the High Court, Gleeson CJ pointed out that the direction was one that was very similar to the direction used in common law jurisdictions.[21] After discussion of various provisions, the HCA decided 4:1 that the common-law style direction was appropriate.[22] The High Court found that the central question was whether the criminal 'act' in the Northern Territory rape provision is simply sexual intercourse, that is a crime of general intent, or whether it is sexual-intercourse-without-consent, that is a crime of specific intent. Those in

---

17 Criminal Code 1899 (Qld), s.24; Criminal Code (WA), s.24; Criminal Code (Tas), s.14; Criminal Code (NT), s.32.

18 See *Arnol v R* [1981] Tas R 157; *Re Attorney-General's Reference No.1 of 1997* [1979] WAR 45; *R v Filewood* [2004] QCA 207, 18 June 2004.

19 Criminal Code 1899 (Qld), s.349; Criminal Code (WA), s.325; Criminal Code (Tas), s.185.

20 Criminal Code (NT), s.414(2) allows a Crown Law Officer to refer any point of law to the Court of Appeal for consideration and opinion.

21 *DPP (NT) v WJI* [2004] HCA 47, 6 October 2004, at [1]–[14].

22 Above *per* Gleeson CJ at [1]–[14], Gummow and Heydon JJ at [15]–[53], Kirby J at [54]–[109].

the majority preferred the latter construction, that the criminal act is sexual-intercourse-without-consent. This interpretation is surprising as it is at odds with the interpretation of the similar provisions in each of the other code jurisdictions. In all the other code jurisdictions the prosecution must prove that the defendant intended to have sexual intercourse with the victim, and separately that the victim did not consent. Thus, in the other code jurisdictions, the prosecution is not required to prove that the defendant had intercourse knowing that the victim was not consenting. The defendant's subjective view of consent usually only becomes relevant in the other code jurisdictions when the defendant raises a mistake defence, and then the mistake must be both honest and reasonable.

The majority judges in the *WJI* case found that pursuant to the Northern Territory code, the accused must intend both to have sexual intercourse with the victim and to have intercourse without the consent of the victim in order to be held criminally responsible for rape. Consistent with this position, they found that if the accused honestly believed that the victim was consenting, that subjective belief would negative the required criminal intent. This outcome is in line with the majority decision in *Morgan*. The majority of the High Court in *WJI* found that despite the existence of a statutory defence of honest and reasonable mistake in the Northern Territory Criminal Code, in relation to rape the statutory defence was displaced because, like common law jurisdictions, the crime of rape was essentially interpreted as a crime of specific intent. Once the provision was interpreted in this way, it logically followed that an honest mistake about consent would negative the specific intent associated with the offence.

Kirby J distinguished the Criminal Code (NT) from codes in other Australian jurisdictions on the basis that it is 'newer', and was developed in recognition of previous debates about the codes.[23] He did this in spite of the fact that the language of the rape and mistake provisions in all four of the Australian criminal codes is very similar. His judgment provides the most thorough discussion in the case of 'foundational' principles of the criminal law. Kirby J noted that although some acts are made criminal without the requirement of intent, this would be an exceptional situation. Reflecting Lord Hailsham's view in *Morgan*, Kirby J. noted that the substantial deprivation of liberty associated with the offence supported his position. He also emphasised the legal neutrality of sexual intercourse in a general sense, stating that 'overwhelmingly the act is consensual' and therefore does not need to be excused. Although claimed by Kirby J as effectively simple truths, these contentions have been contested. MacKinnon has challenged both the idea of neutrality in sexual intercourse and the assumption of consent (1987: 88). Also relevant in response to Kirby J's comments is Kelly's point that the distinction between whether an act is rape or

---

23 Above at [54]–[109].

consensual sex may not be so neat. She suggests that experiences of hetero-sexual sex exist on 'a continuum moving from choice to pressure to coercion to force' (Kelly, 1987: 47). Where on this continuum the particular act falls is not necessarily clear in each particular situation.

In his lone dissenting judgment, Hayne J found that the 'act' of the person accused of having sexual intercourse with a person without their consent was the act of intercourse not intercourse-without-consent.[24] This reflects Lord Simon's dissenting position in *Morgan*. Thus, on Hayne J's conception, the only act that must be intended is the intercourse. According to Hayne J, any other construction would 'represent a radical departure' from what has been understood to be the position in the code jurisdictions for many years. Pursuant to Hayne J's approach, the defendant would have the evidential onus of raising an honest *and* reasonable mistake. Thus, in Hayne J's view, if a defence of mistaken consent arose the prosecution could negative the defence simply by proving beyond a reasonable doubt that the mistake was not reasonable.

Ultimately, the majority decision in *WJI* affirms the majority rationale in *Morgan*. It finds that the central consideration in a rape case should be the self-referential view of the accused in relation to consent with respect to sexual intercourse with the victim. This decision was made notwithstanding numerous recent reforms and recommendations and in the face of contradictory authority in every other code jurisdiction in Australia. The centralisation of the subjective view of the defendant in establishing consent has been replayed in an Australian common law jurisdiction in recent times as well, in the NSW case of *Banditt*.

THE BANDIT ON THE SECOND FLOOR

Banditt was charged with the offence of breaking and entering a dwelling house and committing a serious indictable offence of sexual intercourse without con-sent.[25] Banditt and the victim were cousins and lived in a small country town. Banditt had moved to the town and had been to the victim's house on a previous occasion. He had also met her at the local hotel on a few occasions prior to the alleged offence. According to the victim there had been an earlier occasion when Banditt had tried to kiss her, but she had rebuffed him. According to Banditt there had been a previous occasion of consensual sexual intercourse, but the victim denied this. On the night of the offence, both Banditt and the victim had been at a local hotel and had been drinking there. They had spoken to each other. At some stage the victim left by herself and went home. She gave evidence that she locked her house carefully and went to sleep in her upstairs bedroom. She also gave evidence that at some time during the night she woke up

24 Above at [110]–[147].
25 See *Crimes Act 1900* (NSW), ss.112(1) and 611.

with Banditt on top of her and his penis inside her, and that she was in 'a half-asleep-dream sort of state' for a short period of time.[26] She explained that she thought he was someone else for a moment, but then realised who he was, told him to leave and he left. She then showered and went and complained to a neighbour. It was accepted that the victim was probably at least mildly intoxicated when Banditt had sex with her. Banditt had entered the house by pushing a chair up to the bathroom window and climbing into the bathroom. In spite of having effectively broken into the house, Banditt's defence was that he honestly believed that the victim was consenting. He argued that this was supported by the evidence that as soon as he was aware she was not consenting he withdrew from the house.[27]

Since *Morgan's* case it has generally been accepted in common law jurisdictions that recklessness, in the sense of subjective advertence to non-consent and proceeding regardless, is a form of mens rea for rape (Brown et al, 2006: 752). In New South Wales, the relevant consent provision states that a person who is reckless as to whether the person consents is taken to know that the person does not consent.[28] In *Banditt's* case, the trial judge advised the jury that no issue about consent can arise when the person is sleeping, and that if the victim had given apparent consent in a dreamlike state on the basis that she thought Banditt was someone else, that would also not be valid consent.[29] He also discussed the issue of recklessness and consent and directed that if the defendant goes ahead with intercourse without even considering consent that is recklessness and the defendant would be deemed to know that the victim is not consenting. Later he noted that:

> . . . recklessness is a factor to advert to . . . It does not have to be the product of conscious thought. If the offender does not even consider whether the woman is going to consent or not, then that is reckless and he is deemed to know that she is not consenting.[30]

He then turned to the question of honest mistake and advised the jury that they had to consider what was in the accused's mind. Specifically he directed the jury to consider whether 'he ha[d] *any basis* for a belief that she was consenting or has the Crown persuaded you that he had in fact *no basis* for any such belief'.[31] At the initial trial the defendant was found guilty by the jury.

Banditt appealed to the New South Wales Court of Appeal (NSWCA) on the grounds of alleged errors in the trial judge's directions to the jury on consent.

---

26 *R v Banditt* (2003) 151 A Crim R 215. The facts are set out at [16]–[22].
27 Above at [49]–[50].
28 Crimes Act 1900 (NSW), s.61R.
29 See above at [54]–[67] for a discussion of the summing up at trial.
30 Above at [66].
31 Above at [57] (emphasis added).

Specifically, the appeal was concerned with the trial judge's directions on reck-lessness and mistake. Banditt submitted that the trial judge had imported an objective element into the test of mistake by requiring that his belief have a 'basis'. Further, Banditt's counsel argued that a person does not act recklessly in a situation where he believes that the complainant is consenting to sexual inter-course, even though he is also aware of the possibility that the complainant is not consenting.

James J, in the NSWCA, noted that there are four states of mind relevant to the question of consent and the defendant's knowledge.[32] The first situation was where the defendant knows the victim does not consent, which is clearly rape. The second situation, where the defendant honestly although wrongly believes that the victim does consent, would lead to a verdict of not guilty. The third state of mind is where the defendant does not know whether the victim is consenting, realises that she may not be, and goes ahead with sexual intercourse regardless or notwithstanding this realisation. The judge's view here was that the possibility of lack of consent must be something more than a bare possibility. It must be a possibility with a certain degree of likelihood, although he declined to specify any threshold percentage. For James J, this third scenario demonstrated recklessness and it would lead to a guilty verdict. He described this as advertant recklessness. He also noted a fourth situation that can be understood as inadvertent recklessness. In this fourth scenario, the accused fails to consider whether there is consent and goes ahead with sexual intercourse, treating consent as entirely irrelevant. This would also lead to a guilty verdict. Ultimately, the Court of Appeal dismissed the appeal against conviction.

In 2005 the accused was granted leave to appeal to the HCA. One news-paper headline about Banditt's successful special leave application to the HCA cynically stated: 'Court to judge when yes means yes' (Carson, 2005: 7). The accompanying article suggested that the case would effectively require the HCA to 'set the dating ground rules for amorous and tipsy couples' (Carson, 2005: 7). The basis of the application for leave to appeal was that the NSWCA had endorsed a test of recklessness that was contrary to the position established at common law in *Morgan's* case, 30 years previously. Counsel for Banditt sug-gested that the common law test for recklessness was not advertence to the possibility of non-consent and continuing anyway. Rather he suggested that it required indifference about whether consent is present or not, indifference being a state of mind of not caring. Counsel's point seemed to be that mere advert-ence to the possibility is not enough for criminal responsibility. The reason for this distinction, he suggested, was that there may be good reasons for not establishing for absolute certain whether a person is consenting. The example he gave was the situation of intoxication:

32 Above at [2]–[103].

He is in a conversation with her, she shows by her physical actions that she is receptive to sex, she is in a vaguely awake state . . . she is intoxicated, he is intoxicated . . . what is he to do? Is he to wait till she sobers up before he makes certain that she is able to properly consent?

Further, he argued that 'it is wholly unreasonable for a person to say, "Well, I'd better wait till this person is no longer intoxicated or no longer under the influence of alcohol so that I can make certain that she is really engaging and informed" '.[33] In response, McHugh J commented that feminists might not agree that it is unreasonable to wait. No doubt without irony, counsel suggested that the position would make New South Wales 'worse than the code' states that require reasonableness for a defence of mistake. Worse for whom, one might ask? Leave to appeal was granted and the HCA heard argument in the matter. In the appeal, Banditt's counsel accepted that the jury was satisfied beyond a reasonable doubt that the victim was not consenting. He submitted: 'That is the whole point. Just because she was aggrieved and did not consent, does not mean that he was aware that she was not consenting.'[34]

In its decision, the HCA reviewed recent debates about rape law reform; however, the majority judgment focused on the argument in *Morgan's* case and the interpretation of the term 'reckless'.[35] Ultimately, those involved in the case did not approach the issue of consent as an analysis of what was communicated between the parties. The focus was entirely on the subjective view of the defendant and whether the trial judge's directions on recklessness were appropriate. The HCA found that the trial judge had properly emphasised that 'it was not the reaction of some notional reasonable man but the state of mind of the appellant which the jury was obliged to consider'.[36] The court considered that although the trial judge's directions with respect to the meaning of 'reckless' were satisfactory, generally juries should be directed to apply the ordinary meaning of the term 'reckless'.[37] Although the HCA concluded that Banditt's appeal against conviction should be dismissed, the judgments perpetuate the focus on the defendant's state of mind. Changes to the definitions of consent in New South Wales have had little impact on the way rape is understood. As Schulhofer points out, the woman's unwillingness is not enough to prove rape (1998: 3). The analysis has remained on the subjective, self-referential views of the defendant.

33 *Banditt v R* [2005] HCA special leave application, 22 April 2005, at [5]–[6].
34 *Banditt v R* [2005] HCA appeal argument, 8 September 2005, at [64].
35 *Banditt v R* [2005] HCA 80 at [20]–[27], *per* Gummow, Hayne and Heydon JJ
36 Above at [37]; see also Callinan J at [110].
37 Above at [42], [36]; see also Callinan J at [111]–[112].

CONCLUSION

The two cases discussed above show that legislative reforms to rape law are met by counter-moves by defence lawyers and the judiciary to constantly re-orient consent to an assessment of the defendant's perspective (Ehrlich, 2001: 123–28). This problem has been observed elsewhere as well, for example Sheehy has also noted this pattern in the Canadian context (2002: 15). Clearly, decisions about rape continue to be made in the shadow of *Morgan*. The focus on consent is highly problematic in rape law. It is problematic because, regardless of whether the victim actually consented and despite reforms, it continues to place significant pressure on the prosecution/complainant to demonstrate beyond a reasonable doubt that the defendant was *not* mistaken about consent (Model Criminal Code Officers Committee, 1999: 13; Young, 1998: 442). Further, and conversely, legislative reforms to the definition of consent have not dealt with the benefit afforded to the defendant where a defence of (merely) honest mistake about consent exists.

Reforms in Michigan, which replaced the consideration of consent with a consideration of whether the circumstances of sexual contact were coercive (but allowed the issue of consent to be raised in defence) have not had any impact on the primacy of consent at trial (Graycar and Morgan, 2002: 366).[38] Neither does Rush and Young's proposal that rape should be defined as causing serious injury with sexual penetration fully deal with the problem. They suggest that a person who voluntarily engages in the sexual penetration of another and voluntarily causes serious injury with intention or recklessness as to causing serious injury is guilty of rape (Rush and Young, 1997: 106). It is difficult to see that their proposal would move the focus away from the accused's perception of consent. On their model, the defendant's view that there was consent could presumably be raised to rebut intention to cause serious injury (McSherry and Naylor, 2004: 214). Another possibility is to discard the traditional assumption of innocence (until guilt is proven) in the context of sexual assault prosecutions. In *Morgan's* case, Lord Hailsham pointed out the possibility of a reverse onus offence where intercourse voluntarily entered into would be an offence. In this context he noted that the onus would shift to the defence to prove an honest (and reasonable) mistake that there was consent.[39] This is unlikely to be accepted. Clearly, it is difficult to reformulate the crime of rape without making consent a crucial element of the offence. Given the apparent entrenchment of the concept of consent, it remains an important project to continue to try to refine the definition of consent and the associated rules of evidence.

Slowly, legislative constructions of rape and consent are moving away from

---

38 Note that the South African Law Reform Commission has proposed a similar model (South African Law Reform Commission, 2002: 31–33).

39 *DPP v Morgan* [1976] AC 182 at 209.

privileging the rapist's story. Arguably, this reflects a generalised and gradual shift in criminal law towards acknowledging some responsibility towards victims in relation to the outcome of prosecutions. In light of the above discussion, one important change would be to ensure that any mistake about consent should be both honest and reasonable before a mistake can operate as a defence to rape. This shift is reflected in the VLRC recommendations and changes in New Zealand, Canada and England. In other jurisdictions where a mistake about consent is required to be reasonable, there have been no clear difficulties identified in applying this formulation (McSherry and Naylor, 2004: 224). While the courts continue to defer to the majority in *Morgan* and support an honest mistake defence, however, the final obstacle to a successful rape prosecution will always be the view of the defendant, regardless of changes to the legislative definition of consent. Perhaps we are a little closer to understanding consent as a communication between parties, but there is still some way to go.

BIBLIOGRAPHY

Brown, D., Farrier, D., Egger, S., McNamara, L. and Steel, A., *Criminal Laws*. Federation Press, Sydney 2006.

Carson, V., 'Court to judge when yes means yes', *The Australian*, 30 May 2005, p.7.

Chamallas, M., 'Consent, equality, and the legal control of sexual conduct', *Southern California Law Review*, 61, 1988, pp.777–862.

Colvin, E., Linden, S. and McKechnie, J., *Criminal Law in Queensland and Western Australia*. Butterworths, Sydney 2005.

Cornell, D., 'The philosophy of the limit: systems theory and feminist legal reform', in Cornell, D., Rosenfeld, M. and Carlson, D.G., eds, *Deconstruction and the Possibility of Justice*. Routledge, London 1992, pp.68–94.

Ehrlich, S., *Representing Rape*. Routledge, London 2001.

Faulkner, J., 'Mens rea in rape: *Morgan* and the inadequacy of subjectivism', *Melbourne University Law Review*, 18, 1991, pp.60–82.

Fisse, B., *Howard's Criminal Law*. Law Book Co, Sydney 1990.

Graycar, R. and Morgan, J., *The Hidden Gender of Law*. Federation Press, Sydney 2002.

Heenan, M. and McKelvie, H., *Rape Law Reform Evaluation Project, Report No. 2: The Crimes Rape Act 1991: An Evaluation Project*. Victorian Department of Justice, Melbourne 1997.

Kelly, L., 'The continuum of sexual violence', in Hanmer, J. and Maynard, M., eds, *Women, Violence and Social Control*. Macmillan, London 1987, pp.46–60.

Larcombe, W., 'The "ideal" victim v successful rape complainants: not what you might expect', *Feminist Legal Studies*, 10, 2002, pp.131–48.

Larcombe, W., *Compelling Engagements: Feminism, Rape Law and Romance Fiction*. Federation Press, Sydney 2005.

Mackenzie, G., 'An enduring influence: Sir Samuel Griffith and his contribution to criminal justice in Queensland', *QUT Law and Justice Journal*, 2, 2002, pp.53–63.

MacKinnon, C., 'Feminism, Marxism, method and the state', *Signs: Journal of Women in Culture and Society*, 7, 1983, pp.515–44.

MacKinnon, C., *Feminism Unmodifed: Discourses in Life and Law*. Harvard University Press, Cambridge MA 1987.

McSherry, B. and Naylor, B., *Australian Criminal Law: Critical Perspectives*. Oxford University Press, Melbourne 2004.

Model Criminal Code Officers Committee, *Sexual Offences Against the Person: Discussion Report*. Australian Government, Canberra 1999.

O'Connor, D. and Fairall, P.A., *Criminal Defences*. Butterworths, Sydney 1996.

Taskforce on Women and the Criminal Code, *Report of the Taskforce on Women and the Criminal Code*. Office of Women's Policy, Brisbane 2000.

Rush, P., 'On being legal: the laws of sexual assault in Victoria', *Australian Feminist Law Journal*, 9, 1997, pp.76–89.

Rush, P. and Young, A., 'A crime of consequence and a failure of legal imagination: the sexual offences of the Model Criminal Code', *Australian Feminist Law Journal*, 9, 1997, pp.100–33.

Schulhofer, S., *Unwanted Sex: The Culture of Intimidation and the Failure of Law*. Harvard University Press, Cambridge MA 1998.

Sheehy, E., 'Legalising justice for all women: Canadian women's struggle for democratic rape law reforms', *Australian Feminist Law Journal*, 6, 1996, pp.87–113.

Sheehy, E., 'Evidence law and "credibility testing" of women: a comment on the E case', *QUT Law and Justice Journal*, 2, 2002, pp.1–21.

South African Law Reform Commission, *Sexual Offences Report: Project 107*. South African Law Reform Commission, Pretoria 2002.

Young, A., ' "The wasteland of the law": the wordless song of the rape victim', *Melbourne University Law Review*, 22, 1998, pp.442–65.

Victorian Law Reform Commission, *Sexual Offences Law and Procedure: Final Report*. Victorian Law Reform Commission, Melbourne 2004.

Chapter 7

The personal *is* economic: unearthing the rhetoric of choice in the Canadian maternity and parental leave benefit debates

Gillian Calder

INTRODUCTION*

In January 2004 the Québec Court of Appeal rendered its decision in *Canada (Procureur général) c Québec (Procureur général)*.[1] The court had been asked by the government of Québec to decide the constitutionality of the federal government of Canada's maternity and parental leave benefits, a regime delivered through the (un)employment insurance system[2] in Canada since 1971.[3] In a matter that would ultimately be heard by the Supreme Court of Canada,[4] the Québec Court of Appeal firmly anchored its decision in the rhetoric of choice.

There have been numerous attempts in the early 21st century to put equality issues pertaining to the delivery of maternity and parental leave benefits before Canadian courts.[5] Unlike those efforts, however, the issue before the Québec appellate court was a straightforward division of powers question from the heart of Canadian constitutional law. Who has jurisdiction over these benefits in Canada, the federal government or the provincial governments?

*   Thank you to both Magda Wojda and Jennifer Raso for excellent research assistance and ongoing critique. Various friends and colleagues gave feedback on and inspiration to this chapter's various incarnations, with particular thanks to Rebecca Johnson, Laura Spitz, Hester Lessard and Sharon Cowan. In addition, gratitude is extended to Sue Millns, the women from Stilbaai, the Gender, Sexuality and Law Research Group at Keele University, and to this book's editors, Sharon Cowan and Rosemary Hunter.

1   [2004] QJ No. 277.
2   I use the term '(un)employment insurance' to connote that in 1996 the federal government changed the regime's name from 'unemployment insurance' to 'employment insurance', as part of a neoliberal approach to work in Canada that does not capture the full essence of this regime and its history (Employment Insurance Act, SC 1996, c.23, as amended).
3   Unemployment Insurance Act, 1971, SC 1970–71–72, c.48, as amended.
4   *Reference re Employment Insurance (Can), ss 22 and 23* [2005] SCC 56 (hereinafter: *EI Reference*). For a full case commentary, see Calder (2006).
5   See, e.g. *Canada (Attorney General) v Lesiuk*, 2003 FCA 3; *Miller v Canada (Attorney General)*, 2002 FCA 370, discussed below.

Many felt that the either/or answer this question was likely to generate would do little to disrupt the *status quo*, at least *vis-à-vis* the equality interests of Canadian women. What complicated the issue more than anticipated, however, was the way in which the arguments were put to the court. In deciding the jurisdictional question – and in the absence of an equality framework – the Québec Court of Appeal was asked to consider whether benefits delivered for maternity and parental leave in Canada should be treated differently from other forms of benefits given the 'choice' made by employed parents to have children.

Advocates within and without Québec were surprised both by the question put to the court and by the court's reasoning (Cox, 2004). In straightforward language the Québec Court of Appeal told the parties that maternity and parental leave, while related to employment, was in fact not a matter properly attached to (un)employment insurance. Instead, the court held:

> The pregnancy and parental benefits contemplated in sections 22 and 23 of the *Employment Insurance Act* are not at all part of the unemployment insurance canvas conceived in 1940. These special benefits are not paid further to the loss of a job for *economic reasons*; rather, they are paid further to the interruption of an individual's employment because of *a personal inability to work*. They are, in fact, social welfare payments that cannot easily be considered insurance, which presupposes a catalyst independent of the recipient's will. These benefits must be seen instead as an assistance measure for families and children – that is, as a social assistance measure and a laudable one at that (emphasis added).[6]

The Québec Court of Appeal found that a benefit that rewarded the 'choice' by parents to have children, or to take time away from their jobs to care for children, should be treated in a qualitatively different manner from a benefit provided to workers whose absence from work was for an economic or involuntary reason.

The aim of this chapter is to examine the ways in which 'choice' has shifted the focus of the maternity and parental leave debates – away from what is in the best interests of women negotiating the tensions of their productive and reproductive lives and toward a neoliberal understanding of work. To do this, I explore the Québec Court of Appeal's holding that issues of 'choice' are relevant to, if not determinative of, the way in which these benefits should be delivered in Canadian law. With this grounding I argue that a historically rooted rhetoric of choice is instrumental in obscuring from review systemic inequalities informing this benefit scheme.

6   Above, note 1, at para.75.

I begin by examining how the rhetoric of choice is deployed in feminist legal analysis, using this to show how, despite being overturned by the Supreme Court of Canada, the reasoning of the Québec Court of Appeal is not merely an anomalous moment. The holding reflects instead a broader phenomenon in which choice is increasingly deployed to the disadvantage of women in Canada today. I next discuss the way in which 'choice' has been employed at key moments in the maternity and parental leave debates from the 1940s to the present. I conclude by examining how the Supreme Court of Canada treated the issue of choice, focusing on what this tells us about the way in which women's choices are valued within the current economic climate. To have a benefits regime that enhances women's (and men's) choices when balancing the competing demands of their productive and reproductive lives, the regime must be situated within a broader set of societal shifts in the valuation of caregiving labour. Absent complementary changes, the choices that remain will be hollow ones indeed.

DELIVERING MATERNITY AND PARENTAL LEAVE IN CANADA

In order to understand the significance of the Québec court's finding with respect to the role of 'choice' in the maternity and parental leave benefits regime, I offer a brief discussion of Canadian constitutional history.[7] In this section I address the way the Canadian constitution allocates jurisdiction with respect to issues pertaining to work, social programs and (un)employment insurance. Against this backdrop I discuss the way in which maternity and parental leave benefits became attached to (un)employment insurance in the early 1970s. I conclude by giving a snapshot of how the regime is delivered today. This background enables a fuller discussion of the impact of the rhetoric of choice on the current debates about how maternity and parental leave benefits might be delivered to enhance the equality of women and other caregivers in Canada.

The Canadian constitution attempts to provide for an exhaustive division of powers within Canada with jurisdiction over particular subject matters being allocated to either the federal or the provincial governments.[8] Authority over matters that were of concern to 'the dominion as a whole' was granted to the federal government and authority over matters that were seen to be more 'local'

---

7   For a more detailed analysis of the constitutional issues raised, see Porter (2003) and Campeau (2005).

8   Constitution Act, 1867 (UK), 30 & 31 Vict, c.3, ss.91 and 92.

in nature was granted to the provinces.[9] For the first century of constitutional jurisprudence in Canada, cases largely focused on determining whether legislation enacted by one level of government was outside the scope of its power. Those cases were fraught with tensions particular to the 'formation' of Canada and the negotiation of power between English-speaking and French-speaking Canadians.[10] Constitutional jurisprudence became more complex in 1982 when the Canadian constitution was amended to include a Charter of Rights and Freedoms (the Charter).[11] Constitutional cases post-1982 focus less on which government should or does act, and instead on whether that government has acted in accordance with its rights-based obligations.

The second key component of this background chronicle is how the benefits regime became a part of (un)employment insurance in Canada. From 1940 through to the early 1970s there were numerous attempts by women's and labour groups to amend (un)employment insurance to address the needs of pregnant workers and other caregivers. These attempts took the form of lobbies for legislative reform, legal challenge and strategic litigation and culminated with the addition of the first maternity benefit to (un)employment insurance in 1971. The amended legislation enabled women who took a prescribed leave from work due to pregnancy to receive a benefit in the form of payments from the federal government. Maternity and parental leave benefits remain a part of the (un)employment insurance regime today.

Finally, it is important to understand how maternity and parental leave benefits are presently delivered. The regime is structured so as to deliver a monetary benefit for a period of leave that is protected by provincial employment standards and federal labour codes.[12] A person with insurable income is entitled to these special benefits if she or he has worked 600 hours in the previous 52 weeks. An eligible woman who has given birth to a child is entitled to take a 17-week leave from work and claim benefits for 15 of those weeks. In addition, either birth parent of a newborn child or either parent of an adopted child is entitled to take parental leave with benefits for up to 35 weeks. Benefits for either maternity or parental leave are paid at the regular (un)employment insurance benefit level of 55% of insurable income, to a weekly ceiling.

Recent attempts to reform the delivery of maternity and parental leave have focused at two levels. The first has been the concerted effort by women and labour to advocate for a regime that is delivered in an equality-enhancing way.

---

9   For example, trade and commerce (s.91(2)) was granted to the federal government, while property and civil rights was allocated to the provinces (s.92(13)).

10   For example, see discussion of the relationship between Québec and Canada in *Reference Re Québec Secession* [1998] 2 SCR 217 at paras. 55–60.

11   Canadian Charter of Rights and Freedoms, Part I of the Constitution Act, 1982, being Schedule B to the Canada Act 1982 (UK), 1982, c. 11 (hereinafter the Charter).

12   See, e.g. Employment Standards Act, RSBC 1996, c.113, s.51; Employment Standards Act, 2000, SO 2001, c.9, s.48; Employment Standards Code, RSA 2000, c.E-9, s.50.

There has been remarkable consensus that delivering the benefit through a regime tied to the eligibility requirements of (un)employment insurance is discriminatory (Cox, 2004). The second reform attempt has derived – uniquely – from the province of Québec on the issue of jurisdiction. Québec has attempted to negotiate its own benefits regime with the federal government, one that could be more attentive to the needs of women and other caregivers within Québec. It was the breakdown of these negotiations that led the government of Québec to refer the question of the constitutionality of this regime to the courts,[13] and in which the construction and use of choice as a means of resolving the constitutional question of jurisdiction was problematically raised.

THE RHETORIC OF CHOICE: MOTHERHOOD AND WORK

This next section explores this troubling use of choice by examining how the 'rhetoric of choice' has been conceptualised within feminist legal theory. With this background I move to discuss how 'choice' has come to both shape and limit understanding of the maternity and parental leave benefits regime as a potentially equality-enhancing program.

Rhetoric of choice

The rhetoric of choice permeates feminist discourse and scholarship, particularly in Western societies. Primary among reasons for its resonance is the grounding of choice in concepts like liberation, freedom, empowerment (Johnson, 2002: 56) and bodily integrity (Williams, 1991: 1577). The liberal individual is someone whose 'choices' are deserving of respect, deference and consideration. Particularly in the debates surrounding reproductive choices, and most prominently in the abortion debates through the 1970s and 1980s, choice has played a central role in legal feminism.

Paradoxically, while choice is seen as a means by which options are created, choosers can be (and are) blamed. This rhetorical conundrum results in a form of freedom that obscures systemic constraints as individuals are decontextualised as genderless, rational choosers with prescribed roles and responsibilities (Lessard, 2006). Scholars such as Joan Williams have demonstrated how the use

---

13 In March 2005, the government of Québec negotiated a plan to opt out of the federal regime and from January 2006, maternity and parental leave has been delivered provincially within Québec. This negotiation had no bearing on the issues before the court, and the decision of the court has no bearing on the legitimacy of this program. See Québec Parental Insurance Plan at *http://www.rqap.gouv.qc.ca/Index_en.asp.*

of choice, even within the abortion debate, is part of the way that women and mothers are constructed as either self-interested or self-less, and diverts attention from the constraints within which an individual's choice occurs (1991: 1564). Further, she argues, by wrapping women's decisions about motherhood in the rhetoric of choice, the ideal worker in North American society is constructed in a gendered way (1991: 1620). The proper role of women as caregivers and as mothers is constructed through the rhetoric of choice to be naturally at odds with the reality of the ideal worker.

Similarly, Rebecca Johnson argues that the legal rhetoric of choice is one of the key mechanisms by which the legitimacy of current constructions of gender is shaped (2000: 200). The language of choice is often employed in ways that reinforce the current and unequal distribution of paid work and caregiving responsibilities within families (2000: 205). By leaving decisions within families as matters of choice, the problems of balancing paid and unpaid work become privatised onto the shoulders of women who are making choices, albeit often with their spouses and within their families. The pervasive nature of individualised choice sends the message that the role of law is to protect people's freedom to make choices about their lives, whether or not these choices are situated within a lattice of constraints (Minow, 1992: 2093).

Choice and mothers: story of constraint

It is this conflict between choice and constraint that is at the heart of the maternity and parental leave debates in Canada. An (un)employment insurance system that has historically been structured on a male wage earning model creates the illusion that benefits are available to those who choose to participate in the paid labour market. However, within this model eligibility requirements remain tied to major work force attachment. This definition of attachment prioritises certain kinds of work over others, rewarding the 'choices' of those who participate in the present model. In the balancing of work and family, the rhetoric of choice 'masks a gender system that defines childrearing and the accepted avenues of adult advancement as inconsistent and then reallocates the resulting costs of childrearing to mothers' (Williams, 1991: 1596).

Where conflicts between work and family life are seen as matters of choice, attention is diverted from the very constraints that surrounded those weighty decisions in the first place (Williams, 1991: 1615). On one level, constraints include access to maternity and parental leave (Evans and Pupo, 1993, cited in Madsen, 2002: 37). At another level, these constraints are more systemic. The choices inherent in balancing paid work and motherhood cannot be meaningful without due attention to systemic constraints, including, for example, the gendered division of labour, pay inequities and the lack of adequate daycare.

Choice and neoliberalism

We can see at least three differing ways that the rhetoric of choice is also of persuasive influence in broader debates in Canada today. First, the rhetoric of choice permeates early 21st century equality jurisprudence. Diana Majury argues that in recent case law, 'choice' in the context of marriage and motherhood is translated into the notion 'that women are themselves to blame', which has become a virtually impenetrable shield against equality claims (2006: 225). Where a choice, such as the decision not to marry, leaves a claimant without access to a property division regime otherwise available to married persons, the claimant finds herself unable to prove that her dignity is demeaned so as to warrant a constitutional remedy.[14] In other words, Canadian courts have been increasingly telling women that no discrimination flows from situations where women had a 'choice'.[15]

Second, the rhetoric of choice is employed to construct choices as matters of private responsibility (Lessard, 2006; Madsen, 2002). When faced with competing choices, the state assumes that the 'responsible individual' will make the ones that are in keeping with a privatised notion of family and care. Thus, when delivering a program such as maternity and parental leave, the government relies on women's personal sense of responsibility to their roles as mothers to provide where programs are inadequate. In this sense of choice, the primary responsibility for social reproduction 'resides neither with governments nor ultimately with families but with individuals' (Lessard, 2006: 18). Care is privatised, and in the process, the sexual division of labour is exacerbated, 'shifting more work to women while asserting this is merely a side effect of individual choice' (Cossman and Fudge, 2002: 29–30, cited in Lessard, 2006: 18).

Finally, the rhetoric of choice is employed by policy makers to justify cutbacks in social programs and the further privatisation of care to the family. The citizen at the heart of the neoliberal, free and democratic Canada is the responsible, autonomous chooser, whose choices are not limited by an activist state. These policy makers tell us:

> Freedom cannot exist without personal responsibility. As the state assumes more and more responsibility, our freedom and personal choices are eroded. When the state assumes responsibility for individual choices, it limits freedom. If individuals do not bear the consequences of bad choices, more people will make them and the rest of us will be forced to bear the burden. That, in turn, forces the state to adopt coercive measures to ensure

---

14 Majury is discussing in particular *Nova Scotia (Attorney General) v Walsh* [2002] SCC 83 and *Gosselin v Québec (Attorney General)* [2002] 4 SCR 429.

15 See, e.g. *Walsh*, above, and *Hodge v Canada (Minister of Human Resources Development)* [2004] SCC 65.

that individuals make the choices that the state considers appropriate, and liberty is even further eroded.

(Harris and Manning, 2005: 13)

The neoliberal state, thus, is one that pulls back and leaves the burdens where they 'rightfully' belong, on the shoulders of those who 'choose' to be parents, negotiating the concomitant responsibilities on behalf of all.

CHOICE IN THE MATERNITY AND PARENTAL LEAVE DEBATES

With this discussion of how the rhetoric of choice influences the relationship between caregiving, motherhood and employment generally, I turn to the specific use of choice in the maternity and parental leave debates. Although the decision of the Québec Court of Appeal was surprising to many (Cox, 2004; Monsebraaten, 2004), it also reflects the ideologies underlying women's 'chosen' roles in the labour force that have infused this debate from its outset. This section will look at several key moments which, combined, reflect the power of the rhetoric of choice within Canadian maternity and parental leave debates. I finish with a brief look at what the Supreme Court of Canada had to say about the Québec decision, and what it might mean for parents and other caregivers who continue to face the competing tensions of their productive and reproductive lives.

1940: wives and daughters and the choice to work

The notion that women's choices with respect to balancing motherhood and employment should inform public policy was reflected in the design of the first (un)employment insurance regime. Once federal jurisdiction over unemployment insurance was settled, the framers of the first Unemployment Insurance Act[16] opted for a compulsory, contributory program. The first Act was thus an insurance plan, based on existing models in the United Kingdom and the United States at the time, and not a form of social welfare (Marsh, 1943: 9–26, 56–62; Canada, 1962: 19; see also Evans, 1997: 98). Unlike reliance on needs-based benefits, which were constructed as pejorative, the program was one of employment-based contributory benefits designed to simply replace income that had been earned and paid for and therefore seen as meritorious (Pulkingham, 1998: 8).

The notion of the benefits as properly flowing to those who merited them was based on two, inter-related assumptions. The first was that at the heart of the

16 Unemployment Insurance Act, 1940, SC 1940, c.44, as amended (the 1940 Act).

Canadian workforce was one kind of employee: male, working full-time, and responsible for the support of others. Thus, unemployment insurance was designed for an industrial labour force in a social system in which the vast majority of families were male-headed, one-earner households (Pierson, 1990: 92–93). This assumption informed all aspects of program design, including the way in which elements like benefit rates and eligibility requirements treated men and women in different ways.

The second assumption was that women's unemployment was different from men's, as women could choose whether or not to work (Porter, 2003: 47). Because most women were seen not as employees, but as either wives or daughters, their dependency justified their differential treatment (Pierson, 1990: 90). Drawing on the stereotype that women worked solely for 'pin money',[17] this assumption of choice made the unemployment of women less of a concern to the federal government than the unemployment of men. The scheme rewarded men who worked steadily within the conventions of the time, but made invisible the female employee who had less access to steady or long-term insurable employment (Pierson, 1990: 97).

The notion that women in the paid workforce were there by choice, and therefore less entitled to full protections of the Act, overtly informed the Act. For example, there were explicit exclusions from coverage of particular kinds of employment, such as teaching, nursing and domestic service, effectively excluding many working women.[18] Additionally, women who left work due to sexual harassment or other intolerable work conditions were not eligible for unemployment insurance because the 1940 Act did not grant benefits to voluntary leavers (Pierson, 1990: 102). As such, the first unemployment insurance Act seemed to offer equality, applying equally to all eligible employees, regardless of gender. The reality was that many provisions of the 1940 Act worked differently for men and women, and entrenched in the foundation of the concept of unemployment insurance the notion that women could choose not to work, making their unemployment less of a concern.

1971: the first maternity benefit and the choice of delivery

The second moment of 'choice' came in 1970 when the decision was made to offer a maternity benefit through (un)employment insurance. This decision acknowledged decades of struggle by pregnant workers to highlight that their needs were not being met (Porter, 2003: 108). However, the fact that it was delivered in a regime premised on the male breadwinner as normative meant

17 I am grateful to my colleague Hester Lessard for raising this argument with me. See discussion of the 'pin money' stereotype and its impact on understandings of women's employment in late 19th and early 20th century Canada in Latham and Pazdro (1984).

18 See First Schedule, Part II of the 1940 Act, ss.(f), (g), (h) and (i).

that this new benefit was not attentive to the specific needs of the female labour market participant. The 1970 benefit rewarded certain kinds of choices made by women in paid work, more than it met the systemic need to support social reproduction within the structure of work (Pierson, 1990: 102).

By the late 1960s the issue of pregnant workers had come to inform public debate and was one of the key issues on the agenda for the 1967 Royal Commission on the Status of Women (the Commission). The Commission's mandate was to 'recommend what steps might be taken by the Federal Government to ensure for women equal opportunities with men in all aspects of Canadian society' (Bird, 1990: para.36). The Commission's final report (the Report) provided many women with a 'vehicle to express their aspirations' (Abner, Mossman and Pickett, 1990: para.1), highlighting the agency of individual women in its development. In terms of sex equality, the Report focused on practical goals to be implemented, rather than a detailed legal or philosophical analysis (Abner, Mossman and Pickett, 1990: para.7).

Part of the Commission's mandate, structured as it was in formal equality terms, was guided by the principle that society had a responsibility for women because of pregnancy and childbirth, and special treatment related to maternity would always be necessary (Bird, 1990: para.53). This principle and the recommendations that accompanied it were ultimately implemented through the (un)employment insurance regime. Absent from the debate that led to entrenchment of the benefits in unemployment insurance, however, was the question of whether unemployment insurance was, in fact, the best regime through which to deliver this important new social benefit. The result was a benefit regime infused with an individual notion of choice, in that it only extended to women with employment, and then only to women who could qualify for benefits through the onerous eligibility requirements developed for unemployment insurance.

2000: casting the debate into a rights framework: the choice to litigate

The third moment of choice is evidenced in attempts by advocates to use the Charter to effect change for women attempting to balance the tensions of their productive and reproductive lives. Structuring these arguments through a rights framework has had two problematic results. The first is that courts have reiterated that as long as the benefit is delivered within a formal equality framework, it will not be discriminatory in effect. The second is a reification of the role of choice within that formal equality framework. The decision to deliver a benefit that rewarded certain kinds of labour force attachment, and to deliver that benefit in a regime premised on gendered assumptions about women's labour, has led to a benefit that is not equality-enhancing in substance or effect.

As Nitya Iyer has argued, a benefit that is disproportionately available to certain women based on their labour force participation exacerbates the oppression of poor women, Aboriginal women, women of colour, women with disabilities, single parents and lesbians as mothers (1997: 176). Delivering the benefit through (un)employment insurance serves to reinforce the notion that 'some mothers are better than others' by making it easier for mothers with certain labour patterns to qualify for benefits (Iyer, 1997). Within an equality framework that celebrates choice and obscures constraints, the attempt to litigate change in this area has left much of the regime's most onerous elements undisturbed.

This danger, reifying the individual at the expense of the systemic without attention to the constraints of choice, is a persistent theme in the recent equality challenges brought against the benefits regime. This was shown most profoundly in the Supreme Court of Canada's decision in *Bliss v Canada (Attorney General)*,[19] in which a challenge to the provisions of the first maternity benefit, and in particular how that benefit made it more difficult for pregnant women to attain benefits than other workers, was dismissed by the Supreme Court of Canada. The court devastatingly held that as long as all pregnant persons are formally treated alike by the legislation there is no discrimination (Calder, 2002: 101–7; Porter, 2003: 133–37). The provisions at issue in *Bliss* explicitly entrenched in the maternity leave benefit regime the fear that had permeated the unemployment insurance debates since the 1940s, namely that women were intentional abusers of unemployment insurance (Porter, 2003: 124). The tenor of the judgment demonstrated the fear that women will exercise their choices irresponsibly if they are left unhindered, and that this was embedded in the regime. The *Bliss* decision has been uniformly criticised and its holding that discrimination on the basis of pregnancy was not sex discrimination has been overturned by the Supreme Court of Canada.[20] However, the notions of choice that informed this 1979 decision remain present in recent challenges to maternity and parental leave in the (un)employment insurance context.

Two recent equality decisions are particularly illustrative. In *Canada (Attorney General) v Lesiuk*,[21] the Federal Court of Appeal held that Kelly Lesiuk's dignity was not infringed by eligibility requirements, even if they were set at a level that she was unable to meet due to her caregiving responsibilities.[22] As long as the claimant was treated the same as all other persons who failed to work the requisite hours, and her rights were limited as little as was reasonably possible, then there was no discrimination. Similarly in *Miller v Canada (Attorney General)*,[23] Joanne Miller's inability to claim (un)employment insurance benefits due to taking maternity leave during her eligibility period was held not to be

19 *Bliss v Canada (Attorney General)* [1979] 1 SCR 183.
20 *Brooks v Canada Safeway Ltd* [1989] 1 SCR 1219.
21 Above note 5, leave to the Supreme Court of Canada dismissed 17 July 2003.
22 Above at para.70.
23 Above note 5, leave to the Supreme Court of Canada dismissed 17 April 2003.

discriminatory. Instead, having had access to special benefits, she had in fact 'benefited' under the Act.[24] When compared to all other special benefit recipients, Ms Miller had not faced any discrimination. The legislation, the court asserted, did not perpetuate the view that she was less capable or worthy of recognition or value as a human being. In fact, the opposite was the case.[25] The court affirmed the lower court that one cannot be discriminated against where one has taken advantage of ameliorative provisions of legislation, such as those in place to grant benefits to women during maternity leave. This holding echoes the finding in *Bliss* that legislated 'burdens' and legislated 'benefits' should be treated differently (Martin, 1987: 200). Support for working mothers was seen as a special favour, and not as a reflection of a societal need (Lawrence, 1997: 481).

These cases show that the formal equality approach adopted by the court in *Bliss* that seems so anachronistic has, in fact, endured. They show that assumptions about women and work are ingrained in the law and legal reasoning in a systemic way. Litigation has had little effect on the underlying inequality in the labour market. Social structures remain in place, and the deeply ingrained judicial and societal assumptions about women's choices persist (Bakan, 1997: 51, 53). Using law through rights claims may offer an illusion of improved access to power, but still leaves 'untouched the institutionalisation of power in hierarchical social relations' (Williams, 1990: para.63). A formal equality approach compounded by the view that the choices women make about motherhood are free of systemic constraints, continue to make findings of discrimination untenable.

Choice in the 21st century: dual-earning families

The invocation of choice by the Québec Court of Appeal, thus, can be read in light of a long history of maternity and parental leave debates in Canada, reinforcing the assumption that women and others can avoid adverse impacts by making simple choices about their child care and reproductive lives (Calder, 2003: 339). Embedded in the first Act was the notion that women's dependent position in society made their decisions to work a matter of choice, and as such less worthy of protection. This conceptualisation of women and paid work was reiterated even when the needs of pregnant workers ultimately forced change within (un)employment insurance. Additionally, strategic litigation has solidified an understanding of the maternity and parental leave benefits in a formal equality framework. Diana Majury and Hester Lessard have both argued that the use of the Charter in the current neo-liberal context has led, paradoxically, to regressive outcomes for women attempting to challenge their place in the

---

24 *Miller v Attorney General of Canada*, CUB 50489 (24 November 2000) at 16, affirmed by the Federal Court of Appeal, above note 5.

25 Above at 17.

Canadian family (Lessard, 2006; Majury, 2006). This analysis is resoundingly reinforced in the maternity and parental leave debates, and informs the Québec Court of Appeal decision in 2004.

As noted at the outset, the language of the Québec Court of Appeal was simple: an insurance regime should distinguish between economic events and personal choices. Even though the government of Québec pursued its jurisdictional argument with the objective of offering a more progressive benefit, the damage resulting from evoking the rhetoric of choice is palpable. The jurisdiction question put to the Supreme Court of Canada was the wrong question, and no matter what the court decided, it was not going to offer an answer that could bring about substantive change in the regime. It was either going to reinforce the *status quo*, or it was going to dismantle the current benefit's application to the entire country and let each province decide whether or not they would take steps to provide a benefit to women whose labour force attachments were disrupted by 'choice'. Although a provincial regime might allow Québec to be more attentive to the needs of women, the outcome for women in other provinces was unlikely to be so advantageous.

By framing the question in terms of choice, the Québec Court of Appeal neglected questions about the unequal gender-based costs of caregiving, the societal interest in caring for children and the disadvantages attendant on being a parent (Johnson, 2000: 209). By constructing issues of social reproduction as personal, the Québec Court of Appeal privatised the problems of women and, in the process, reinforced an understanding of gender by asserting different expectations and responsibilities for men and women (Johnson, 2000: 200). This process reflects not only a change in the way that the state is organised, but an entrenched understanding of where responsibility for the welfare of citizens lies. Recognising the significance of the production of a labour force, by women, to the working of a capitalist society furthers the importance of centring social reproduction in any analysis of social policy.

THE SUPREME COURT OF CANADA'S CHOICE

In October 2005 the Supreme Court of Canada rendered its decision and overturned the Québec Court of Appeal. In the unanimous holding of the court, the Québec Court of Appeal had erred in its finding that the maternity and parental leave benefits regime was properly a matter of provincial jurisdiction. In a decision relying on a traditional federalism analysis, the court affirmed that the regime is properly part of (un)employment insurance, fitting with the pith and substance of a head of power that was added to bring unemployment issues into federal jurisdiction in 1940. With care and attention to the needs of women, the court characterised the benefit in a manner that saved the federal regime, and in the process, the *status quo*.

I have argued elsewhere that within this judgment there lie the seeds of optimism (Calder, 2006). The court, in my view, went further than the question posed in finding that the regime is properly a matter of federal jurisdiction. It noted that 'a growing portion of the labour force is made up of women, and women have particular needs that are of concern to society as a whole.'[26] In contrast to the language of the Québec Court of Appeal that had framed women's childbearing decisions as personal, the Supreme Court of Canada held that 'an interruption of employment due to maternity can no longer be regarded as a matter of individual responsibility.'[27] Benefits are not determined on the basis of whether the loss of employment is for 'meritorious' reasons. Instead, 'the benefits relate to the function of the reproduction of society', something for which we all have a collective responsibility.[28]

However, even though the language of the Québec Court of Appeal was not endorsed by the Supreme Court of Canada, the court did not discredit the distinction drawn by the Québec Court of Appeal between the different reasons that one is absent from work. The court only went so far as to say that the distinction was not relevant for jurisdictional purpose, both should be included in the federal (un)employment insurance regime. They did not discuss whether the benefit for maternity or parental leave meets the needs of women across Canada attempting to balance the tensions of their productive and reproductive lives. The way in which the question was posed did not give the court an opportunity to disrupt the rhetoric of choice in any profound way. The question of how to describe women's choices with respect to motherhood and whether or not those choices should be given weight was left for another day.

CONTEXTUALISING CHOICE: CENTRING WOMEN'S SOCIAL REPRODUCTIVE LABOUR

Ultimately, centring questions of choice in this debate draws away from what is, in my view, the key question: whether the program as it is presently structured is or is not meeting the needs of women attempting to balance their productive and reproductive lives. Delivering a benefit for maternity and parental leave through (un)employment insurance has done little to resolve the inherent tension in a capitalist society between production for individualised gain and collective responsibility for social reproduction, and in the process reified a regressive notion of choice. Without systemic change, a benefit regime like this one will only preserve the *status quo* at best.

This is the case, I argue, because women's domestic obligation is taken for

---

26 *EI Reference* at para.66.
27 As above.
28 Above at para.73.

granted in the formulation of social policies (Picchio, 1992: 112) and social reproduction has been left outside of political analyses of the economy and neglected as a site for political struggle (Calder, 2006). The simple dichotomy used by the Québec Court of Appeal to differentiate between economic and personal reasons for being absent from work was inherently flawed. So is a division of powers analysis that constructs the maternity and parental leave benefits regime as social assistance, severing the relationship between production and reproduction in the process. If social reproduction was centred in an analysis of this regime, one would find that women's reproductive labour is not just a private or familial service, but 'an important and socially indispensable labour that contributes to the production of the population and its labour-power ... that it produces workers who are ready and willing to sell their capacities to work in the labour market on a daily and generational basis' (Luxton, 2002: 6). Unpaid labour in the form of care in the home is not just the private action or 'choice' of individuals; it is and should be subject to economic analysis as part of the generational reproduction of society (Calder, 2003: 352). A theoretical perspective that centres social reproduction offers a means by which a policy change that addresses both women's productive and reproductive labour can be analysed. The maternity and parental leave benefits regime should be a means by which the social reproductive labour of women and men who take time out from their work, both paid and unpaid, to give birth to and care for children is valued.

There are those who would argue that ultimately the problem is not the attachment of the benefit to (un)employment insurance, but rather the miserliness of the benefits regime that needs to be remedied (Cox, 2004). What I have argued, however, is that the core of the problem is continuing to link eligibility for benefits to labour market participation, and in turn, the assumption that women's labour market participation is based on choice. What remains unchallenged under this regime is the question of the state's responsibility for adequate childcare, pay equity, restructuring the gendered division of labour and attention to social reproduction when programs are delivered. If we value social reproductive labour and recognise the benefit to society in general of parents, and in particular women, who care for young children, then it does not make sense to require a certain standard and kind of labour force attachment in order to be eligible for a maternity and parental leave benefit, a standard that leads to the disenfranchisement of many people who arguably need the benefit the most.

BIBLIOGRAPHY

Abner E., Mossman, M.J. and Pickett, E., 'No more than simple justice: assessing the Royal Commission Report on Women, Poverty and the Family', *Ottawa Law Review*, 22, 1990, pp.573–605.

Bakan, J., *Just Words: Constitutional Rights and Social Wrongs*. University of Toronto Press, Toronto 1997.

Bird, F., 'Introduction: special introduction: special issue commemorating the 20th anniversary of the Royal Commission on the Status of Women in Canada', *Ottawa Law Review*, 22, 1990, pp.543–54.

Calder, G., *Gender, Social Reproduction and the Canadian Welfare State: Assessing the Recent Changes to the Maternity and Parental Leave Benefits Regime*. York University (LLM Thesis), Toronto 2002.

Calder, G., 'Recent changes to the maternity and parental leave benefits regime as a case study: The impact of globalization on the delivery of social programs in Canada', *Canadian Journal of Women and the Law*, 15, 2003, pp.342–66.

Calder, G., 'A pregnant pause: federalism, equality and the maternity and parental leave debate in Canada', *Feminist Legal Studies*, 14, 2006, pp.99–118.

Campeau, G., *From UI to EI: Waging War on the Welfare State*. UBC Press, Vancouver 2005.

Canada, *Report of the Committee of Inquiry into the Unemployment Insurance Act 1962*. Supply and Services Canada, Ottawa 1962.

Cossman, B. and Fudge, J., eds, *Privatization, Law, and the Challenge to Feminism*. University of Toronto Press, Toronto 2002.

Cox, R., *The Recent Quebec Appeal Court Decision on the Constitutionality of Maternity and Parental Benefits as Employment Insurance Benefits: Some Feminist Reflections*. National Association of Women and the Law, Ottawa 2004.

Evans, P. and Pupo, N., 'Parental leave: assessing women's interests', *Canadian Journal of Women and the Law*, 6, 1993, pp.402–18.

Evans, P., 'Divided citizenship? Gender, income security and the welfare state', in Evans, P.M. and Wekerle, G.R., eds, *Women and the Canadian Welfare State*. University of Toronto Press, Toronto 1997, pp.91–116.

Harris, M. and Manning, P., *A Canada Strong and Free*. Fraser Institute, Vancouver 2005.

Iyer, N., 'Some mothers are better than others: a re-examination of maternity benefits', in Boyd, S.B., ed., *Challenging the Public/Private Divide: Feminism, Law, and Public Policy*. University of Toronto Press, Toronto 1997, pp.168–94.

Johnson, R., 'If choice is the answer, what is the question? Spelunking in *Symes v Canada*', in Chunn, D.E. and Lacombe, D., eds, *Law as a Gendering Practice*. Oxford University Press, Don Mills 2000, pp.199–222.

Johnson, R., *Taxing Choices: The Intersection of Class, Gender, Parenthood, and the Law*. UBC Press, Vancouver 2002.

Latham, B.K. and Pazdro, R.J., eds, *Not Just Pin Money: Selected Essays on the History of Women's Work in British Columbia*. Camosun College, Victoria 1984.

Lawrence, M., 'Approaches to gender equality in the workplace: *Dumont-Ferlatte v Canada (Employment and Immigration Commission)*', *Ottawa Law Review*, 29, 1997, pp.477–95.

Lessard, H., '*Charter* gridlock: equality formalism and marriage fundamentalism', *Supreme Court Law Review*, 33, 2006, pp.291–316.

Luxton, M., *Feminist Perspectives on Social Inclusion and Children's Well Being*. The Laidlaw Foundation, Toronto 2002.

Madsen, L., 'Citizen, worker, mother: Canadian women's claims to parental leave and childcare', *Canadian Journal of Family Law*, 19, 2002, pp.11–74.

Majury, D., 'Women are themselves to blame: choice as a justification for unequal treatment', in Denike, M., Stephenson, M.K. and Faraday, F., eds, *The Law Project: Reinvigorating Equality*. Irwin Law, Toronto 2006, pp.209–43.

Marsh, L., *Report on Social Security for Canada*. University of Toronto Press, Toronto 1943.

Martin, S.L., 'Persisting equality implications of the "Bliss" case', in Martin, S.L. and Mahoney, K.E., eds, *Equality and Judicial Neutrality*. Carswell, Toronto 1987, pp.195–206.

Minow, M., 'Choices and constraints: for Justice Thurgood Marshall', *Georgia Law Review*, 80, 1992, pp.2093–2108.

Monsebraaten, L., 'A call to arms for women's rights lobby', *Toronto Star*, 14 March 2004.

Picchio, A., *Social Reproduction: The Political Economy of the Labour Market*. Cambridge University Press, Cambridge 1992.

Pierson, R., 'Gender and the unemployment insurance debates in Canada, 1934–1940', *Labour/Le Travail*, 25, 1990, pp.77–103.

Porter, A., *Gendered States: Women, Unemployment Insurance, and the Political Economy of the Welfare State in Canada, 1945–1997*. University of Toronto Press, Toronto 2003.

Pulkingham, J., 'Remaking the social division of welfare: gender, "dependency", and UI reform', *Studies in Political Economy*, 56, 1998, pp.7–48.

Williams, J., 'Gender wars: selfless women in the republic of choice', *New York University Law Review*, 66, 1991, pp.1559–1634.

Williams, T., 'Re-forming "women's" truth: a critique of the Report of the Royal Commission on the Status of Women', *Ottawa Law Review*, 22, 1990, pp.725–59.

Chapter 8

Decision making at the end of life: the choice is yours, or is it?

Hazel Biggs

INTRODUCTION

In healthcare decision making the relationship between choice and consent is complex. In theory choice implies that there is a range of alternative options and consent suggests that there is the possibility of refusal. Recent case law demonstrates that both of these concepts are problematic with regard to end-of-life decision making.

Generally choice is exercised through the notion of individual autonomy, which is regarded as the cornerstone of medical ethics, and is given legal expression through the law of consent. The basis of this is encapsulated in the now famous dicta of Cardozo J that 'every human being of adult years and sound mind has the right to decide what shall be done with his own body',[1] illustrating that consent is central to the administration of any healthcare intervention. Furthermore, English law is clear that '[a]n adult patient who suffers from no mental incapacity has an absolute right to choose whether to consent to medical treatment, to refuse it or to choose one rather than another of the treatments being offered',[2] demonstrating the interrelationship between choice and the right to consent. The presence of a valid consent therefore legitimates what would otherwise amount to a civil wrong or a criminal assault[3] and a patient must be given the opportunity to consent to or refuse a proposed treatment option in order to ensure that the clinician involved does not incur criminal or tortious liability.

In practice the law expands upon this fundamental premise so that not only must consent be obtained to authorise medical treatment, but where a competent adult patient chooses to refuse treatment by declining to consent that

---

1   *Schloendorf v New York Hospital* 105 NE 92 (1914).
2   *Re T* [1992] 4 All ER 649 at 652.
3   *Re R (Wardship) (A Minor: consent to Treatment)* (1992) 7 BMLR 147, *per* Lord Donaldson MR at 155.

refusal must also be respected.[4] The principle applies even if the patient will inevitably die as a consequence of refusing treatment:

> ... it is unlawful, so as to constitute both a tort and the crime of battery, to administer medical treatment to an adult, who is conscious and of sound mind, without his consent ... such a person is completely at liberty to decline to undergo treatment ... even if the result of his doing so will be that he will die.[5]

This chapter will argue that despite the fundamental acceptance of choice and consent in relation to healthcare decision making generally, when it comes to end-of-life decisions real choice is limited and the rhetoric of choice does not accord with the reality. Choice is, for example, limited by resources, by law and, where women are concerned, often by protectionist, paternalistic social attitudes. It is, for example, only possible to choose to spend your dying days at home in your own environment if there is somebody there willing and able to care for you. In addition, despite evidence and public opinion polls that repeatedly demonstrate high levels of public support for voluntary assisted dying for the terminally ill, these choices remain prohibited by law. As a result only a limited range of options is permitted at the end of life and many are denied the opportunity to seek the kind of death they might prefer.

Recent high profile cases demonstrate that where women seek assisted dying they encounter a collusion of social and judicial attitudes that deny not only their right to choose, but also their autonomy. In this context, the chapter will consider why women's choices are questioned with the consequence that their ability to exercise autonomous choice is compromised. It will also argue that just because a person is perceived as occupying a vulnerable position, this does not mean they are unable to make an autonomous choice, nor should it mean that they are prevented from giving a valid consent and acting upon a choice that is truly their own. The chapter will begin with an exposition of the concept of choice in the context of healthcare before going on to focus on choice at the end of life and to examine the ways in which some choices are restricted by the law.

CHOICE AND CONSENT IN HEALTHCARE

At the present time the mantra of choice is pervasive in English politics, healthcare and medical law. For example, recent developments in healthcare policy

---

4   For example, *Re T (Adult: Refusal of Treatment)* [1992] 4 All ER 671; *Re C (Adult: Refusal of Medical Treatment)* [1994] 1 All ER 819; *Re MB (An Adult: Medical Treatment)* [1997] 2 FLR 426; *Re B (Adult Refusal of Medical Treatment)* [2002] 2 All ER 449.

5   *Airedale NHS Trust v Bland* [1993] 1 All ER 821, *per* Lord Keith at 860.

include the patient's right to make choices based on sound information, and to choose where to be treated and by whom.[6] With regard to end-of-life care, recent government guidance has insisted that choice should be central to the provision of terminal and palliative care and that those who need it should be encouraged and empowered to decide for themselves what kind of care they wish to receive, including the type of institution they prefer and the philosophy under which care is delivered (*Building on the Best*, 2003; Department of Health, 2006b).

Choice is clearly important from the perspective of service provision and is of increasing significance with regard to medical law, where it has been emphasised in a number of recent cases. Of particular note here is *Chester v Afshar*,[7] which encompassed a range of issues around consent and information giving. The House of Lords concluded that because the claimant had not received complete information regarding her medical treatment she had effectively been denied the opportunity to make a proper choice. She was successful in her claim even though she consented to the surgery, and would probably still have agreed to it had she been fully appraised. One of the things that distinguished her case from previous, similar cases[8] was the fact that she was denied the opportunity to make a considered choice and perhaps to elect to have the surgery at a different time, which may have spared her the side effects she suffered.

In some respects *Chester v Afshar* represents a turning point in medical law in relation to choice and consent. How far it will have an influence on medical practice and the availability of choice generally is debatable, however. More specifically, the concept of therapeutic discretion dictates that, although doctors are under a legal duty to treat their patients according to their best interests, it is their own interpretation of those best interests that frequently determines the choices available to patients. For example:

> There are limits on patients' choices not only because of legal constraints about what options are allowed but also because of the professional judgement of doctors . . . They recommend the treatment that is best for an individual patient, having regard to that patient's needs and the treatments and resources available.
>
> (BMA, 2004: 88)

Having formed an opinion about each patient's clinical needs the doctor will then exercise discretion to decide what treatment options to advise. In this way the range of therapies the patient is given to select from may be incomplete

---

6   A vast array of literature has been published by the Department of Health to this effect including Department of Health (2004) and (2006a).
7   *Chester v Afshar* [2004] 3 WLR 927.
8   *Sidaway v Board of Governors of the Bethlem Royal Hospital* [1985] 1 All ER 643.

because it represents only those options that the clinician has judged to be suitable, potentially beneficial to the patient and within budget. The patient will therefore have the opportunity to consent to one or more treatment options from a list proffered by the clinician, but the list may be incomplete because the doctor has already made a judgement about which are the *best* options to make available. Where this is the case, not only is the choice limited, it is also not fully informed because the patient is not given the opportunity to select from every possible treatment option, which challenges the validity of any consent obtained.

These are important concerns that have an impact on and may compound some of the difficulties often experienced in the context of end-of-life decision making. Despite the apparent shift to prioritise choice in health care the therapeutic options available are not unlimited and individual patients may find their choices constrained in a variety of ways and for a variety of reasons, particularly in relation to end-of-life care. Sometimes the choices that individual people seek, such as medically assisted dying, are prohibited by law,[9] while those who make apparently legitimate choices experience resistance and obstruction.[10] This chapter will critique a number of cases involving people who sought to make particular choices about the medical care they would receive at the end of their lives. It will explore the limits of choice at the end of life through the experiences of several women, and one man, whose considered choices have become the subject of legal challenge. In each case the choice available was constrained, either by the law or the medical profession or both.

WHATEVER YOU CHOOSE WE'LL DECIDE FOR YOU!

The exercise of therapeutic discretion was a central theme in the most recent case in which the issue of choice in end-of-life decision making was involved.[11] The case was distinctive because, unlike many recent end-of-life cases,[12] this one concerned a male patient, Leslie Burke, who, rather than seeking endorsement for a decision that would end his life, wanted to ensure that treatment was not withdrawn from him.

Mr Burke is a victim of spino-cerebellar ataxia, a progressively degenerative congenital condition which will inevitably cause his death. He challenged guidance issued by the General Medical Council (2002) outlining the circumstances in which artificial nutrition and hydration (ANH) might legitimately be

---

9 R *(on the application of Pretty) v DPP* [2002] 1 All ER 1.
10 *Re B (Adult: Refusal of Medical Treatment)* [2002] WL 347038 (Fam Div); *Re Z (Local Authority: Duty)* [2005] 1 WLR 959.
11 *Burke v GMC* [2005] 2 WLR 431 at 504.
12 For example, *NHS Trust A v M, NHS Trust B v H* [2001] Fam 348; R *(on the application of Pretty) v DPP* [2002] 1 All ER 1; *Re B (Adult: Refusal of Medical Treatment)* [2002] WL 347038 (Fam Div).

withheld or withdrawn from a patient such as himself. Despite this, and media reporting to the contrary (Batty, 2005; Harris, 2005), the case was not about the 'right to life'. It is inevitable that Leslie Burke will die from his condition even with continued ANH, so his legal challenge was not brought with the intention of trying to extend his life. Rather, it revolved around concerns about the circumstances he might encounter prior to his death.

In the final stages of his illness Leslie Burke is expected to lapse into a coma and die, but before this he will become progressively more physically debilitated until eventually he loses all physical control and the ability to communicate. Throughout this time and until the very terminal phases of the disease process he is likely to retain cognitive awareness, which raises the possibility that he will lose decision-making capacity while his intellect remains unimpaired. Under the Mental Capacity Act 2005, a person will be deemed not competent to consent to or refuse treatment if they are unable to understand the information relevant to the decision, retain that information, use or weigh it as part of the process of making the decision, or communicate their decision. As a result Leslie Burke will be rendered incompetent even while he retains the intellectual capacity to understand his predicament and its implications, but cannot engage with his medical carers.

The generic term 'locked in syndrome' is used to describe patients who experience this phenomenon where theoretically they have the intellectual ability to make decisions for themselves, but in practice they are unable to communicate those decisions. Leslie Burke was concerned because it is at this stage of his deterioration that the clinicians caring for him will probably consider withdrawing ANH. His legal challenge was born out of the fear that if ANH were to be withdrawn while he is still mentally alert he might experience symptoms associated with the withdrawal of food and fluids. Understandably, he sought to avoid the likely discomfort and distress that would accompany that eventuality.

It has been accepted since *Airedale NHS Trust v Bland*[13] in 1993 that where treatment is futile it may be lawfully withheld or withdrawn even though death is a foreseeable result and the patient's life might be prolonged if treatment were continued. The situation here is subtly different since Leslie Burke will die regardless of whether ANH is withdrawn or withheld. The GMC Guidance stipulates that having regard for the views of the patient, it is the responsibility of the consultant or GP caring for a patient such as Leslie Burke to decide 'whether to withhold or withdraw life prolonging treatment' (GMC, 2002: para.32). It also includes the provision that this may be appropriate even where 'death is not imminent' if it is judged that 'providing artificial nutrition or hydration may cause suffering or be too burdensome in relation to possible benefits' (GMC, 2002: para.81). Leslie Burke challenged the guidance on several

---

13 *Airedale NHS Trust v Bland* [1993] 1 All ER 821.

grounds and sought declarations from the court that it is unlawful. Specifically, he argued that the guidance was incompatible with domestic law and amounted to a breach of Articles 2, 3 and 8 of the European Convention on Human Rights (ECHR) if its application resulted in death through starvation or dehydration, particularly if the patient had previously expressed a desire to continue receiving ANH. He also claimed that unless the provision of ANH amounted to degrading treatment in itself then its withdrawal would contravene Article 3, and further that the guidance failed to safeguard the rights of patients under Articles 2, 3 and 8, especially in cases where there was a lack of agreement between clinicians and relatives or carers about withdrawal of ANH, in which circumstances he claimed that the matter should properly be referred to a court.

At issue for Leslie Burke was not whether or not the treatment was futile in terms of whether it would or would not prolong his life. It is very clear that the continuation of ANH after he loses the capacity to communicate will not appreciably extend his lifespan. The broader question, however, is whether the provision of ANH would benefit him by allowing him to avoid the indignity and suffering that might accompany its withdrawal. Here it seems certain that if there is any possibility of Leslie Burke experiencing symptoms of thirst and starvation, which could be avoided by the continuation of ANH, then surely providing the treatment would be of benefit to him. In addition, as Article 3 of the ECHR 'requires the victim to be aware of the inhuman and degrading treatment which he or she is experiencing or at least to be in a state of physical or mental suffering',[14] not to do so would fly dangerously close to violating Burke's Article 3 rights.

In an extensive first instance judgment, Munby J upheld all of Leslie Burke's claims and granted the declarations he sought. The ruling located the views of the patient at centre stage, endorsed established case law[15] and decreed that:

> If the patient is competent (or, although incompetent, has made an advance directive which is both valid and relevant to the treatment in question) his decision to require ANH which he believes is necessary to protect him from what he sees as acute mental and physical suffering is . . . in principle determinative.[16]

Put simply, Munby J emphasised each patient's right to choose the form of treatment received based on her or his understanding of what would best serve his or her best interests.

---

14 *NHS Trust A v M, NHS Trust B v H* [2001] Fam 348, *per* Butler-Sloss LJ at 362.
15 *Re T* [1992] 4 All ER 649; *Re MB (Adult: Medical Treatment)* [1997] 2 FCR 541.
16 *Burke v GMC* [2005] 2 WLR 431 at 504.

The relevance of best interests in a case like this is multi-faceted. Not only does therapeutic discretion rely upon the clinical analysis of best interests, as discussed above, but best interests criteria are central to decision making for patients who have lost capacity to participate in the decision-making process. Since Leslie Burke was primarily concerned about decisions that will be taken after he has lost capacity through an inability to communicate, Munby J's approach was appropriate and satisfied his requirements. The Court of Appeal however, overturned Munby J's judgment and denied the significance of best interests criteria on the grounds that at the time of the hearing Mr Burke was capable of making his own decisions and choices, and that it would clearly be unlawful for life-prolonging treatment to be withdrawn from him in those circumstances. Arguably however, rather than the court at first instance 'extending well beyond the approach to patients in the position of Mr Burke',[17] the Court of Appeal has missed the central point of Leslie Burke's claim.

At first instance *Burke* trumpeted the patient's right to choice at the end of life and in medical treatment more generally. In doing so, however, it was seen as a challenge to the professionalism of doctors because it confronted head on the notion that patients have no right to demand particular kinds of medical intervention.[18] So controversial was the fact that the High Court judgment apparently placed patient autonomy and choice above therapeutic discretion that one irate commentator even claimed that it amounted to a 'draconian restriction on the exercise of doctors' professional skills' (Gillon, 2004: 811).

The idea that patients might be empowered to exercise greater control over medical decision making is clearly threatening to some within the medical profession. For example, Samanta and Samanta explain that the first instance decision in *Burke* 'could have severely restricted clinical judgement and discretion in relation to artificial nutrition and hydration and by implication other forms of treatment considered clinically useless' (2005: 1284). Their words demonstrate the complex dynamic between clinical judgement, or discretion, and the patient's own involvement in the assessment of their best interests. Concerns like these imply that the potential interference with clinical discretion that may result from prioritising patient autonomy in relation to end-of-life decision making is detrimental, and serve to illustrate the latent paternalism that still exists in some sections of the medical profession.

Further, the implication that Munby J's reasoning might be applied more widely and extended to other forms of treatment indicates an implicit nod towards the complicated issues associated with the allocation of scarce resources and the effects that the exercise of choice might have on others. The idea that a balance needs to be struck between the choices of individual patients and their possible impact upon others is gaining currency. For example, Margaret Brazier

---

17 R *(on the application of Burke) v General Medical Council* [2005] 3 WLR 1132 at 1140–41.
18 J *(Child in Care: Medical Treatment)* [1992] 4 All ER 614.

has recently argued that '[r]esponsibility for one's choice demands consideration of how those choices will affect others' (Brazier, 2006: 401). Though logical and in some senses compelling, such arguments are easily employed to bolster paternalistic attitudes that can be destructive of patient autonomy and choice, as is evidenced in the following examples where women have chosen specific end of life options.

INCAPABLE OF CHOICE – YOUR CHOICE IS WRONG!

The case of Ms B[19] involved a woman seeking to have her end-of-life choice respected and was also characterised by a difference of opinion between a patient and her doctors as to what was in her best interests. Here the patient suffered from a congenital malformation of the blood vessels in her neck and she suddenly and quite unexpectedly became paralysed from the neck down following complications. The damage was irreversible with no prospect of recovery. Ventilator support was required to keep her alive, but she was not dying. Prior to the rapid deterioration in her condition, Ms B had executed a living will outlining the circumstances in which she would want treatment to be withdrawn. Her stipulations were that she wished treatment to be withdrawn if she was 'suffering from a life threatening condition, permanent mental impairment or permanent unconsciousness'[20] and, although those exact circumstances had not arisen, once her prognosis was known she soon decided that she no longer wanted to live that way and asked that the ventilator be withdrawn.

In theory there should have been no problem with Ms B's request. As noted earlier, it is settled law that an adult patient who suffers from no incapacity has 'an absolute right to choose whether to consent to medical treatment, to refuse it or to choose one rather than another of the treatments being offered'.[21] It should, therefore, have been fairly straightforward for her to make her choice to withdraw her consent, articulate that fact and thereby authorise the removal of the ventilator. In practice it was not that simple.

Withdrawing the ventilator would inevitably result in Ms B's death and, because of the gravity of her choice to refuse further ventilation, those caring for her were understandably concerned to ensure that it was a considered and safe decision. Therefore, despite the fact that her mental capacity had not previously been questioned, they sought a psychiatric evaluation of her mental capacity in an effort to confirm that she was competent to make this decision. An initial assessment by two hospital psychiatrists confirmed that she was perfectly capable of deciding for herself and exercising her choice. Subsequently, however, the psychiatrists changed their minds and Ms B was offered

19 *Re B (Adult: Refusal of Medical Treatment)* [2002] WL 347038 (Fam Div).
20 As above at para.4.
21 *Re T (Adult: Refusal of Treatment)* [1992] 4 All ER 649 at 652–53.

rehabilitation instead of treatment withdrawal, an option that was not made available to her by the clinical team.

Ms B was very clear about what she wanted, however, and insisted on a further, independent psychiatric evaluation of her competence. This conclusively demonstrated that she was not depressed and had full mental capacity. The way seemed clear for the ventilator to be disconnected and for Ms B's life to be brought to an end. Yet the controversy continued as the team continued to harbour concerns about her competence. Also, over the protracted period of time that Ms B had been in hospital, she had been cared for by the same medical team whose members had become emotionally attached to her such that they felt unable to participate in disconnecting the ventilator. In desperation Ms B applied to the court for a declaration to confirm that her decision should be respected and that she had been unlawfully treated since the date of the independent psychiatric examination.

There can be little doubt that the health care team acted in good faith and according to what they regarded as Ms B's best interests when they declined to disconnect her from the ventilator. However, their understanding of her best interests seems to have been coloured by their own opinions and concerns which were applied in a paternalistic manner that overrode her autonomy and choice. Following a bedside hearing the court confirmed conclusively that Ms B was fully competent to decide for herself and entitled to have her choice to refuse consent upheld. The clinicians were required to refer the patient to a different hospital if they felt unable to participate in removing the ventilation and nominal damages of £100 were awarded against the hospital in recognition of the trespass caused by treating her against her will. Ms B died shortly afterwards.

In some ways, although Ms B had to battle for her autonomy to be respected, she was fortunate that the realisation of her choice to die turned on nothing more than the competent refusal of medical care. In effect this provided her with the opportunity to exercise a choice, even if she had to fight through the court for it to be recognised. The position is less favourable for others.

CHOICE, BUT NO CHOICE

English law does not permit medically assisted dying either through active euthanasia, which is regarded as homicide, or assisted suicide, which is contrary to the Suicide Act 1961. While it is not a crime for a person to commit suicide,[22] anybody who aids, abets counsels or procures the suicide of another contravenes the Suicide Act and risks a custodial sentence of up to 14 years' imprisonment.[23] At the present time, therefore, medically assisted suicide is simply not a choice

22 Suicide Act 1961, s.1.
23 Suicide Act 1961, s.2(1).

permitted by law. However, in a health care environment that promotes individual autonomy and patient choice, there is growing evidence that many people wish to be able to choose the time and manner of their dying by being assisted to die. Public opinion polls consistently demonstrate that between 71% and 87% of people favour a change in the law to permit assisted dying.[24] Indeed, the European Court of Human Rights recently recognised this as a central concern in the community:

> . . . in an era of growing medical sophistication combined with longer life expectancies, many people are concerned that they should not be forced to linger on in old age or in states of physical or mental decrepitude which conflict with strongly held ideas of self and personal identity.[25]

Diane Pretty was one such person. She suffered from motor neurone disease (MND), a progressive and ultimately fatal condition. The most likely cause of her death would be paralysis of the diaphragm or food aspiration. The illness would not affect her mental capacity and she would retain full mental capacity and awareness of her situation throughout, while gradually becoming physically incapable of caring for herself. Mrs Pretty did not want to experience the kind of death that awaited her and would have preferred instead to take her own life by suicide. However, the debilitating nature of MND meant that she was too infirm to administer lethal medicine or bring about her death by other means. Because suicide is not a crime, Diane Pretty initially assumed that as she was not able to take her own life due to her infirmity she would be able to enlist the help of somebody else. As a result she sought the assistance of her doctors and requested assisted suicide. It was then that she discovered that the law prohibits assisted suicide and that her doctors were understandably unwilling to help and risk jeopardising their careers and their liberty. Given this her husband, Brian, then agreed that he would be prepared to assist.

Mrs Pretty wanted to be able to choose the time and manner of her dying. She wished to be assisted to die if her suffering became unbearable, but she did not want to expose her husband to potential prosecution, conviction and imprisonment if he assisted her. She therefore sought an assurance from the courts that the Director of Public Prosecutions (DPP) would not pursue a case against him if he was implicated in her suicide. Administratively this claim was destined for failure since although the DPP is able to exercise discretion as to whether or not to prosecute after the event, the office has no constitutional power to grant immunity of this type in advance of a crime being committed. Any such decision would also be subject to a potential judicial review rendering any assurance given to the Prettys ineffective.

24 *Hansard*, 12 May 2006, Column 1185.
25 *Pretty v United Kingdom* (Application no. 2346/02) ECHR at para.65.

In addition Mrs Pretty claimed, inter alia, that section 2 of the Suicide Act 1961 was discriminatory and incompatible with her rights under Articles 2, 3, 8, 9 and 14 of the European Convention on Human Rights in that it prevented her from achieving what an able-bodied person might achieve for herself. Neither claim was successful. Of the Human Rights claims advanced, only the Article 8 claim came close to succeeding. The ECHR recognised the validity of the appeal to the right to respect for her private and family life under Article 8 of the Convention,[26] but rejected her claim because it was detrimental to 'the protection of health or morals, or the protection of the rights and freedoms of others'.[27]

The case raises several issues in relation to consent and choice. Obviously it demonstrates that choice is constrained by the law, as is to be expected in a liberal society. Perhaps less obvious, however, is the point that not only are the individual's choices limited, as Diane Pretty discovered, but they are in some senses subordinated to the perceived needs of others in society. Diane Pretty was mentally competent, fully aware of her situation and sought to exercise her autonomy by deciding when and where her life might end. She was capable of making her own choices and of giving a valid consent but was ultimately prevented from so doing, not because the ECHR was entirely unsympathetic to her claim, but because to uphold it would pose a threat to 'the protection of the rights and freedoms of others'.[28] The potential vulnerabilities of unnamed others in society dictated that Diane Pretty would not get the kind of death she chose, and she died of her illness in May 2002. However, there was another option she could have pursued.

THE TRAVELLER'S CHOICE

Assisted suicide is not lawful in England, but it is an available option in other jurisdictions, most notably Oregon, the Netherlands and Switzerland amongst others. Most of these have strict regulations that limit the availability of assisted suicide to those who reside in the state, but Switzerland has no such prohibition. As a result in excess of 40 British nationals have travelled to Zurich and received assisted suicide through the organisation known as *Dignitas*. The first case to receive notoriety involved 74-year-old Reginald Crewe, who travelled to Switzerland with his wife and daughter and a television crew in 2003. He was in fact the second Briton to make the trip, with the first and the vast majority of the others receiving virtually no publicity. More recently, however, other cases involving women have been brought to the public attention, one of which will be discussed in detail.

---

26 As above at paras. 74–78.
27 European Convention on Human Rights, Art.8(2).
28 As above.

The patient known as Mrs Z found herself at the centre of a controversial court case in 2004 because she had chosen to travel to Switzerland for an assisted suicide.[29] Mrs Z suffered from cerebellar ataxia which rendered her disabled and meant that although she lived at home with her husband she required extensive support from her local authority. Previously she had tried, and failed, to take her own life and she subsequently persuaded her husband and family that it was her fervent wish to travel to Switzerland for an assisted suicide. The local authority was informed of this by Mr Z and, on the understanding that Mrs Z was a 'vulnerable adult', the authority obtained a High Court injunction restraining him from committing a criminal offence by removing his wife to Switzerland and effectively aiding and abetting her suicide. As a part of that process the official solicitor was engaged to act on behalf of Mrs Z and a psychiatric assessment of her legal capacity was ordered prior to a further hearing.

At that hearing Hedley J examined the scope of the local authority's duty towards Mrs Z. He confirmed that the duty of care existed because of her vulnerability, but that it extended, inter alia, to establishing whether she possessed the mental capacity to make the decision and if so, whether she had been unduly influenced in her decision. If she had not been so influenced and the decision was indeed her own then there was a duty to enable her to lawfully give effect to her choice. Further, if there were grounds to suspect that a criminal offence may be committed, there was a duty only to draw that to the attention of the police.

The judgment confirmed that since the 1961 Act suicide is no longer 'punishable as a criminal act'[30] and that a competent person who decides to take their own life may do so with impunity. When a vulnerable person is involved the state has a duty to protect them, but for those who are mentally competent, individual autonomy and self-determination will trump any protective action invoked. Accordingly, since the psychiatric report on Mrs Z found her to be mentally competent, she had 'the right to take what others may see as unwise or even bad decisions in respect of themselves' and she alone would bear responsibility for her decisions.[31] In these circumstances there was no obligation to seek the continuation of the injunction. Ultimately the injunction was lifted and Mr and Mrs Z did travel to Switzerland where she died with the assistance of *Dignitas*.

Hedley J observed that 'by making arrangements and escorting Mrs Z on the flight, Mr Z will have contravened s 2(1)' of the Suicide Act 1961,[32] but clearly Mrs Z would be unable to exercise her choice unless her husband committed

29 *Re Z (Local Authority: Duty)* [2005] 1 WLR 959.
30 As above at 963.
31 As above.
32 As above at 964.

a crime. Theoretically, relatives and friends who accompany *Dignitas* suicide patients could be prosecuted under section 2 of the Suicide Act, and some have been interviewed by the police in connection with their conduct. However, thus far the Crown Prosecution Service has declined to take such action.

CONCLUSIONS – WOMEN'S CHOICES AND WIDER IMPLICATIONS

Taken in context these few examples seem to demonstrate a groundswell of support for more and better choice at the end of life. Patients have a legal and ethical right to exercise their autonomy through the law of consent, but that right is frequently constrained by the lack of choice. For example, in the case of medically assisted dying, choice is limited because assisted dying is not a lawful option in the United Kingdom. Other medical choices may be rejected because they do not accord with an established view of what amounts to proper medical treatment in the circumstances, or because the clinical team is unwilling or unable to comply, as evidenced in *Burke*. To a large degree it is understandable that medical professionals will seek to prevent patients in their care from making choices that will end their lives, especially if the patient is not terminally ill. The case of Ms B is a clear example of the tensions that can arise when a patient seeks to exercise a choice that involves a life-limiting decision which may be regarded as unnecessary by her or his medical carers and in many respects, this case epitomises the central issues associated with choice in end-of-life decision making. Ms B made a decision that her doctors and nurses disagreed with and as a result they were not prepared to act upon it. Consequently, her capacity to make a decision of such gravity was questioned, which not only delayed any action that might be taken as a result of her choice, but also devalued the decision itself. The reasons why a medical team might respond in this way to such a decision are complex and a matter of academic interpretation, but the evidence reviewed during the case gives some insights that may be valuable in understanding the broader implications of contested decisions at the end of life.

Ms B herself testified about her own response to the situation. 'I felt that I was being treated as if I was being unreasonable by putting people in an awkward position . . . I felt my path was being blocked and I was being pressurised to accept this option . . . that my rights were being eroded.'[33] Clearly she felt that there was some antagonism to her position and that she was powerless to resist. However, the root of the antipathy is perhaps understandable when one also considers the situation of the medical professionals who would also be

---

33 *Re B (Adult: Refusal of Medical Treatment)* [2002] WL 347038 (Fam Div) at para.50.

finding the situation 'stressful and distressing',[34] particularly as they had 'clearly become emotionally involved'.[35] In these circumstances, where the patient has rejected advice given in good faith in favour of an option that appears to be contrary to her best interests, it is unsurprising that the medical team found it difficult to form an objective view that would enable them to respect Ms B's autonomy. The result was that Ms B was presented with the option of one-way weaning, which Dame Elizabeth Butler-Sloss described as 'designed to help the clinicians and other carers and not in any way designed to help Ms B'.[36]

It could be argued that the clinicians were simply exercising their professional autonomy and applying clinical or therapeutic discretion according to their understanding of the patient's best interests. However, there is no justification for applying best interests criteria to decision making when the patient herself is competent to consent to or refuse the available treatment. The medical team appear to have been trying to protect Ms B from herself, believing in some way that she was vulnerable to making unsound decisions simply because of her medical condition. Some interesting resonances arise here. Diane Pretty was denied her choice because assisted suicide is prohibited by the Suicide Act 1961, but also because to permit her to have her life ended in that way might endanger other, vulnerable people. By implication, the ECHR was arguing that although Mrs Pretty might be regarded as having the mental capacity to safely consent to assisted suicide, others might not. As such, if Mrs Pretty were permitted to exercise her choice it might not be possible afterwards to protect the health and morals of others who could be vulnerable. Similarly, the local authority that obtained the injunction initially restraining Mr Z from taking his wife to Zurich acted on the assumption that because Mrs Z was unwell and infirm she was vulnerable to persuasion and possibly abuse. This was despite the fact that Mrs Z was the instigator of the idea and Mr Z had voluntarily informed the local authority of the plan.

The nature of vulnerability is under-explored in this context, but it does appear to have a gendered dimension. The examples discussed seem to indicate that women patients are regarded as vulnerable and their decisions compromised merely because they are ill. However, the simple fact that a patient is a woman does not mean that she is vulnerable. Neither does the fact that she is very unwell or terminally ill. Very ill female patients who suffer no mental incapacity are as capable of making valid decisions about their health care as any other individual in a similar position. They are no more prone to succumb to pressure or the views of others when making decisions. However, they do appear to be more likely to have their decisions questioned by those in a professional caring role, and to have their legitimate choices subverted by the

34 As above at para.77.
35 As above at para.98.
36 As above.

paternalistic attitudes of professional carers and authorities. As the cases of Ms B and Mrs Z demonstrate, women in this position may be perceived as particularly vulnerable to irrational decision making, or to be susceptible to outside influences, which may provide one explanation for why so many of the end-of-life decision making cases that come to court involve women. It has been argued that it is possible that women may be more inclined to choose life-limiting treatment options in order to avoid becoming burdensome, or simply because they are less comfortable in the role of the cared for rather than the carer (Biggs, 1998). This is an interesting and important phenomenon, but it does not mean that their decisions are necessarily due to undue pressure from others, nor does it inherently devalue any decision made or any choice taken.

The key principle at play is individual autonomy and there is a wealth of literature that demonstrates that women and men tend to exercise their autonomy in different ways and for different reasons (Frazer et al, 1992; Gilligan, 1982; Held, 1993; Weir, 1996). Within the traditional liberal understanding of the concept, a person who exercises autonomy and self-determination exhibits features that are more readily associated with masculinity than femininity, such as detachment and selfishness, as in the case of Leslie Burke. By contrast, women's decisions tend to adopt a more relational approach that relies upon and takes into account the ways in which they are connected to others (Gilligan, 1982; Held, 1993). Yet the fact that women are motivated to make their end-of-life treatment choices by reasons that may be associated with their gender does not mean that the choices they make or the decisions they take are less safe. Women may well be influenced in their decision making by their relationships and interactions with others, but so long as there is no coercion or undue influence there is no inherent reason why those decisions should not be regarded as autonomous and reliable (Biggs, 2003).

In practice, however, the distrust of the motivations underlying women's end-of-life decision making, and the medical and judicial scepticism about the veracity of those decisions revealed in the cases discussed in this chapter, suggest that the courts will continue to be called upon to adjudicate disputes involving end-of-life decision making by women.

BIBLIOGRAPHY

Batty, D., 'Man loses "right to life" battle', *The Guardian*, 28 July 2005, and at *http://society.guardian.co.uk/health/story/0,,1537875,00.html*

Biggs, H., 'I don't want to be a burden! A feminist reflects on women's experiences of death and dying', in Sheldon, S. and Thomson, M., eds, *Feminist Perspectives on Health Care Law*. Cavendish, London 1998, pp.279–96.

Biggs, H., 'A Pretty fine line: life, death, autonomy and letting it B', *Feminist Legal Studies*, 11, 2003, pp.291–301.

BMA, *Medical Ethics Today (2nd ed)*. BMJ Books, London 2004.

Brazier, M., 'Do no harm – do patients have responsibilities too?', *Cambridge Law Journal*, 65, 2006, pp.397–422.

Building on the Best: Choice, Responsiveness and Equity in the NHS. The Stationery Office, London 2003.

Department of Health, *Better Information, Better Choices, Better Health*. DH Publications, London 2004.

Department of Health, *Choice Matters: Increasing Choice Improves Patients' Experiences*. NHS, London 2006a.

Department of Health, *Introductory Guide to End of Life Care*. DH Publications, London 2006b and at *http://www.endoflifecare.nhs.uk*.

Frazer, E., Hornsby, J. and Lovibond, S., *Ethics: A Feminist Reader*. Blackwell; Oxford 1992.

General Medical Council, *Withholding and Withdrawing Life-Prolonging Treatments: Good Practice in Decision-Making*. GMC, London 2002.

Gilligan, C., *In a Different Voice: Psychological Theory and Women's Development*. Harvard University Press, Cambridge MA 1982.

Gillon, R., 'Why the GMC is right to appeal over life-prolonging treatment', *British Medical Journal*, 329, 2004, pp.810–11.

Harris, J., 'Court of appeal clarifies GMC guidelines on right to life', *The Lawyer.com*, 28 July 2005 and at *http://www.thelawyer.com/cgi-bin/item.cgi?id=116284&d=122&h=24&f=46*

Held, V., *Feminist Morality*. University of Chicago Press, London 1993.

Samanta, A. and Samanta, J., 'End of life decisions', *British Medical Journal*, 331, 2005, pp.1284–85.

Weir, A., *Sacrificial Logics*. Routledge, London 1996.

Chapter 9

Consent in violent relationships

Rosemary Hunter

INTRODUCTION

> The ideal legal subject upheld in liberal theory is a rational, choosing
> person, capable of decision, an autonomous individual. The individual
> is without particularities of identity such as gender. Such a figure of neu-
> trality is a deliberate legal creation to overcome differences – whether of
> cultural origin, race, gender, or other particularities. This imaginary figure
> legitimates law's generality and, sometimes, law's violences.
>
> (O'Donovan, 1997: 47)

As O'Donovan notes here, the capacity to consent is the hallmark of the liberal
legal subject. Especially in civil litigation, agreement between the parties, rather
than the imposition of a judicial determination, is the institutionally preferred
method of disposition. Liberal societies believe that individuals are in the best
position to determine their own solutions and should be given maximum freedom to do so. Private agreements are thought both to enhance individual
autonomy and freedom of choice, and to maximise social welfare, since parties
will (at least theoretically) only agree to arrangements that make them both
better off (Neave, 1994: 111). As O'Donovan also notes, however, consent
regimes impute equality of bargaining power between the parties. The person
who makes a consent agreement is the abstract, formally equal, legal person,
rather than a person in a particular social relationship with the other party
(O'Donovan, 1997: 47). Although consent allows for the operation of particularity to the extent that consenting subjects are taken to be capable of protecting
and promoting their own personal interests, it excludes particularity to the
extent that the situated position of a party may *prevent* them from protecting
and promoting their own personal interests.

Feminist critics of alternative dispute resolution – particularly mediation processes in family law – have objected to the institutional preference for settlement
on the basis of the empirical absence of equality of bargaining power between
supposedly 'consenting' parties. They have argued that mediation fails to even
out and consequently perpetuates power imbalances between the parties to a

relationship, especially where that relationship has been characterised by one party's violence towards the other (e.g. Alexander, 1992; Astor, 1994b; Astor, 1995; Astor and Chinkin, 2002: 349–55; Bottomley, 1985; Grillo, 1991; Neave, 1994). Most of this literature contends that mediation is totally inappropriate in cases where the violent partner is still attempting to exercise power and control over his ex-partner, and/or where the target of violence is still afraid of the perpetrator or believes him to be very powerful (e.g. Astor, 1994a; Bliss and Melvin, 1998: 77–78; Girdner, 1990; NADRAC, 1997: 64–65).

The liberal paradigm of the autonomous, consenting legal subject puts women who have been targets of violence – and feminist legal scholars – in a double bind, however. On the one hand, it is arguable that the legal system ought to recognise that survivors of violence have a diminished capacity to consent in legal transactions with their abusers. On the other hand, such a recognition risks diminishing women's status as fully human and fully functioning citizens – a return to the days when women were not seen as legal persons and were legally incapable of engaging in independent public activity or of giving or withholding consent to a range of transactions (O'Donovan, 1997: 55–57). In response to initiatives such as the construction of 'battered woman syndrome' and 'no drop' policies in prosecuting violent men, for example, feminist legal scholars have been concerned to stress battered women's agency rather than their helplessness, and to resist efforts by the legal system to take over decision-making for them (e.g. Gondolf and Fisher, 1988; Mills, 1998; Mills, 1999; Stubbs and Tolmie, 1999). How are we to avoid falling into what O'Donovan (1997: 49), drawing on Judith Butler, refers to as the 'contradictory claims of powerlessness and self-determination' for survivors of violence in the legal system?

This is a question that I argue cannot be answered in the abstract, and that I propose to address instead in particularised, practical terms. There are two reasons for this. First, abstract reasoning about the meaning and nature of consent inevitably takes place within the parameters of the liberal legal paradigm, which is the very source of the problem. Liberal legal philosophy offers a bounded range of answers to questions about consent and consenting subjects.[1] It provides little middle ground between the absolutes of powerlessness and self-determination. Victims of violence either have sufficient agency to consent, or they do not and therefore cannot consent. Consent itself appears to be indivisible. Individuals are classified according to their capacity to consent, rather than instances of (apparent) consent being classified according to their surrounding circumstances. There is no room in the liberal account of consent to think

---

1 I am here drawing on Mary Douglas's arguments about the way in which institutions organise social knowledge, provide tools for classification and hence do much of our thinking for us. Thus, according to Douglas, 'Any problems we try to think about are automatically transformed into [institutional] problems. The solutions they proffer only come from the limited range of their experience' (1986: 92).

about how occasions of consent might be structured so as to render them more or less valid, or meaningful to their subjects.

In this context, we might recall Ann Scales's warning against adopting law's vocabulary, epistemology and political theory (1986: 1376). Scales argues that feminists should pay attention to context rather than looking for the supposed 'essence' of a concept such as consent. We should focus on distinguishing between 'occasions of respect' and 'occasions of oppression' in order to get to 'the moral crux of the matter', and in doing so, should consider the results of a particular activity or transaction rather than simply the process by which it occurred (1986: 1387–88, 1402). In the case of violence against women, the results we might want to achieve are ones that acknowledge the existence of violence and seek to ensure the future safety of women and their children. In relation to consent processes, therefore, 'occasions of respect' are those in which agreements achieve these outcomes, while 'occasions of oppression' are those in which violence is ignored or sidelined, and the agreement reached serves to perpetuate abuse.

The second reason for addressing the question of consent in violent relationships at a practical rather than theoretical level is that while removing the possibility of consent in these situations may be a theoretical option, pragmatically it is impossible to dispense with consent. Institutions do not simply promote consent because it is considered philosophically desirable. It is also an institutional imperative. No court has the capacity to try all of the cases that are brought before it, or even all of the cases involving violence. Court systems are heavily dependent on out-of-court negotiations and settlement processes in order to cope with their caseloads (Galanter, 1974: 121–22). Adjudication is a scarce public good, which occurs only when all other dispute resolution options have been exhausted. Settlement is the *expected* outcome in civil cases, including those involving violence. Furthermore, one of the ways in which adjudication is rationed is through price, and that price may be particularly unaffordable for a survivor of violence. In addition, a trial may be more daunting or more traumatic for a survivor, or its outcome worse, than out of court negotiations. Thus, to eschew consent in favour of judicial determination is not a realistic option most of the time. As a consequence, it is more useful to think about how consent processes can become 'occasions of respect', than to imagine doing away with them altogether.

The particular consent regimes that I examine in this chapter are those relating to domestic violence protection orders, and family law litigation concerning arrangements for children and property division after separation. As part of a research project on 'women's experience in court', I observed court proceedings in Melbourne, Australia in these two jurisdictions over an 18-month period in 1996–97. Domestic violence protection orders were dealt with in Magistrates Courts – the lowest level courts in the state court hierarchy, which also process a high volume of summary criminal and low-value civil matters. Family law, children and property matters were dealt with by a federal superior court, the

Family Court of Australia. In addition to observations inside and outside the courtroom, I reviewed 124 files of matters listed for hearing in the Family Court, and interviewed 18 lawyers and domestic violence support workers, and 13 women litigants who were survivors of violence and who had been through the relevant proceedings, sometimes repeatedly. Consent processes turned out to occupy a significant portion of my observations, and hence also became the subject of interview questions and discussions.

DOMESTIC VIOLENCE PROTECTION ORDERS

I observed 100 applications for domestic violence protection orders – called 'intervention orders' under the Victorian Crimes (Family Violence) Act 1987 – in nine suburban Magistrates Courts. The usual procedure was for an applicant to obtain an interim order on an ex parte basis, after which the defendant would be served with the order, and given the chance to come to court to contest the making of a final order, on a fixed date in two to four weeks' time. The majority of applicants and defendants came to court without legal representation. In some courts, domestic violence court support programs had been established to assist applicants who would otherwise be unrepresented, but these did not run in all courts or every day. In a small majority of cases, the defendant did not appear at all on the return date, and the final order was then made on an uncontested basis.

If a defendant did appear at court on the return date, however, he would be given every encouragement, by counter staff and by the magistrate, to consent to an order rather than to contest the matter. In order to persuade defendants to consent, the practice had developed of allowing them to consent to an order while denying the allegations made in the complaint. This option proved extremely popular. Of the 30 final order applications observed in which the defendant appeared and a decision was made, 17 (57%) were disposed of by consent without admissions, while only six (20%) were disposed of by consent with admissions, and seven (23%) were contested. Proponents of consent without admissions argued that it represented a win-win-win solution for all parties. It saved time for the court; the applicant got her order more quickly, at less cost, and without having to go into the witness box and endure a potentially traumatic hearing with an uncertain result; and the defendant was able to 'save face' to some extent.[2]

---

2 E.g. discussion with Magistrates, Moonee Ponds Magistrates Court, 1 November 1996; Hana Assafiri, Coordinator, Immigrant Women's Domestic Violence Service, interviewed 24 June 1997; Susan Borg, barrister, interviewed 17 October 1997; Flora Culpen, community legal education worker, interviewed 17 March 1997; Judith Peirce, solicitor, interviewed 21 August 1997; Solicitor S1, interviewed 16 January 1996; Solicitor S2, interviewed 28 October 1997; Support Worker SW1, interviewed 23 December 1997; Wearing (1992: 110–11, 184). Court clerks

On the other hand, the procedure of allowing the defendant to consent without admissions had a number of drawbacks. First, the practice violated the usual rules of settlement in civil cases in that it was entirely unilateral. The defendant was given the option to consent without admissions. The applicant was never asked whether she agreed to the order being made on that basis, or whether she would prefer to tell her story and prove her case. Thus, the question of her capacity to exercise agency in this situation was prematurely foreclosed.

Of the six women I interviewed who had obtained orders by consent without admissions, only one was entirely pleased with the result, saying that she was just happy to have the order and to be far away from the defendant.[3] Two specifically noted that they had not been asked whether *they* were consenting. One of these said she was happy to have the order, but was very angry about the defendant's denials, which she considered to be cowardly. She would have liked to have been given a choice, for the magistrate to have asked for her opinion.[4] The other said she had expected her ex-boyfriend to deny the allegations, since he was also facing criminal proceedings in respect of his assaults on her, but she did not know that she had any alternative.[5] A third was not at all happy with the outcome of her application. The magistrate had tried to convince her that it was good to have the order regardless, but she thought that was ridiculous, and could not understand how the magistrate could give the order but still accept the defendant's denials.[6] The husband of the fourth woman had sent a letter to the court agreeing to the order but denying the allegations, and she had not been able to say anything. She argued that he should have been compelled to come to court to say why he was denying the allegations, and was angry that his word had been accepted against hers, so that she got the order, but was not believed.[7] Some of the lawyers and support workers interviewed thought that women ought to be given the option to accept or reject an order based on the defendant's denials,[8] although one considered that obtaining the 'consent' of a woman from a non-English speaking background in these circumstances would be farcical.[9]

The second major drawback of the practice of consent without admissions related to its institutional and public consequences. If the great majority of intervention orders are granted either ex parte or by consent without admitting the allegations, there is an overall lack of institutional affirmation of women's

interviewed by Wearing also considered that orders to which the defendant had consented were less likely to be breached (1992: 111) – a highly dubious proposition.

3   Woman Litigant WL6, interviewed 23 December 1997.
4   Woman Litigant WL4, interviewed 23 December 1997.
5   Woman Litigant WL1, interviewed 8 September 1997.
6   Woman Litigant WL10, interviewed 23 December 1997.
7   Woman Litigant WL2, interviewed 18 December 1997.
8   Flora Culpen, above note 2; Judith Peirce, above note 2; S1, above note 2.
9   Hana Assafiri, above note 2.

stories of abuse.[10] There are few findings by magistrates that these stories are *true*. The lack of such affirmation, in turn, fuels the spectre of false allegations which plagues this jurisdiction (see, e.g. House of Representatives, 2005: 56–57; Kaye and Tolmie, 1998; Melville and Hunter, 2001; Römkens, 2001: 282, 287–88). Further, there is a lack of public, legal condemnation of abusive behaviour. What happened is not clearly labelled as unlawful,[11] and abusive men are not required to take responsibility for their actions.[12] More generally, the existence of violence against women and the scale of the violence fail to enter the realm of public knowledge. Men's denial and minimisation of violence is echoed by the state, not just in individual cases, but on a grand scale. Consent without admissions thus contributes significantly to making the social 'problem' of violence disappear from view.[13]

The third substantial drawback of intervention orders obtained by consent without admitting the allegations was the subsequent effect of these orders in Family Court proceedings. The existence of family violence was one of the factors the court was required to take into account in determining what orders to make in the best interests of the child,[14] but intervention orders made by consent without admissions were routinely discounted in the Family Court as evidence that violence had occurred. As two of the women interviewed pointed out, in these cases, the court tended to believe the husband's denials rather than the need for an order to protect the safety of the wife and children.[15]

THE FAMILY COURT

In the Family Court, once a party filed an application for final orders in relation to children and/or property division, the court process would provide ample encouragement and opportunities for dispute resolution through directions hearings, interim hearings and orders, counselling appointments in children's matters, conciliation conferences in property matters, and pre-trial conferences, before a full adversarial hearing before a judge could occur. At any stage during this process, the parties could hand up Minutes of Consent Orders embodying the agreement they had reached, which would usually be endorsed by the court without question.[16] Consequently, only about 6% of cases filed ultimately

---

10 Flora Culpen, above note 2; Judith Peirce, above note 2.
11 Hana Assafiri, above note 2.
12 Flora Culpen, above note 2.
13 SW1, above note 2.
14 Family Law Act 1975 (Cth), former s.68F(2)(i).
15 WL2, above note 7; WL10, above note 6.
16 Indeed, Margaret Harrison has observed that the court's role is 'most commonly reduced to a forum which ratifies lawyer-negotiated agreements' (1986: 243).

received a judicial determination (Family Court of Australia, 1997: 64–66; Hunter, 1999: 153, 157, 160).

Cases involving allegations of domestic violence – including very serious allegations (Hewitt et al, 1996: 24) – were no exception to this rule. A series of studies have, indeed, pointed to the prevalence of consent orders in cases involving violence. For example, in a study by the Family Court Research Unit of 83 domestic homicide cases in Victoria in 1987–1990, it was found that of the ten cases that had previous contact with the Family Court, half had involved consent orders relating to the children or property (Hore et al, 1996: 20–23). In another study of women's experiences of negotiating child residence and contact arrangements against a background of domestic violence, the researchers found that four of the five cases in which the perpetrator of violence had custody of the children were a result of consent orders or private agreement, and all four women said they had relinquished custody due to the father's bullying or demands (Kaye et al, 2003: 100–101, 109). In a third Australian study looking at Family Court files in which it was alleged that court orders had been contravened, 50 of the 55 cases involving domestic violence had consent orders (Rhoades, 2002: 85). Similarly, a US study of divorces in one circuit court over a 12-month period found that cases involving both children and spousal violence were most likely to be settled by agreement, a result the authors described as 'astounding' (Logan et al, 2003: 276).

Breakdown of consent orders

In my own research, 80 of the Family Court files reviewed involved allegations of violence by the husband towards the wife, and at least 46% of these resulted in consent orders, although the outcome was unknown in a further 21%. Of the 20 cases observed that reached the stage of a final, contested hearing, six settled at the door of the court. The limited validity of 'consent' in these cases, however, was demonstrated in the strikingly 'non-stick' nature of the agreements reached. At least 30% of the 80 matters (and again, there was a large unknown component – 29%) subsequently returned to court for further proceedings. Of the 13 cases observed in which it was possible to determine the fate of consent orders made either during the observation period or at an earlier stage, only two agreements had held, and these were both agreements which had contained terms designed to ensure the safety of the mother. Consent orders in the other 11 cases had all broken down, either because the wife/mother could not realistically comply with what she had 'agreed' to, because the husband/father chose not to comply with the orders, and/or because the husband/father was not satisfied with the compromise he had made, and pressed for a more complete victory.

The women I interviewed had similar experiences. One of the women described being coerced by her barrister into signing consent orders giving access to her two children to her ex-husband, but her ex-husband ignored the conditions imposed in the orders, and she subsequently suspended access after he threatened to kill her. When he was sent to gaol for assaulting her, he agreed to have no contact with the children so long as she sent him photos from time to time, but as soon as he was released, he commenced new proceedings, and the matter had still not been finally resolved.[17]

The same phenomenon has been observed in other studies (e.g. Hewitt et al, 1996: 24; Logan et al, 2003: 276; Rendell et al, 2000: 83). Women who have been targets of violence agree to arrangements that they know to be unsafe and unworkable (e.g. Kaye et al, 2003: 108–109; Rhoades et al, 2000: 71; Rhoades, 2002: 86), and not surprisingly, these agreements break down, resulting in further applications for final orders, or for variation of the consent orders, or enforcement proceedings against the mother. In her study of contravention applications in the Family Court, Rhoades found that a common outcome of applications alleging contravention of consent orders was an investigation of the circumstances by means of a Family Report, and subsequent variation of the orders to provide more appropriate arrangements for the children and the mother (Rhoades, 2002: 87) – surely an inefficient, dangerous and traumatic method of achieving a satisfactory outcome.

Reasons for consent

As suggested earlier, the reasons why settlement occurred in cases involving domestic violence were a combination of clients' circumstances and the court's expectations, as well as lawyers' practices and the legal doctrine in the shadow of which bargaining took place. For example, the women interviewed referred to financial considerations as the strongest reason for settling.[18] One said she did not have a choice about settlement because she could not afford to go to trial. In her pithy summation, 'you take as much justice as you can afford to get'.[19]

Other studies have noted the use of fear, coercion and bullying by violent men, with women agreeing to unfair property settlements and unsatisfactory contact arrangements in the hope of preventing further violence (Family Law Council, 1998: 29; Kaye et al, 2003: 109; Women's Coalition Against Family Violence, 1994: 95). One woman quoted by Kaye et al (2003: 110) said: 'I consented so hey lady, you're happy with everything. By consenting that means you're happy – wrong. By consenting you're just buying peace. It's got nothing to do with whether you were happy about the arrangements or not.'

In my own study, there was also evidence of coercion in the process of arriving at consent orders. In five of the cases observed, the consent orders agreed to

---

17 WL2, above note 7.
18 Woman Litigant WL9, interviewed 19 December 1997; Woman Litigant WL12, interviewed 19 December 1997.
19 Woman Litigant WL5, interviewed 19 December 1997. See also Erlanger et al (1987: 120).

suggested that the mother had at best been badly advised given the context of violence, or at worst completely overborne. In two of these cases, the appalling history of violence in the relationship, the ongoing dangerousness of the father, and the damaged and terrified state that the mother was in would have amply justified orders for no contact between the father and his children. Nevertheless, the women in both of these cases consented to contact orders. In one, the mother's claim for damages for ongoing physical injuries and sexual and emotional abuse was also dismissed as part of the property settlement.[20] In the other, the mother eventually did seek an order for no contact, and was successful in the Full Court of the Family Court.[21]

In one of the other cases, it was alleged that the father had subjected the mother to every form of violence imaginable, and continued to harass and intimidate her. The mother sought variation of the contact arrangements to better suit the children's activities, and orders for the father to sign passport applications for the children, as she wished to take them on a visit to her parents overseas. The consent orders resolving this application, however, made absolutely no concession to the children's activities in the contact arrangements, and restrained the mother from removing the children from the country.[22] In a fourth case, the mother had been forced to leave the child with the father, and was applying for orders for more extensive contact than the father would allow. Late in the morning, it was reported to the judge that the parties were preparing Minutes of Consent Orders, but the child's representative did not agree to the terms currently proposed. The child's representative was very concerned that the agreement proposed to leave the child with the father, as there was evidence that the father and his family were turning the child against the mother, and in the process subjecting the child to severe emotional abuse. However the child's representative could see that the mother was being worn down by the insistence on the father's side that the child stay with them. By the middle of the afternoon, the judge was told that the parties had 'resolved' the matter, along the lines earlier indicated, while the child's representative looked very unhappy. Clearly in these cases, the woman's 'consent' was merely a product of her continued subordination to the perpetrator of violence.

At the same time, the court's 'settlement culture' exerted strong pressure towards resolution by means of consent orders (see, e.g. Armstrong, 2001: 151; Hunter et al, 2000: ch.7; Jaffe et al, 2003: 3; Rhoades, 2002: 83, 87). One solicitor, for example, said she advised all of her clients before going to court that they would be required to try to settle the case, and a barrister referred to the statistical inevitability that '95.6% of cases settle'.[23] In one of the cases

---

20 Case FC15, Family Court of Australia, Melbourne Registry, 5 December 1996.
21 Case FC16, Family Court of Australia, Melbourne Registry, 6 January 1997.
22 Case FC18, Family Court of Australia, Melbourne Registry, 9 April 1997.
23 S1, above note 2; Barbara Phelan, barrister, interviewed 29 October 1997.

observed, which had involved serious incidents of physical violence and the husband threatening the wife with a gun, the judge encouraged the parties to engage in settlement discussions, and gave them a lecture on the importance of talking to each other and reaching agreement, since they had many years of joint parenting ahead of them.[24]

The court's encouragement of settlement was also manifested in the process of approving consent orders. Judges usually congratulated the parties on reaching agreement and commended them for acting so cooperatively in relation to their future parenting, thus sending a strong message that this was what the court hoped for and expected.[25] One of the women interviewed had found this little speech utterly galling. She said her ex-husband had strung out the settlement negotiations (in relation to property issues) all day, mucking around, playing games and wearing her down, so that by the time they got into court to have the orders approved she was very angry. She wanted to ask for costs, but her solicitor said the Family Court does not like to blame anybody. Then the judge commended them for reaching an amicable agreement, and she had to sit there and say nothing.[26]

Lawyers were an integral part of the court's settlement culture, and played a crucial role in achieving settlements (see, e.g. Hunter et al, 2000: ch.7). For example, one of the solicitors I interviewed noted that all of his cases settled well before they reached a final hearing, and he also briefed barristers who were good settlers.[27] Clients who did not see the 'sense' in settling were often pressured by their lawyers to do so (e.g. Erlanger et al, 1987: 593; Rhoades et al, 2000: 72; The Family Court Lobby Group, 1990: 22). One interviewee noted that 'you see women in the waiting area of the Family Court being pressured every day',[28] and this was certainly true of my observations. In one of the cases I observed that ultimately settled, there were clearly some sticking points along the way, and the barristers on both sides worked very hard to get their clients to reach an agreement.[29] In another case, the barristers negotiated the final terms of consent orders between themselves at the bar table, in consultation with the judge but with almost no reference to their clients, while in a third case, the matter was 'resolved' between the barristers and solicitors, who then proceeded to have the Minutes of Consent Orders translated to the non-English speaking

24 Case FC1, Family Court of Australia, Melbourne Registry, 20–21 and 24 June 1996.
25 E.g. Cases FC4, Family Court of Australia, Melbourne Registry, 29 July 1996; FC6, Family Court of Australia, Melbourne Registry, 16 December 1996; FC10, Family Court of Australia, Melbourne Registry, 7 February 1997; FC12, Family Court of Australia, Melbourne Registry, 7 April 1997; FC14, Family Court of Australia, Melbourne Registry, 9 August 1996.
26 WL5, above note 19.
27 S2, above note 2.
28 Clare McNamara, community legal centre solicitor, interviewed 14 June 1996.
29 Case FC19, Family Court of Australia, Melbourne Registry, 17 April 1997.

mother.[30] Her participation in actually reaching the agreement appears to have been minimal.

As well as the court's emphasis on settlement, women who had been targets of violence also faced doctrinal uncertainty in relation to domestic violence during the period of my fieldwork. It was not yet clear how recent amendments to the Family Law Act would be interpreted by the court, and in this somewhat unpredictable climate, women felt compelled to consent to agreements because it was by no means guaranteed they would achieve any better results from adjudication (see also Mnookin and Kornhauser, 1979: 969–71). For example, the barrister of one of the women interviewed had persuaded her to sign consent orders on the basis that the judge was going to grant access to her ex-husband anyway, and consent orders would give her greater control over the conditions of access. She later felt that she had been 'shafted'.[31] The argument that consent orders provided the client with greater certainty and control over the outcome than they would have if the matter was to be decided by a judge, was frequently used by solicitors as a means of persuasion to settle, telling clients that they were taking a big risk and anything could happen if they went before a judge rather than reaching an agreement.[32]

The results of consent

Some of the lawyers interviewed said that they attempted to protect and empower women who had been victims of violence in the settlement process, for example by demonstrating their understanding of the client's position, acknowledging the limited capacity of some clients to make independent decisions, not exploiting the client's dependence and vulnerability, and ensuring the client was emotionally supported and given enough time to think.[33] I also observed two cases in which the husband's lawyer appeared to be 'crunching' him to agree to a settlement that respected the position of the wife to a far greater degree than the husband's instructions would have conceded.[34] At the other end of the spectrum, though, there were many lawyers who appeared to be quite prepared to prey on the vulnerability of abused clients or to ignore their needs in order to achieve a settlement.[35] Women in Kaye et al's study also reported many examples of negative experiences with lawyers, including not acceding to their concerns, not following their instructions in negotiations, and pressuring them to agree to arrangements that were not in accordance with their wishes (2003: 74–75).

30 Cases FC6, above note 25; FC20, Family Court of Australia, Melbourne Registry, 24 April 1997.
31 WL2, above note 7.
32 Barbara Phelan, above note 23; S1, above note 2; S2, above note 2.
33 E.g. Barrister B1, interviewed 17 October 1997; Barbara Phelan, above note 23.
34 Cases FC10, above note 24; FC12, above note 25.
35 See examples given above. Also S1, above note 2.

While I observed consent orders being made in 11 cases, the orders in only four of those cases incorporated protections for the safety of the wife/mother and children in the context of the husband/father's past and continuing violence. These orders supported the wife's position (maintaining residence of the children, allowing her to relocate interstate, withdrawing the husband's application to penalise the wife for breaching contact orders) and minimised the need for contact between the parties (by allowing the wife to relocate, temporarily suspending the husband's contact with the children, providing for contact only at the child's request, or providing handover arrangements that kept the parties well apart), thereby reducing the capacity for the husband to engage in ongoing harassment and abuse of the wife. In the other seven cases, as discussed above, the orders at best made no concessions to safety, and at worst perpetuated the husband's/father's abuse and control.

In addition, and consistent with its encouragement of settlement, the court in the course of approving minutes of consent orders generally failed to scrutinise the nature of the 'consent' that had been given or the safety of the proposed orders. Family Court Registrars interviewed by Rhoades et al said that if minutes of consent orders were presented to them, they would generally make the orders without inquiry (2000: 97–98; see also Erlanger et al, 1987: 598). In my observations, although judges did sometimes scrutinise consent orders to ensure that they did not present unacceptable risks to the child,[36] they never queried consent orders on the basis that they failed to ensure the mother's safety or perpetuated abuse against her.

DISCUSSION

It is clear from the preceding descriptions that consent regimes in intervention order proceedings and in the Family Court operate somewhat differently and with different results. Thus, rather than proposing a one-size-fits-all solution, I will suggest local responses tailored to the specificities of each situation.

In relation to intervention orders, the main reasons why consent orders become 'occasions of oppression' rather than 'occasions of respect' are that the applicant is given no notice of the defendant's intentions on the return date, and that the defendant is permitted to consent to an order without admissions, without any reference to the applicant. In order to overcome these features, legislative and procedural amendments are required to mandate notice by the defendant ahead of the return date as to whether he consents to an order or intends to contest it,[37] and to abolish the option of consent without admissions. These changes may in turn require a greater level of representation and support

---

36 E.g. Case FC4, above note 25. See also *T v N* (2003) 31 Fam LR 257.
37 See, e.g. Domestic Violence Act 1995 (NZ), s.76; Restraining Orders Act 1997 (WA), ss.31–32.

for applicants from lawyers and court support program workers, either to deal with contested cases, or to negotiate consent orders with appropriate terms to ensure the woman's safety.

In relation to family law, various commentators have suggested that women in violent relationships cannot and should not be expected to agree to consent orders (e.g. Hewitt et al, 1996: 24; Jaffe et al, 2003: 3; Logan et al, 2003: 277). On the other hand, the Australian Family Law Council has doubted whether anything can be done to change the situation, since it is unclear:

> . . . how, if at all, a Court can take into account the disabling effects of a history of family violence on a person's capacity to exercise proper judgement in proceedings or negotiations leading to an order, especially orders made by consent.
>
> (Family Law Council, 1998: 30)

These competing positions illustrate the policy paralysis engendered by the liberal paradigm.

As indicated above, however, consent orders in family law cases involving domestic violence become 'occasions for oppression' when the woman's legal representatives fail to take the history of violence into account and/or to ensure that the terms of the orders agreed protect her and her children's safety, and when the court rubber-stamps consent orders that fail to do these things. The evidence also suggests that consent orders in cases involving domestic violence are often a waste of time and resources, as the level of breakdown is so high. The court's encouragement of settlement in these cases appears perverse. The research further suggests that two types of interventions are effective in these cases. One is consent orders that support the position of the survivor of violence and include measures to ensure her safety. The other is court orders based on an investigation of the allegations of violence and the impact of violence on the children, and which provide for appropriate arrangements and ensure safety.

Again, legislative amendment could promote these results – in this instance, an amendment to specify women's and children's safety as the primary objective in cases where domestic violence is alleged (Bowermaster, 1998: 462; Eriksson and Hester, 2001: 793; Laing, 2000; Rendell et al, 2000: 121–22).[38] This legislative change would give women an additional bargaining chip in settlement negotiations, and would also educate lawyers about the importance of recognising and responding to violence, and impact on the court's practices in both decision making and approving consent orders. Legal and professional education

---

38 Other jurisdictions, for example, incorporate a rebuttable presumption against residence or unsupervised contact being awarded to a violent spouse (see Jaffe and Crooks, 2004: 921, 927; Lemon, 2001), or provide that where violence is alleged, the focus of a children's matter should be on whether and how contact can be exercised safely for the children and the other partner (see, e.g. Sheeran and Hampton, 1999).

that emphasises the need to represent survivors of violence in negotiations in a way that is empowering rather than dominating, and that promotes their safety and autonomy, could also contribute to the achievement of more satisfactory results from consent processes in family law.

In conclusion, it appears that a particularised, empirical approach enables the identification of solutions to the problem of consent in violent relationships that might remain invisible if discussion of the issue remained at an abstract, theoretical level. Rather than focusing on the characterisation of the woman (as fully capable or wholly incapable of consent), such an approach focuses on the characteristics of the process. Given that consent regimes will continue to operate, understanding the details of their operation allows us to distinguish occasions of respect from occasions of oppression and to see how the former can be maximised. This is important not just in terms of providing a better process, but also in terms of achieving better substantive outcomes from the legal system for survivors of violence, and for the development of theorising about consent that is grounded not in liberal categories but in the concrete realities of women's lives.

BIBLIOGRAPHY

Alexander, R., 'Mediation, violence and the family', *Alternative Law Journal*, 17, 1992, pp.271–73.

Armstrong, S.M., ' "We told you so . . .": women's legal groups and the Family Law Reform Act 1995', *Australian Journal of Family Law*, 15, 2001, pp.129–54.

Astor, H., 'Violence and family mediation: policy', *Australian Journal of Family Law*, 8, 1994a, pp.3–21.

Astor, H., 'Swimming against the tide: keeping violent men out of mediation', in Stubbs, J., ed., *Women: Male Violence and the Law*. Institute of Criminology, Sydney 1994b, pp.147–73.

Astor, H., 'The weight of silence: talking about violence in family mediation', in Thornton, M., ed., *Public and Private: Feminist Legal Debates*. Oxford University Press, Melbourne 1995, pp.174–96.

Astor, H. and Chinkin, C., *Dispute Resolution in Australia*, 2nd ed. Butterworths, Sydney 2002.

Bliss, N. and Melvin, T., 'Mediation in the shadow of domestic violence', in Fisher, T., ed., *Proceedings of the 4th National Mediation Conference*. School of Law and Legal Studies, LaTrobe University, Melbourne 1998, pp.75–80.

Bottomley, A., 'What is happening to family law? A feminist critique of conciliation', in Brophy, J. and Smart, C., eds, *Women in Law: Explorations in Law, Family and Sexuality*. Routledge & Kegan Paul, London 1985, pp.162–87.

Bowermaster, J.M., 'Relocation custody disputes involving domestic violence', *University of Kansas Law Review*, 47, 1998, pp.433–63.

Douglas, M., *How Institutions Think*. Syracuse University Press, Syracuse, New York 1986.

Eriksson, M. and Hester, M., 'Violent men as good enough fathers? A look at England and Sweden', *Violence Against Women*, 7, 2001, pp.779–98.

Erlanger, H.S., Chambliss, E. and Melli, M.S., 'Participation and flexibility in informal processes: cautions from the divorce context', *Law & Society Review*, 21, 1987, pp.585–604.

Family Court of Australia, *Report to the Chief Justice of the Evaluation of Simplified Procedures Committee*. Family Court of Australia, Melbourne 1997.

Family Law Council, *Violence and the Family Law Act: Financial Remedies: Discussion Paper*. Family Law Council, Canberra 1998.

Galanter, M., 'Why the "haves" come out ahead: speculations on the limits of legal change', *Law & Society Review*, 9, 1974, pp.95–160.

Girdner, L., 'Mediation triage: screening for spouse abuse in divorce mediation', *Mediation Quarterly*, 7, 1990, pp.365–76.

Gondolf, E.W. and Fisher, E., *Battered Women as Survivors: An Alternative to Treating Learned Helplessness*. Lexington Books, Lanham, MD 1988.

Grillo, T., 'The mediation alternative: process dangers for women', *Yale Law Journal*, 100, 1991, pp.1545–1610.

Harrison, M., 'Attitudes to lawyers and the legal process', in McDonald, P., ed., *Settling Up: Property and Income Distribution on Divorce in Australia*. Prentice Hall, Sydney 1986, pp.241–58.

Hewitt, L., Brown, T., Frederico, M. and Martyn, R., 'Family violence in the Family Court', *DVIRC Newsletter*, August 1996, pp.19–25.

Hore, E., Gibson, J. and Bordow, S., *Domestic Homicide*. Family Court of Australia, Melbourne 1996.

House of Representatives Standing Committee on Legal and Constitutional Affairs, *Report on the Exposure Draft of the Family Law Amendment (Shared Parental Responsibility) Bill 2005*, *www.aph.gov.au/house/committee/laca/familylaw/report/fullreport.pdf*

Hunter, R., *Family Law Case Profiles*. Justice Research Centre, Sydney 1996.

Hunter, R. with Genovese, A., Melville A. and Chrzanowski, A., *Legal Services in Family Law*. Justice Research Centre, Sydney 2000.

Jaffe, P.G. and Crooks, C.V., 'Partner violence and child custody cases: a cross-national comparison of legal reforms and issues', *Violence Against Women*, 10, 2004 pp.917–34.

Jaffe, P.G., Lemon, N.K.D. and Poisson, S.E., *Child Custody and Domestic Violence: A Call for Safety and Accountability*. Sage, Thousand Oaks, CA 2003.

Kaye, M., Stubbs, J. and Tolmie, J., *Negotiating Child Residence and Contact Arrangements Against a Background of Domestic Violence*. Families, Law and Social Policy Research Unit, Socio-Legal Research Centre, Griffith University, Brisbane 2003.

Kaye, M. and Tolmie, J., ' "Lollies at a children's party" and other myths: violence, protection orders and fathers' rights groups', *Current Issues in Criminal Justice*, 10(1), 1998, pp.52–72.

Laing, L., *Children, Young People and Domestic Violence*. Australian Domestic and Family Violence Clearinghouse, Sydney 2000.

Lemon, N.K.D., 'Statutes creating rebuttable presumptions against custody to batterers: how effective are they?', *William Mitchell Law Review*, 28, 2001, pp.601–76.

Logan, T.K., Walker, R., Horvath, L.S. and Leukefeld, C., 'Divorce, custody, and spousal violence: a random sample of circuit court docket records', *Journal of Family Violence*, *18(5)*, 2003, pp.269–79.

Melville, A. and Hunter, R., ' "As everybody knows": countering myths of gender bias in family law', *Griffith Law Review*, *10*, 2001, pp.124–38.

Mills, L.G., 'Mandatory arrest and prosecution policies for domestic violence: a critical literature review and the case for more research to test victim empowerment approaches', *Criminal Justice and Behavior*, *25*, 1998, pp.306–18.

Mills, L.G., 'Killing her softly: intimate abuse and the violence of state intervention', *Harvard Law Review*, *113*, 1999, pp.550–613.

Mnookin, R. and Kornhauser, L., 'Bargaining in the shadow of the law: the case of divorce', *Yale Law Journal*, *88*, 1979, pp.950–97.

National Alternative Dispute Resolution Council (NADRAC), *Fairness and Justice in Alternative Dispute Resolution: Discussion Paper*. NADRAC, Canberra 1997.

Neave, M., 'Resolving the dilemma of difference: a critique of the role of private ordering in family law', *University of Toronto Law Journal*, *44*, 1994, pp.97–131.

O'Donovan, K., 'With sense, consent, or just a con? Legal subjects in the discourse of autonomy', in Naffine, N. and Owens, R.J., eds, *Sexing the Subject of Law*. Law Book Co, Sydney 1997, pp.47–64.

Rendell, K., Rathus, Z. and Lynch, A. for the Abuse Free Contact Group, *An Unacceptable Risk: A Report on Child Contact Arrangements Where There is Violence in the Family*. Women's Legal Service Inc, Brisbane 2000.

Rhoades, H., 'The "no contact mother": reconstructions of motherhood in the era of the "new father" ', *International Journal of Law, Policy and the Family*, *16*, 2002, pp.71–94.

Rhoades, H., Graycar, R. and Harrison, M., *The Family Law Reform Act 1995: The First Three Years*. University of Sydney and Family Court of Australia, Sydney 2000.

Römkens, R., 'Law as a Trojan horse: unintended consequences of rights-based interventions to support battered women', *Yale Journal of Law and Feminism*, *13*, 2001, pp.265–90.

Scales, A.C., 'The emergence of feminist jurisprudence: an essay', *Yale Law Journal*, *95*, 1986, pp.1373–1403.

Sheeran, M. and Hampton, S., 'Supervised visitation in cases of domestic violence', *Juvenile and Family Court Journal*, *50(2)*, 1999, pp.13–25.

Stubbs, J. and Tolmie, J., 'Falling short of the challenge? A comparative assessment of the use of expert evidence on the battered woman syndrome', *Melbourne University Law Review*, *23*, 1999, pp.709–48.

The Family Court Lobby Group, *'In Whose Best Interest?' A Report of the South Australian Phone In on Women, Domestic Violence and the Family Court*. The Family Court Lobby Group, Adelaide 1990.

Wearing, R., *Monitoring the Impact of the Crimes (Family Violence) Act 1987*. LaTrobe University, Melbourne 1992.

Women's Coalition Against Family Violence, *Blood on Whose Hands? The Killing of Women and Children in Domestic Homicides*. Women's Coalition Against Family Violence, Melbourne 1994.

Contributors

Hazel Biggs is Professor of Medical Law at Lancaster University. Her research interests include medical law, specifically legal and ethical issues at the beginning and end of life and clinical research, criminal law and feminist legal theory. She has published extensively in each of these areas, including *Euthanasia, Death with Dignity and the Law* (Hart, 2001), and, with Robin Mackenzie, 'End of life decision-making, policy and the criminal justice system: who cares about carers?', *Genomics, Society and Policy, 12(1)*, 2006, pp.118–28.

Anél Boshoff is an Associate Professor at the Law Faculty of the University of Johannesburg, South Africa. She obtained her LL.D degree in 2000 with a thesis entitled 'The interpretation of fundamental claims in a diverse society'. She has published widely within her main areas of research, namely jurisprudence, legal ethics, interpretation theory, gender studies and family law.

Gillian Calder is an Assistant Professor of Law at the University of Victoria, Canada. Her primary areas of research interest are Canadian constitutional law, feminist and equality theories, performativity and law, and law's discursive impact on understandings of family. Recent publications include: 'A pregnant pause: federalism, equality and the maternity and parental leave debate in Canada', *Feminist Legal Studies, 14*, 2006 pp.99–118.

Sharon Cowan is a lecturer in law at the School of Law, Edinburgh University, where she is a member of the Centre for Law and Society. Her research interests include feminist legal theory, sexuality gender and the law, criminal law, criminal justice and medical law. She is currently working on a book on feminist perspectives on consent in the criminal law. Recent publications include ' "Freedom and capacity to make a choice": a feminist analysis of consent in the criminal law of rape' in Munro, V. and Stychin, C., eds, *Sexuality and Law: Feminist Engagements* (Routledge Cavendish, Abingdon, Oxford 2007, pp.51–71).

Heather Douglas is a Senior Lecturer in the Law School, University of Queensland, Australia. She researches primarily in the area of criminal law with a special interest in the way in which the criminal law deals with domestic violence. She recently completed her PhD, which examined the impact of aspects of the criminal law on Indigenous Australians.

Maria Drakopoulou is a Senior Lecturer in Law at the University of Kent, United Kingdom. She is also a founding member and articles editor of the journal *Feminist Legal Studies*. Her main areas of research interest are feminist theory, legal theory and legal history. Her most recent publication is 'On the founding of law's jurisdiction and the politics of sexual difference, the case of Roman law', in McVeigh, S., ed., *Jurisprudence of Jurisdiction* (Routledge Cavendish, Abingdon, Oxford 2006). She is currently working on a book on the genealogy of feminist legal thought.

Louise du Toit is a Senior Lecturer in the Department of Philosophy at the University of Johannesburg. She obtained a D Litt et Phil from the same institution. She has published numerous articles on topics ranging from sexual difference and rape to questions of identity and ethnicity.

Rosemary Hunter is Professor of Law at the University of Kent, United Kingdom. She is a prominent feminist, socio-legal scholar, whose research interests include access to justice, anti-discrimination law, domestic violence, dispute resolution and women in the legal profession. Her last edited collection was *Changing Law: Rights, Regulation and Reconciliation* with Mary Keyes (Ashgate, Aldershot 2005).

Karin van Marle is Professor of Law at the University of Pretoria. Her research interests include feminist theory, critical legal theory and postapartheid jurisprudence. Recent publications include 'Exploring ubuntu: tentative reflections', *African Human Rights Law Journal*, 2005, pp.195–220 (co-authored with Drucilla Cornell), an edited collection, *Sex, Gender, Becoming. Postapartheid Reflections* (Pretoria University Law Press, Pretoria 2006), and a collection co-edited with WB Le Roux, *Postapartheid Fragments: Law, Politics and Critique* (UNISA Press, Pretoria 2007).

Index

Lightning Source UK Ltd.
Milton Keynes UK
26 March 2010

151955UK00001B/55/P